POLISH-AMERICAN FOLKLORE

Folklore and Society

Series Editors
Roger Abrahams
Bruce Jackson
Marta Weigle

*A list of books in the series appears
at the back of the book.*

POLISH-AMERICAN
FOLKLORE

Deborah Anders Silverman

University of Illinois Press

Urbana and Chicago

Publication of this book was supported by funds from
William R. Greiner, Walter M. Drzewieniecki, the Kosciuszko
Polish Home Association, Inc., Arthur S. Parks, William R.
Parks, Jenny Pokrzywka, and James T. Strychalski.

Library of Congress Cataloging-in-Publication Data
Silverman, Deborah Anders, 1954–
Polish-American folklore / Deborah Anders Silverman.
p. cm. — (Folklore and society)
Includes bibliographical references and index.
ISBN 0-252—0256-9-5 (cloth : alk. paper)
1. Polish Americans—Folklore. 2. Polish Americans—Social
life and customs. 3. Polish Americans—Ethnic identity. I.
Title. II. Series.
GR111.P65S55   2000
398'.089'9185073—dc21   99–006985

C 5 4 3 2 1

For Bruce Jackson and Ronald Ambrosetti

CONTENTS

Illustrations follow pages 50 and 108

ACKNOWLEDGMENTS

Folklorists never work alone. Fieldwork requires collaboration on a scale unimaginable to scholars in many other academic disciplines, and so my professional debts are many. First, I heartily thank Bruce Jackson, Charles Keil, Dennis Tedlock, and James Leary for their many helpful suggestions for improving earlier drafts of this manuscript and Tad Tuleja, for his incisive comments regarding Polish-American folk celebrations. I also am grateful to Ronald Ambrosetti, who first encouraged my research interest in Polish-American folklore while I was a graduate student at the State University of New York College at Fredonia; Mia Boynton of Ithaca, New York, and the late John Smythe for their advice and suggestions for potential informants; Daniel Kij of Lackawanna, New York, former president of the Polish Union of America, and the late Alois Mazur, for assistance in translation and providing the names of additional contacts; and *Polish American Journal* editor Mark Kohan of Hamburg, New York, and polka columnist Steve Litwin of Binghamton, New York, for valuable discussions of Polish-American folk music.

I also wish to thank those who welcomed me into their social clubs: Ann Mikoll and the Chopin Singing Society of Buffalo, New York; Raymond Budniewski and the officers of the Kosciuszko Club of Dunkirk, New York; and Ron Polak and the Polka Pals of Buffalo, New York. Chet Tarnowski, Joe Rozen, Stephanie Rozen, Alex Uszacki, and Sophie Urbanik, all of Dunkirk, New York, graciously allowed me to share in the warmth of their family holiday gatherings while completing my field-work. In addition, I am grateful to the Mark Diamond Research Fund at the State University of New York at Buffalo for partially underwriting the expenses associated with my research.

To Judith McCulloh, assistant director and executive editor at the University of Illinois Press, I offer many thanks for her helpful sugges-tions, patience, and enthusiasm for my project. Terry Sears, managing editor, provided expert advice on manuscript preparation, while Mary Giles, associate editor, put the final polish on my manuscript with her skillful editing.

Finally, I owe a great debt to my family, including my husband, audio engineer Edward Silverman, for his many years of loving encourage-ment, his proofreading expertise, and his invaluable technical assistance on so many fieldwork expeditions; our children, Scott and Beth, for their patience while Mom was busy with the family's "third child"; and my parents, Arthur and Adriana Anders, and my husband's parents, Her-bert and Rose Silverman, for their unflagging interest and enthusiasm about my research. And to my many Polish-American interviewees, I say *"dziękuje bardzo"* for aiding me in rediscovering my ethnic heritage.

A GUIDE TO POLISH
PRONUNCIATION

Vowels

In the Polish language, the vowels are pure, consisting of one sound only; they are never drawled, as is sometimes the case in English. Thus, we have the following vowels:

a as in father   *ó* as in loop
e as in let   *u* as in too
i as in feel   *y* as in it
o as in bought

There are also two nasalized vowels, ą and ę, which cannot be exactly described by English sounds but rather by French sounds. Both vowels are single nasalized sounds:

ą as in the French "bon"
ę as in the French "un" (a clear *e* as in pen and the ending with a trace of *n*)

Consonants

Most Polish consonants are to be read as in English, but with the following suggestions:

c followed by any vowel except for i is pronounced as "ts" *c* followed by i or accented as *ć* is pronounced as the "ch" in church, with the i sound stressed

ch sounds like the *kh* of the Scottish loch

cz as in choo-choo

dz sounds like the *J* of John

dż as in the *j* of jam

ł sounds like *w* in English

š or s followed by i is pronounced "ssh"

sz as in the *sh* of sheep

w as a v

z as in zebra

The letters *q, v,* and *x* are not in the Polish language. Daniel Kij, Alois Mazur, Arthur Anders, Martha Andrzejewski, and Al Clark provided assistance with English translations from Polish in this text.

Source: This pronunciation guide is based on Pogonowski, *Polish-English/English-Polish Dictionary,* 286–90; Raysman, *Say It in Polish,* n.p.; and Knab, *Polish Customs,* 288.

POLISH-AMERICAN FOLKLORE

INTRODUCTION

Polonia. More than eight million Americans of Polish descent can claim Polonia, which means "Poland" in Latin, as their "homeland," the birthplace of their ancestors. Polonia is the Polish-American community, which can be found within cities, towns, and villages throughout the United States. As such, Polonia is a unique culture that straddles two worlds, mainstream America and Poland. Sociologist Helena Znaniecka Lopata observes, "Polonia is an ethnic community located in the American national culture society with the United States as its political system, but it was founded on the Polish national culture society."[1]

In its early years, the American Polonia was a haven for newly arrived immigrants from Poland who met with suspicion or outright rejection from white Anglo-Saxon Protestant Americans. That was especially true for the masses of Poles who left their partitioned country after 1870, seeking relief from the economic and political persecution imposed by the governments of Prussia, Russia, and Austria.

These immigrants, mostly peasants, exchanged one set of problems for another when they arrived on America's shores. Unlike the earlier Scotch and Irish immigrants, they spoke no English, and their Roman Catholic religion was a foreign element in a land that was predominantly Protestant. Their response to these challenges was to forge a new ethnic identity through folklore, a strategy often employed by individuals or groups to establish an identity.[2]

What, then, does this new Polish-American ethnic identity look like, three or four generations after the mass migration of the nineteenth century? The published record yields few answers, because book-length ethnographic studies of American Polonia have focused largely on historical or sociological, rather than folkloristic, concerns. Among the historians, Wacław Kruszka, John Bukowczyk, James Pula, Victor Greene, and Joseph Wytrwal have produced outstanding histories of the American Polonia as a whole; excellent accounts of the immigrants' early years in Chicago and Buffalo, respectively, have been written by Dominic Pacyga and William G. Falkowski, Jr.[3] In sociology, Helena Znaniecka Lopata and coauthors William Thomas and Florian Znaniecki have dealt with American Polonia; studies based on fieldwork in the Polish-American communities of Buffalo, Boston, Los Angeles, and Detroit have been written by Niles Carpenter and Daniel Katz; and other assessments are by Eugene Obidinski (Buffalo), Ewa Morawska (Boston), Neil Sandberg (Los Angeles), and Paul Wrobel (Detroit).[4]

In the field of Polish-American folklore, the record is fragmented. There are no recent book-length studies, grounded in fieldwork, that cover all folklore genres, although folklorists have published journal articles or books devoted to a specific folklore genre.[5] In the late 1950s, Helen Stankiewicz Zand was a leader in this regard, publishing a series of journal articles in *Polish American Studies* focusing on the early immigrants' folk beliefs, rites-of-passage customs, holiday celebrations, and proverbs. Her writing, however, was not based on fieldwork in Polish-American communities but rather, on her memories of life in Buffalo's Polonia.[6] The genre of Polish-American folk music (including the folk songs and polkas) is represented by contributions from Harriet Pawlowska, Charles Keil, Susan Davis, Janice Kleeman, James Leary and Richard March, Paula Savaglio, and Robert Walser. Richard Spottswood has edited a collection of Polish immigrants' songs for a Library of Congress series of recordings.[7] In the genre of oral narratives, Catherine Harris Ainsworth has collected folk tales and religious legends in western New York state's Polonia, and William Clements, Mac Barrick, James Leary, and Lydia Fish are among those who have examined the "Polack" joke.[8] Among other folklore genres, Elizabeth Goldstein and Gail Green conducted research on foodways in upstate New York, Susan Davis looked at Polish-American wedding customs, Dennis Kolinski and Kate Koperski researched folk religious beliefs and practices in Wisconsin and Buffalo, respectively, and Mia Boynton and Kate Koperski interviewed folk artists in Buffalo.[9]

Members of the ethnic group also have published articles or books on Polish-American folklore. Most notable among these efforts was *Polish Folklore*, a quarterly journal edited by Marion Moore Coleman and published in the late 1950s and early 1960s by Alliance College in Cambridge Springs, Pennsylvania, a college founded by Polish immigrants. As the editor noted in the first installment, the journal's mission was preservation, a continuation of her own previous efforts to collect the lore of Poland as preserved in this country.[10] The journal focused on the folklore of the old country, especially folk tales and religious legends, as remembered by Polish immigrants, rather than the folklore's role in the new lives of the immigrants and their descendants in America.

Another in-group preservation effort was a series of "Treasured Polish" publications from Polanie Publishing Company of Minneapolis, describing folk rhymes, games, folk songs, recipes, and Christmas customs of rural Poland in the nineteenth century. Like the journal *Polish Folklore*, these volumes lack the attention to context that more recent ethnographic works contain.

This book is intended to fill the gap in scholarship in the field of Polish-American folklore. Based upon extensive fieldwork in western New York state's Polonias, interviews with other Polish-Americans throughout the northeastern United States, and library research focusing on Polonias throughout America, my study looks at the ways in which today's Polish-Americans are imaginatively revising their immigrant ancestors' folklore to create a sense of ethnicity in multicultural America. It is a dynamic, contextual process, what Stephen Stern and John Allan Cicala call "creative ethnicity."[11]

My fieldwork, which began in 1991 with follow-up interviews of individuals whom I first taped in 1978, expanded over the next five years to encompass more than 150 people. Because I believe that wisdom in a folk community is not the exclusive property of the tribal elders, I made painstaking efforts to ensure variety. I spoke to leaders of Polonia as well as ordinary people interested in their Polish heritage; the young as well as the old; men and women, middle class as well as working-class Polish-Americans; Polish-Americans in interethnic marriages as well as those who married within the ethnic group; and those still living within Polonia's traditional geographic boundaries as well as those now outside its borders. I audiotaped and photographed many people in their homes; others were taped at public events such as folk festivals, polka dances, and holiday gatherings.

The wealth of folklore that I obtained through these methods can be categorized in several genres, each discussed in its own chapter, including folk celebrations of holidays, rite-of-passage events, personal experience narratives and other verbal lore, folk religion, folk medicine, folk music and dance, folk crafts, and foodways. I devote a separate chapter to representations of folklore in the public arena because of Polonia's increasing interest in presenting its folklore to outsiders.

What makes this study unusual is a finding that flies in the face of conventional assumptions about the transmission of folklore within ethnic groups: that it is transmitted within a geographically united folk community. Many interviewees have moved outside the boundaries of the traditional Polonia into multiethnic neighborhoods (chapter 2), yet they retain a surprisingly strong attachment to the ethnic group's lore regardless of their class, gender, age, or geographic location.

These Polish-Americans exemplify a phenomenon noted in 1959 by sociologist Amitai Etzioni about third-generation Jews, that a group can maintain its cultural and social integration and identity without having an ecological basis.[12] Etzioni noticed that third-generation Jews had moved to suburbs where Jews composed no more than one-third of the population. Yet these Jews maintained their common traditions, reinforced through various means of communication such as ethnic newspapers, organizations, clubs, and synagogues. Etzioni believed that for these individuals, the Jewish ethnic group was a "reference group," reinforced in certain social situations, rather than a "community."[13]

Helena Znaniecka Lopata, who has conducted extensive sociological research among Polish-Americans, refers to such ethnic "reference groups" as "superterritorial ethnic communities."[14] She distinguishes the superterritorial ethnic community from several other territorially based sub-units in American Polonia. At the local level, there is the neighborhood, where Polish-Americans interact daily in a social network of parishes, clubs, and services. Above that is the settlement, comprising more than one neighborhood, followed by the local ethnic community, the regional ethnic community, and, finally, the superterritorial ethnic community.[15] In this book, "community" will refer to the superterritorial ethnic community, which I refer to as "Polonia without walls," unless otherwise noted. The Polish-Americans in this community, like the Jews cited by Etzioni, retain ties to their ethnic folklore by reading, listening to, and watching ethnic mass media; participating in ethnic social clubs and churches; attending ethnic group events; and discussing ethnic folklore on the Internet. I offer examples in the chapters that follow.

My study also led me to another surprising conclusion: Intermarriage does not necessarily weaken one's attachment to his or her ethnic traditions. In fact, the non-ethnic spouse may eagerly join in embracing those traditions, strengthening their transmission to the next generation. I found that many Polish-Americans with non-Polish-American spouses continue to practice Polish-American traditions with the enthusiastic support of their spouses. In one home, for example, I observed a Swedish-American wife and her Polish-American husband making pierogi (dumplings filled with cheese or other ingredients) in preparation for the family's Polish-American Christmas meal. These observations apply to foodways (chapter 14) as well as other folklore genres, as noted throughout the book.

What is emerging now, as I attempt to sketch in these pages, is a new Polonia without walls, a folk community whose lore is appealing not only to those whose ancestors were Polish immigrants but also to newcomers from other ethnic and racial groups. They are attracted by a resilient yet dynamic Polish-American folk culture that values the family and home, providing a sense of rootedness and stability in an era of economic and social uncertainty.

1

LIFE IN THE OLD COUNTRY
AND THE MASS MIGRATION TO AMERICA

The American Pole cannot and should not be molded according to
the Old World model. Striving to develop independently, soundly,
and naturally, he must, like a plant, adapt to local conditions.
—Rev. Wacław Kruszka, 1901

Father Kruszka was a visionary who recognized at an early date that
America's Polish immigrants were indeed a new entity rather than
another ingredient for the melting pot.[1] Yet the ethnic roots of these
Polish-Americans extended far back into history, to the ancient Western Slavic tribes that developed their culture between the sixth and tenth
centuries A.D. Poland's consolidation as a nation came in the years 960–
966 A.D. under the leadership of Mieszko I (960–992), ruler of the Polanie, one of several pagan Slavic tribes living between the Oder and
Vistula Rivers and beyond.[2] In 963, Mieszko's territory was attacked by
the Germans, who invaded under the pretext of converting the pagan
Poles to Christianity. To assure the independence of his people and
eliminate the Germans' claim for invasion, Mieszko decided to adopt
the Christian faith immediately.

At the time, Rome and Greece were the increasingly divergent centers of Christianity. Because Mieszko wished to consolidate relations with
the Latin West, he chose Rome and asked the Slavic nation of Bohemia,
already Christianized, to serve as the intermediary.

The Polish leader sent messengers to Bohemia asking Boleslaus, its
duke, for the hand of his daughter Dabrowka. She consented, conditional upon Mieszko's acceptance of Christianity. Their marriage in 965
was followed by his conversion the following year, then the conversions

of members of the royal court and, eventually, after extensive mission-
ary work, all of the Polish people. The impact of Mieszko's conversion
upon Polish folklore cannot be underestimated; the superimposition
of Catholicism upon paganism gave Poles a "double faith" that is reflected to this day in holiday celebrations such as Dyngus Day and Christmas Eve.[3]

Mieszko's reign inaugurated the first of four periods of history before
the first partition of Poland in 1772. The first, the Kingdom Period (960–
1138 A.D.), was a time of growth for the new nation. It was followed by
the Duchy Period (1138–1320), when the kingdom was divided into
smaller units lacking a central power; the Empire Period, Poland's Gold-
en Age (1320–1572), when the kingdom was reunified; and the Period
of Elective Kings (1572–1772).[4] In this final period, the country was
weakened by its system of elective kings, often foreign, and by the introduction in the Sejm (Parliament) of the *liberum veto,* which allowed any
deputy to stop passage of any bill.[5]

For more than eight hundred years, then, Poland was governed by a
monarchy, a class structure that put most of Poland's people at the mercy
of a privileged few. Before the partitions of 1772, 1791, and 1795 Poland had three social classes: the *szlachta* (gentry), the *chłopi* (peasant
folk), and the *mieszczaństwo* (burghers).[6]

The szlachta comprised about 10 percent of the population. It was the
only class represented in the Sejm and enjoyed many rights, such as
participation in the election of kings and freedom from arbitrary arrest
or confiscation of land. No matter how impoverished, such nobles enjoyed the same high status as the most powerful magnates in the land.
The preeminence of the szlachta was due largely to the agrarian socio-
economic structure of Poland before the Industrial Revolution.

Polish agriculture traditionally specialized in the production of grains
for export based on manor farms that relied on serf labor, a system known
as *folwark pańszczyzniany.* This system of serfdom bound approximately 80
percent of the population—the peasants—to land owned by the szlachta. As a result, these two classes developed a certain interdependence as
well as a great deal of animosity, a fact partitioning powers later used to
win the peasants' support for their governments.

This agricultural system largely ignored Poland's third class, the burghers who lived in towns. Composing about 10 percent of the population,
the burgher class emerged during the fourteenth and fifteenth centuries with the rise of Poland's towns. The Jews, Germans, and other non-

Poles in this class worked as shopkeepers and merchants, but unlike the gentry they had no representation in the Sejm.

Land, then, was the key to Poland's economy before the Industrial Revolution.[7] Even a peasant had some right to cultivate a small plot of land on a lord's manor, although such rights varied sharply, depending on whether the peasant belonged to a noble's lands (as did 64 percent of the peasant class), church lands (17 percent), or crown lands (19 percent).[8] Peasants on crown lands generally had more firmly established rights to the land, lighter labor obligations to the lord, and could appeal legal cases to special royal courts.

The "Peasants' Hell"

Life in general, however, was so difficult for peasants that Poland became known in Europe as the "peasants' hell."[9] For a typical Polish peasant, home was a place made of stone, logs, or boards, plastered over with mud and whitewashed. The roof was thatched or mud-covered, with straw laid over it and often with moss growing on top. The interior was usually divided into two rooms, one serving as the living, eating, and sleeping quarters for the family and the other housing livestock and poultry.[10]

Small as the family's plot of land might have been, it meant a great deal psychologically as well as economically to the peasant, who distinguished between the *gospodarz* (peasant landowner) and the *komorniki* (tenant farmers on another's land), who were "rated as the humblest people in the village, a little better than beggars."[11]

Because of the soil's productive function, the concept of fertility as expressed through crops and children was important to a peasant's life.[12] A patriarchal family structure revolved around the land. Usually, the father provided a dowry for his daughters in the form of clothes, household goods, and livestock; sons were reliant upon their father's generosity with the family's property. The father was viewed as a temporary land manager in a complex system of property inheritance: "Each time a son marries, the father makes over to him a portion of the farm. Ordinarily the result is that when the last son marries, the father is left landless, or virtually so."[13] At that point, the father and mother would receive *dozywocie* (support for life) by settling in with the son or daughter in whom they had the greatest confidence, but all too often such a retirement would be a "bed of thorns."[14]

Given their strong bond with the land, it is understandable that Polish peasants held a worldview limited to their *okolica* (from *oko,* meaning "eye"), the area within eyesight, or, from a sociological perspective, the area in which a person's reputation is contained.[15] The concept is analogous to *campanilismo* (from *campana,* the Italian word for "bell") among Italian peasants, an idea defined as "a view of the world that includes reluctance to extend social, cultural, and economic contacts beyond points from which the parish or village bell could still be heard."[16]

The okolica offered stability but also discouraged deviations from customary patterns: "Fixed in one place for centuries, the peasants thought of themselves mostly in the simple terms of their own village circle, within which they were at home and outside of which they were only strangers. Always their interests had been local, limited to the little area within the shadow of their own church tower."[17]

It was within this little village circle that Polish folklore flourished in its many regional variations for generations. It was strongly agricultural and religious in character; rites of passage and seasonal celebrations, in particular, still reveal this influence.[18] But this folklore of the okolica would undergo dramatic changes as the result of the partitioning of Poland. While the partitions brought no improvement to the peasant's hell, they did provide an opportunity for escape from intolerable economic and political conditions.

Poland Disappears: The Partitions

By the eighteenth century, the Kingdom of Poland was greatly weakened as a world power due to its elective monarchy, the nobility who protected their own vested interests through use of the liberum veto in the Sejm, and numerous wars and invasions that devastated the Polish economy.

The election of kings by Poland's Sejm was especially destructive to the sovereignty of the state, because Russia, Austria, and Prussia took an increasing interest in influencing the outcome of the elections in the years leading up to the first partition in 1772.

Poland lost about one-third of its territory and half of its population in 1772. Austria annexed most of Galicia, Prussia took the provinces of Ermeland and Pomerania and the region at the mouth of the Vistula River, while Russia claimed the outlying eastern border regions.

The loss of such vast territories in tandem with the French Revolution was enough to awaken the Polish Sejm to action. The much-heralded constitution of May 3, 1791 advocated constitutional monarchy based on Montesquieu's interpretation of the English constitution, elements of the Austrian and Prussian Enlightenment, and ideas from the American and French Revolutions. The liberum veto was abolished, and representation in the Sejm was opened to the burgher class.

At about the same time, industrialization began in Poland, with factories employing serf labor located on the szlachta's lands; progress in farming technology resulted in increased production. Such signs of vitality alarmed Poland's neighbors, especially Russia, which invaded Poland in 1792, resulting in the second partition a year later, when lands went to Prussia and Russia.

After an unsuccessful insurrection led by Thaddeus Kosciuszko in 1794, Russia, Prussia, and Austria completed the third and final partition in 1795. The heart of Poland, including Warsaw, went to Prussia, Austria expanded its Galician acquisitions, and Russia took the remaining territory east of a line from Grodno to Brest-Litovsk. In terms of population, Austria gained roughly four million people, Prussia, three million, and Russia, about seven million. The old kingdom had been divided as follows: to Russia, 62 percent of the land and 45 percent of the population; to Prussia, 20 percent of the land and 23 percent of the population; and to Austria, 18 percent of the land and 32 percent of the population.[19] Until the end of World War I more than 125 years later, partitioned Poland looked as shown in figure 1.

As a result of the final partition, many Polish patriots became exiles, including composer Fredric Chopin and poet Adam Mickiewicz. During this period, the exiles developed a romantic nationalist ideology best expressed by the Polish national anthem, "Jeszcze Polska Nie Zginęła," which was composed in 1797: "Our Poland shall not perish while we live to love her." Mickiewicz and writer Julius Słowacki created a new doctrine, Polish messianism, which claimed Poland was a martyred Christ figure, crucified by the partitioning powers.[20] The exiles fought with Napoleon's forces, hoping for his support for an independent Poland, but with his defeat and the Congress of Vienna in 1815, the boundaries as established by the partitions were maintained.

The patriots also organized underground resistance movements in all three sections of Poland, with revolts in 1830 in Russian Poland, in Krakow and Galicia in 1846, in 1848 in Prussian-held Poznania, and the

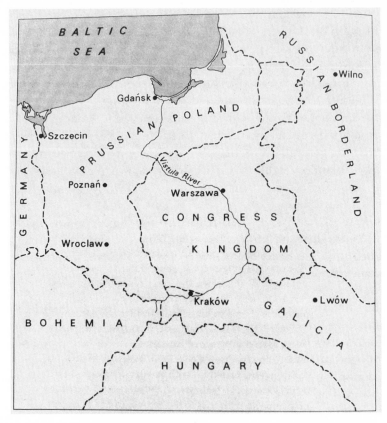

Figure 1. Map of Partitioned Poland circa 1870. Source: Edward R. Kantowicz, *Polish-American Politics in Chicago, 1888–1940* (Chicago: University of Chicago Press, 1975), 4. (Used with the permission of the University of Chicago Press)

"January Insurrection" in Russian Poland in 1863. All were systematically repressed by the foreign powers and led Poles after 1863 to replace their romantic nationalist ideology with realism in the form of "organic labor," support for internal economic and social progress rather than revolution.[21]

The Emigration of Adventurers and Political Exiles

For some Polish patriots, proponents of a national rather than folk culture, emigration to America was the answer.[22] These political refugees were not Poland's first emigrants, however; they were preceded by adventurers such as the fabled sailor Jan z Kolno (John from Kolno), who arrived as commander of the Danish king's ship in Labrador in 1476. His exploits are chronicled in "The Kaszubs before Vienna" by Polish poet Hieronim Derdowski (1852–1902):

I Jaś z Kielna świętego
  tędzim beł wiarusem
Co w Ameryce bywoł jesz
  przed Koląbusem,
I tak liczne rozmnożełw
  niej kaszubście plemnię,
Że tu druge ju mąmę
  obiecaną zemnię.

(Johnnie from sacred Kolno
  was a sturdy guard's name
Who went to America before
  Columbus came,
And so abundantly propagated
  the Kashubian band,
That we now have here our
  second promised land.)[23]

Later adventurers included a contingent of Polish glassblowers, pitch-makers, and potash workers at Jamestown, Virginia, in 1608; in 1619 they staged a successful strike when denied the right to vote alongside their English-born peers.[24] The earliest family to settle in America was the Zborowskis of New York, who amassed a fortune via real estate speculation.[25] Other prominent Poles included Peter Stadnicki, whose Holland Land Company was responsible for the founding of Buffalo, New York.[26]

These adventurers during America's colonial period (1608–1776) composed the first wave of Polish emigrants; they were followed between 1776 and 1870 by many political refugees of the gentry class, such as Thaddeus Kosciuszko and Count Casimir Pulaski, both of whom played leading roles in America's Revolutionary War, and Ernestine Potowski-Rose, who successfully lobbied for a married women's property law in New York state in 1849.[27] Neither the adventurers nor the political émigrés established distinct Polish-American communities; rather, they were absorbed into mainstream American society, where they continued to advocate the cause of an independent Poland.

Life under the Partitioning Powers

But their relatives back in Poland continued to suffer from the effects of overpopulation, small landholdings, primitive agricultural methods, meager farm productivity, insufficient industrial development, low wages, and excessive taxation.[28] Although the serfs were emancipated in Prussian Poland starting in 1807, in Austrian Poland in 1848, and in Russian Poland in 1861, life remained difficult. Because Poland was ruled by three different foreign powers, the conditions that set the stage for the mass migration to America varied in each region.

In Prussian Poland, large landowners were encouraged by the government to transform the rural economy into a system of large-scale commercial agriculture.[29] With a system of protective subsidies, low taxes, and scientific farming methods, agricultural productivity skyrocketed; thus, fewer Polish agricultural laborers were needed, and employment in other fields was limited.

Cultural repression was another problem for Prussian Poles. In 1864 the teaching of Polish was prohibited in Prussian schools. That was followed by Otto von Bismarck's Kulturkampf campaign. Launched in 1872 to centralize the German empire against regionalism and Catholicism, Kulturkampf lasted until 1885. It pitted state against church, centralism against autonomy, and authorities against citizens, surfacing with particular sharpness in the Polish territory. By 1885 there were mass expulsions of Poles from the area as the Prussian government brought in Germans to "colonize" the region. As might be expected, the Kulturkampf years were those of peak Prussian Polish migration. About 1.2 million people emigrated to the United States, Canada, and elsewhere between 1870 and 1914.[30]

Like their counterparts in Prussia, Russian Poles suffered under a repressive government. Following the unsuccessful revolt of 1830, the czar instituted Russification. The area was ruled directly by Russia, the Polish language was prohibited in schools, and Polish universities were closed, resulting in the emigration of Polish intellectuals.

After the January Insurrection of 1863, Russia executed hundreds of Poles, deported thousands more to Siberia, confiscated some 1,600 estates and gave them to czarist officials, transformed the Polish Bank into a subsidiary of the Imperial Bank, and took strong measures against the Catholic Church.[31]

As in Prussian Poland, the Russian government encouraged the development of commercial agriculture, which resulted in the displacement of many rural Poles. But offsetting this development, the government also began rapid industrialization both in Russia and its Polish lands during the nineteenth century, absorbing much of the surplus labor from the countryside. Coal mining, iron, steel, textile manufacture, and sugar refining became mainstays of the Russian Polish economy by the century's end.[32] However, the Russo-Japanese War of 1904, the strikes and lockouts in 1905 and 1906, and a shift in industrial production from Russian Poland to Russia all impelled both rural and industrial workers to emigrate. Approximately 1.3 million people left the region between 1870 and 1914, with most Russian Poles arriving in America during the 1890s.

In comparison with the Poles living under Russian or German rule, Austrian Poles, known as Galicians, enjoyed a good deal of autonomy. The province's administration passed into Polish hands in 1868, and Polish was recognized in Galicia as the official language the following year. As a result of this show of confidence by the Austrians, Galicians supported the government. Many entered government service, where they received training for self-rule some fifty years later. Universities were revived and the Academy of Sciences opened, making Galicia the artistic and intellectual center for divided Poland.

Economically, though, Galicia was the most backward of the three Polish regions, with overpopulation and poor soil as its main problems. As late as 1830, when the other two Polish provinces were gearing up for the Industrial Revolution, 80 percent of Galicia's inhabitants lived in the country, often in dire poverty. Peasant landholdings were small, and farming methods were antiquated; many Galicians sought seasonal farm work in Germany or emigrated overseas. About 1.1 million Austrian Poles left their homeland between 1870 and 1914.[33]

A New Era: The Peasant Migration *Za Chlebem* (for Bread)

Because of the economic hardships in partitioned Poland, peasants began trickling into America in the mid-nineteenth century. The earliest community established by the peasant Poles was that of Panna Maria, Texas, founded in 1854 by the Rev. Leopold Moczygęba and three hundred Upper Silesian farmers. Other sporadic settlements before the massive immigration that started in the 1870s included Polonia, Wisconsin (founded in 1855), Parisville, Michigan (founded in 1857), and the Polish parishes founded during the 1860s in Milwaukee, western Wisconsin, and Chicago.[34] Of the thirty thousand Poles in America during the Civil War, four thousand fought for the Union and another one thousand for the Confederacy.

Agents from steamship companies and merchant vessels, anxious to have a full load on a return trip from Europe, actively sought prospective immigrants in Polish villages, as did several American states and potential employers seeking cheap labor. Perhaps the most powerful enticements were letters from previous immigrants, mailed to loved ones back home or published in Polish newspapers. These letters were known as "bowing letters" because they featured greetings, or "bows," to family members far away.[35] A typical bowing letter, written in 1912 by a barely literate immigrant chambermaid, features a standard ceremonial opening invoking God's assistance, followed by a poem and information about her life in America. In addition to the formulaic opening, there is also repetition of certain phrases, another characteristic of cultures such as that of peasant Poland which are primarily oral:

> I am beginning this letter with the words: "Praised be Jesus Christus," and I hope that you will answer: "For centuries of centuries. Amen."[36]
>
> DEAREST OLEJNICZKA: I greet you from my heart, and wish you health and happiness. God grant that this little letter reaches you well, and as happy as the birdies in May. This I wish you from my heart, dear Olejniczka.
>
> The rain is falling; it falls beneath my slipping feet.
> I do not mind; the post-office is near.
> When I write my little letter,
> I will flit with it there,
> And then, dearest Olejniczka,
> My heart will be light [from giving you a pleasure].
> In no grove do the birds sing so sweetly
> As my heart, dearest Olejniczka, for you. . . .
>
> Dearest Olejniczka, I left papa, I left sister and brother and you, to start out in the wide world, and today I am yearning and fading away like the world without the sun. . . . I went up on a high hill and looked in that far direction, but I see you not, but I see you not, and I hear you not. . . .
>
> And now I write you how I am getting along. I am getting along very well, very well. I have worked in a factory and I am now working in a hotel. I receive 18 (in our money 32) dollars a month, and that is very good. If you

would like it, we could bring Wladzio over some day. We eat here every day what we get only for Easter in our country. We are bringing over Helena and brother now. I had $120 and I sent back $90.[37]

Many other immigrants sent home money or steamship tickets for the journey.[38] One writer urged his brother to join him in his successful new life in America "because in our country I experienced only misery and poverty, and now I live better than a lord in our country. I work my nine hours and I have peace; I have enough to drink and to dress well, and I have money."[39] Such letters, "every word received like a jewel," would put an entire village "into a state of tingling excitement" and be widely circulated throughout an entire community after being read by the original recipients.[40]

Like the Italian peasants who emigrated to the United States at the same time, a young, single Polish man generally would come with others from his village to an American city where a friend already lived. The young man, who might have been a blacksmith, carpenter, or shoemaker back home, would find a factory job as an unskilled laborer, staying with friends or relatives or at one of the many boardinghouses run by Polish wives. He would send for his family as soon as he could afford to do so.

Following the Franco-Prussian War of 1870, the trickle of immigrants became a flood. Thousands of peasant Poles journeyed to the United States by way of Castle Garden and later Ellis Island, settling in the New England, Middle Atlantic, and North Central states, especially Connecticut, New York, New Jersey, Illinois, and Michigan.

As a number of scholars have noted, it is difficult to determine the exact number of Polish immigrants, because Poland was under foreign

Table 1. Major Polish-American Population Centers

City	1905	1920
Chicago	250,000	400,000
New York	150,000	200,000
Pittsburgh	70,000	125,000
Buffalo	70,000	100,000
Milwaukee	65,000	100,000
Detroit	50,000	100,000
Cleveland	30,000[a]	50,000[a]

a. Toledo, Philadelphia, Baltimore, and Boston were below these figures.

domination during most of the immigration period, which meant that immigrants would list Prussia, Russia, or Austria as their birthplace rather than Poland.[41] In addition, the U.S. Immigration and Naturalization Service changed its form of identification for Polish immigrants several times, and there was heavy travel back and forth between Poland and America. Most important, who was to be included as a "Polish-American," only those of foreign stock or those with at least one ancestor from Poland? Despite these drawbacks, it can be estimated that by 1920 between 2.5 million and 3.6 million Poles lived in the United States, including more than one million (86 percent) in American cities (table 1), a figure that did not vary much over subsequent decades.[42]

2

"THE OLD NEIGHBORHOOD ISN'T THE SAME ANY MORE": THE EVOLUTION OF POLISH-AMERICAN ETHNICITY

With each tick of the timeclock, the past receded, the accent softened, the English improved, and to one degree or another the mass of Polish immigrants put on America and shed the Old World.
—Verlyn Klinkenborg, *The Last Fine Time*

Framed by the tall, imposing twin spires of the church, a typical urban Polish-American neighborhood between 1870 and 1910 might be described as follows: "The homes were simple story-and-a-half wooden cottages set in narrow gardens enclosed by wooden fences. The long uniform rows were broken at intersections by two-and-a-half story buildings which housed a grocery store, a saloon or sometimes a drug store. One or two streets were given over to business places, combined homes and offices of professional men and homes of more prosperous citizens."[1]

The cottages were, in reality, crowded multiple dwellings for two or three families. The interiors evoked the Old World, with many holy pictures framed in gilt or polished wood, some forming the center of an altar with an eternal lamp, the Easter palm, and a herb bouquet blessed on Assumption Day. Homes also featured a small font for holy water inside the door; the inscription K+M+B (the initials of Kaspar, Melchior, and Balthazar, the three kings [chapter 4]) from Epiphany Day over the doorway; beds piled high with *pierszyny* (feather-filled comforters); potted plants in windows; a garden with sunflowers, hollyhocks, lilac, sweet jasmine, and such vegetables as carrots, cucumbers, parsley, dill, and chives; a henhouse; and a woodshed.[2]

The heart of Polonia's okolica, however, was the ethnic Roman Catholic parish, the first institution established by the new immigrants. For example, St. Stanislaus, Buffalo's first Polish parish (and western New York's), was founded in 1873, followed two years later by Dunkirk's first Polish church, St. Hyacinth's. Neighborhoods were known by the name of the local parish, a measure of the importance of the church in the okolica; thus, the community surrounding St. Stanislaus Church was called *Stanisławowo*.[3]

Once the ethnic church and the allied parish schools were in place, a network of voluntary associations sprang up to aid the Polish immigrants, harking back to the land banks and village cooperatives of rural Poland. These new Polish-American voluntary groups included national fraternal bodies such as the Polish Roman Catholic Union (1873) and its chief rival in the formation of a Polish-American identity, the Polish National Alliance (1880), the Polish Union of the United States of North America (1890), the Association of the Sons of Poland (1903), and the Polish White Eagle Association (1906).

The fraternal benevolent associations, mutual aid societies, and building and loan associations offered financial protection to immigrants in the days before welfare, workers' compensation, and employee benefits. In return for paying regular dues, members could draw out modest accident, sickness, or death benefits; obtain small business loans or home mortgages; and even obtain mourners or pallbearers. By the 1910s, eight hundred thousand Poles, approximately three-quarters of the immigrants, belonged to at least one of the seven thousand immigrant societies in Polonia.[4] The mutual aid societies functioned as social and cultural centers in the community:

> The center was usually a large hall filled with tables and chairs. Here Polish songs, rhythmic folk dances, lively music, and stirring dramas were developed and perpetuated; gems of Polish literature were read and reread, and many episodes from Polish history were related. The walls of the center were adorned with framed lithograph pictures of Polish revolutionary heroes. The atmosphere . . . clouded with foul cigarette or cigar smoke, was hardly inviting to the eye or nose. But this was the place to hear local gossip.[5]

Polonia's many newspapers and periodicals, initially only in Polish but later in the English language as well, also provided Polish-Americans with information pertaining both to their communities and the homeland.

The early Polish-American okolica was both self-sufficient and isolated. Lumberyards, churches, schools, newspapers, dry goods stores, drugstores, feed stores, furniture stores, bakeries, butcher shops, grocery shops, shoe shops, barber shops, hardware stores, print shops, and funeral homes all were contained within Polonia. "The only time you had to go downtown was to buy a suit of clothes or to go to the fruitstands that the Italians ran, or to high school—but you didn't really belong there," one man told me.[6]

Communication between Polish immigrants and white Anglo-Saxon Protestant Americans was of a business or political nature, not social; WASPs did not stay in neighborhoods overrun by immigrants, but moved to uptown districts or suburbs, foreshadowing a move that later generations of Polish-Americans themselves would make.

Yet the Poles' isolation was not complete; they settled near other East Europeans, a cushion against culture shock.[7] As one immigrant who came to Dunkirk, New York, in 1914 noted, "Dunkirk was Polish, but there were also different ethnics, because I can remember we blended with Czechs, Lithuanians, Germans, Slovenians, and Russians. I can remember speaking all these different dialects."[8]

New Occupations, New Factions

The Polish-American okolica was situated near the available jobs. Some immigrants opted to remain in farming, taking over worn-out farms abandoned by Yankees in the Connecticut Valley, where they raised onions and tobacco, or they had truck gardens on Long Island, farmed in Massachusetts and New Jersey, and grew corn and wheat in the South and West.[9]

Many others, however, who arrived with "little more than calluses on their hands" and "muscle-power," as described by Joseph Wytrwal, took industrial jobs. They became unskilled laborers in the textile mills of New England, the railroads and lumber mills of the West, the coal mines of Pennsylvania and West Virginia, the slaughterhouses of Chicago, and the steel mills of Buffalo, Akron, and Youngstown. Others were employed in shoe and clothing manufacturing, automobile assembly, furniture factories, and oil and sugar refineries. Polish women went to work in textile mills, clothing factories, cigar factories, packinghouses, canneries, hotels, and restaurants; served as domestic servants; did laundry and cleaning; or kept boardinghouses.[10]

The changes from rural to urban life and farming to industrial occupations had implications for Polish-American folklore: Agricultural festivals and prolonged holidays no longer held a major place in the scheme of life. As Roger Abrahams has noted, Americans have clung to such seasonal festivals long after their direct involvement in agriculture has passed; therefore, although the techniques of observance may remain the same, their messages are launched in different contexts, thus imparting different meanings.[11] This phenomenon as exemplified in Polonia's public festivals will be examined in chapter 15.

In addition to the major change to industrial occupations, Polish immigrants also were contending with another new force, regionalism. Shedding their village identities, the former peasants still chose to associate in the New World with others from their region of Poland. Even a small city such as Dunkirk, New York—with a total population of fewer than twenty thousand—had two distinct Polish communities for many years. One was founded in the 1870s by Prussian (German) Poles, and the second was established in 1902 by Austrian (Galician) and Russian Poles. Ethnic slurs hurled by the groups included "Galaniery" to refer to the Galicians, "Cossacks" or "Bolsheviki" for the Russians, and "Tabakiery" for the Prussians. "They called them *Tabakiery*'because those German people would even go into church with their snuff boxes and use snuff in church, you know? And that's what '*tabakiery*' means, 'tobacco'."[12] Other epithets included "Zmiętuje" (small fish), applied to the Prussian Poles, and "Gorky" (hill people), a negative term for Russian and Austrian newcomers who resided on the hilltop where the second Polish community was located. Boys from one community dared not cross the railroad tracks dividing the two Polonias for fear of being beaten by their counterparts in the other ward.[13]

Factionalism also was manifested in acrimonious class struggles within Polonia over the formation of a unique Polish-American identity. In the final quarter of the nineteenth century, nationalists in the Polish National Alliance (PNA) clashed bitterly with religionists from the Polish Roman Catholic Union (PRCU). The nationalists, numerically the smaller faction, argued that Polonia's main objective should be the restoration of independence to Poland, with religion of only secondary importance. Religionists, however, insisted that a Pole could be only Roman Catholic and that although Poland's independence was a worthwhile goal, Polonia's primary function was to maintain a Catholic identity.[14]

Complicating matters was the fact that in the American Catholic Church, parish ownership was given to the diocesan bishop, who was not usually a member of the ethnic group. The ethnic religionists, stressing Catholic loyalty, agreed to diocesan title, but nationalists condemned that as outside interference.[15] By the 1890s, friction had escalated into verbal and physical assaults over parish ownership in parishes in Chicago, Buffalo, and other cities. These battles were widely reported by the partisan Polish-American newspapers of both camps. Pro-religionist publications such as Buffalo's *Polak w Ameryce* (The Pole in America) and the PRCU's *Naród Polski* (The Polish Nation) locked horns with nationalist organs, including the PNA's *Zgoda* (Harmony) and Milwaukee's *Kuryer Polski* (The Polish Courier).[16] Some nationalists went so far as to establish, under the leadership of the Rev. Francis Hodur of Scranton, Pennsylvania, a separate church called the Polish National Catholic Church. Eventually, the Polish National Catholic Church claimed members in Buffalo, Chicago, Scranton, and Baltimore and in Michigan, New Jersey, and Connecticut. The schism in Scranton was so deep that Polish National Catholics were known as "kickers," whereas the remaining Roman Catholics were called "suckers."[17]

Tensions in Polonia eased considerably in 1908, when the Roman Catholic Church hierarchy in America appointed the Rev. Paul Rhode as the country's first Polish-American bishop. This gave America's Poles the *równoprawnienie* (equality) they had long demanded. Because Bishop Rhode proved to be both a loyal Roman Catholic as well as ardent nationalist, conceiving of his role as *the* Polish representative in the American Church, he was able to mollify both factions.

The Second Generation's New Ethnic Identity

Up until World War I, Polish immigrants struggled with differences involving religion and regional origin as they attempted to craft a new identity in America, initially as Poles. By the 1920s, however, with the emergence of the second generation born in the United States, they were no longer calling themselves Poles. They were Polish-Americans. John Bukowczyk has noted that Polonia's leaders in the 1920s deliberately embraced Americanism, founded political and civic clubs, and plunged into naturalization work to counteract the nativism and Americanization fever sweeping the country at that time. In that manner, they were demonstrating that they were "American enough not to be perennially suspect."[18]

Young, second-generation Polish-Americans were significantly different in their outlook on ethnic identity. In a study of Buffalo's Polonia in 1927, more considered themselves Americans (53.6 percent) than American Poles (26.8 percent), Polish American (11.8 percent), or Poles (7.8 percent).[19] As Bukowczyk has observed, "These Polish-Americans in their late teens or early twenties might still speak Polish at home, might want to maintain Polish community life, and would not marry outside their group. But most differed from their immigrant parents in many other ways. The majority did not object to the idea of interethnic marriage; and most, while retaining Polish customs, had absorbed a great deal of American culture."[20]

This hybridization of culture is most readily apparent in the development of the Polish-American polka during the Roaring Twenties (chapter 11). Another manifestation of the evolution of the folk community was the transformation of its material culture. The crowded cottages, woodsheds, and henhouses of the immigrants gave way to one- or two-family homes with driveways and garages; the interiors no longer contained a holy water font or many holy pictures; and the huge featherbeds, the Assumption Day bouquet, and the *gromnica* (large blessed candle) so prominent in immigrants' homes were relegated to back rooms.[21]

Despite their desire to be considered as Americans during the 1920s and 1930s, Polonia's members continued to encourage the use of Polish in their parochial schools and an interest in Polish-American organizations. In fact, the Rev. Justyn Figas of Buffalo began broadcasting "Father Justyn's Rosary Hour" in 1931, a radio program that eventually was syndicated and heard on more than fifty stations. As a supplement to the parochial schools of the period, Polish-Americans founded Saturday "Polish schools" to promote secular Polish culture and Polish nationalist ideology. One former student described his school:

> AL CLARK: All day Saturday I had to go to Polish school.
> SILVERMAN: And that's when you concentrated on learning Polish, learning to speak it and read it?
> CLARK: Yeah, we had to read and write and understand Polish. Everything was in Polish. In fact, they had these little skits, little plays, and you had to learn your words, you know, do sort of a minor theater. And another thing, they stressed the fact that you were in America, but you had to speak a certain amount of Polish at home.[22]

Although instruction in the Polish language was emphasized, Polonia's leaders realized that its use had declined dramatically; editors of Polish-American newspapers were publishing in English rather than Polish to attract the younger Polonians who no longer spoke Polish.[23] Wacław Kruszka, in a humorous description of the Polish dialect used in Polonia, pointed to the dialect's corruption:

> A *grynhorn* [greenhorn; a person newly arrived from the old country], of course, has difficulty understanding such a dialect and is often appalled by it, reproaching his immigrant countrymen for corrupting the native language with adopted words. . . . But soon the same *grynhorn* . . . begins to express himself by saying that today he will go to the city by *kara* [car, in Polish, *wagon kolejowy*] for *biznesem* [business, in Polish, *interes* or *sprawunek*]. . . . He soon learns to polonize other English words and says that he was in a *salunie* [saloon, in Polish *karczma*] where at the *barze* [bar] stood the *barkiper* [barkeeper; *szynkarz*] who served *wiski* [whiskey; *gorzałki*], and next they had *luncz* [lunch; *przekąska*] and *potrytowali* [treated; *częstować*] each other to a beer.[24]

In arguing that such language evolution was immigrants' innovative and necessary response to their new environment, Kruszka was decades ahead of contemporary folklorists who believe that today's ethnic Americans are similarly engaged in "creative ethnicity," selectively and imaginatively representing their ethnicity through folklore.[25]

More Challenges for Polonia: Ethnicity in Suburbia

The Polish-American community's sense of ethnicity continued to respond to changes provided by the Great Depression and World War II. Although the loss of economic opportunities during the depression tended to keep young Polish-Americans within the established Polonia, World War II and its aftermath encouraged the well-documented flight of Polonians to suburbia. Those who remained behind in the increasingly decaying inner-city neighborhoods were portrayed by novelist Verlyn Klinkenborg in *The Last Fine Time*. He describes the world of Buffalo's Polish East Side in 1947, a pivotal era when young Eddie Wenzek, newly returned from the war, is about to transform the workers' tavern owned by his parents into a swank nightspot, "George & Eddie's," where highballs and french-fried shrimp are served. The neighbors view Eddie as a highly eligible bachelor: "What few flaws he has (he is not enough Polish, he has lost the tongue, but then what child is enough Polish these days, the only ones are the DPs the priests sponsor and that is not such a good thing anyway, eating lard on bread) are minor compared to his promise, which is the promise dearest to a Polish-American heart: property, filial respect, a cash business."[26] Klinkenborg continues to fill in details of his father-in-law's later life: his marriage, children, and the neighborhood's new racial groups and increasing poverty that result in higher crime, eventually forcing Eddie to sell his restaurant and flee to the suburbs. His homestead on the East Side, 722 Sycamore, falls victim to the city's wrecker ball in 1972.

The Last Fine Time is a descriptive, albeit somewhat romanticized, portrait of one phase of Polonia's life, but it fails to realize that the Polish-American community has continued to thrive in new surroundings. Since 1990, for example, Buffalo's Polish-American community on the East Side has lost Ruda's Polkas and Polish Gifts store and the Chopin's Singing Society, a leading cultural organization, to the nearby suburb of Cheektowaga, which has a large Polish-American population. In addition, although several of the city's East Side Catholic churches have been closed by the Diocese of Buffalo, many Polish-American parishes exist in Cheektowaga and other suburbs.

Those third- and fourth-generation Polish-Americans who have dispersed to the suburbs, as well as those who remained in Polonia, are selectively using the folklore of their ancestors to make statements about their identity, a phenomenon several scholars have noted.[27] As one Polish-American man observed, "The old neighborhood isn't the old neighborhood any more. It's becoming standard people in the suburbs. We have this group of older Polish-Americans who are still living in the old neighborhood and it's not like it used to be, but they're pretending it is. But it's not really like that any more. I think we have ethnicity developing on different levels in different ways."[28]

The efforts of these ethnic Americans have been labeled as the "ethnic revival" of the 1970s and 1980s, a response in part to the Black Power movement. But as Helena Znaniecka Lopata has rightly argued, an unfortunate tendency to lump all ethnic communities together has emerged from observation of the ethnic revival.[29] All too often, scholars have failed to note that within an ethnic group there are variations in ethnicity due to differences of class, the salience of affective ties, intermarriage, and one's location in the life-cycle. The much-publicized "ethnic revival" of the 1970s, for example, could be partially explained as the coming of age of large numbers of Baby Boomers who married and started families, thus becoming more interested in the ethnic folklore of their childhood because they hoped to pass traditions along to their own children.

In my research, I have encountered many Polish-American grandmothers who continue traditional family celebrations until a life-cycle change such as illness or death makes it necessary for a daughter, daughter-in-law, or niece to assume those responsibilities. At that point, there may be changes in the menu and the event's format, date, or location, or the tradition may be discontinued. There is concern among musicians in the polka music world, for example, because of a lack of young adult fans. That might be due to competition from rock music, but it might also be caused by changes in lifestyle brought about by family commitments that keep these adults at home with young children on weekend evenings rather than in taverns. These examples of life-cycle changes point to the need for additional research on the relationship between folklore usage and life-cycle position.

Class differences within the ethnic group, which Milton Gordon has called the "ethclass," have been addressed to some extent.[30] Among Polish-Americans, for example, Charles Keil has noted two distinct communities: a "pretending" Polonia of "make-believe" szlachta (aristocracy become intelligentsia) who prefer the polonaise, and a Polonia of "believing" chłopi (peasants become workers) who enjoy polka music.[31]

Likewise, John Bukowczyk and Helena Znaniecka Lopata have marked a class split in Polonia between those interested in promoting Poland's "high" or "national" culture and proponents of the "folk" culture of the peasant immigrants.[32] In Poland, the national culture gained ascendancy over the folk culture as the result of industrialization, urbanization, and mass education following World War I. That explains why many recent Polish immigrants, products of the middle class, look askance at established Polish-American communities founded on the working-class folk culture of the peasants and refuse to settle there. I will examine these class differences, especially apparent in Polonia's musical and dance preferences, in chapter 15.

Another important issue that scholars have begun to address is the emotional advantages of ethnicity. As Daniel Bell has pointed out, "Ethnicity has become more salient because it can combine an interest with an affective tie. Ethnicity provides a tangible set of common identifications—in language, food, music, names—when other social roles become more abstract and impersonal."[33]

Anya Peterson Royce also argues that ethnicity provides an affective experience outside the nuclear family; likewise, Michael M. J. Fischer believes that ethnicity is a deeply rooted emotional component of identity.[34] My fieldwork has borne out these observations, particularly regarding the Easter and Christmas celebrations now held in social clubs as well as families, a convenience and an emotional bond for those whose adult children live far away (chapters 3 and 4).

The relationship between affective ties and ethnicity is particularly important in considering intermarriage, a widespread phenomenon by the end of the twentieth century.[35] Intermarriage presents a thorny dilemma for folklorists: Does it necessarily mean a decrease in the transmission of ethnic folklore? According to my research, Polish-American women who are in their sixties or older and have married outside the ethnic group tend to cook foods of their husbands' ethnic group. The older women from other ethnic groups who marry Polish-American men prepare traditional Polish foods. A German-American wife describes her family's foodways thus:

> JEAN BROGCINSKI: I had to learn to cook Polish because he likes pierogi and
> *gołąbki* [cabbage rolls] and mushroom soup and all those for Christmas.
> Anything to please my husband!
> SILVERMAN: So who taught you the Polish cooking?
> BROGCINSKI: Mostly from neighbors or friends that knew how to do it, and I
> perfected it myself then.[36]

Yet in intermarriages of the successive generation, those currently in their twenties and thirties, I found many couples passing on the traditions of both parents' ethnic backgrounds. The following comments from a thirty-five-year-old Polish-American man who has an Irish-American spouse are typical: "I think it's very important to show the children that there are some customs and traditions that they should get involved with. They've been doing pretty good the last couple of years. They've accepted a little bit of the foods. We have pierogi, bread, fish."[37]

The couple, who have two young daughters, celebrates the traditional Polish Christmas Eve supper with its blessed *opłatek* (wafer) and the Easter *święconka*, featuring food blessed in church; visit the tomb of Jesus set up in their Polish parish at Eastertime; and cook traditional Polish foods such as "pigs in a blanket" (*gołąbki*), seasoned ground beef wrapped in cabbage leaves. They also, however, are members of the local Irish Society, attend an annual Irish picnic, and are teaching traditional Irish songs to the children.

The effects of class, life-cycle location, affective ties, and intermarriage upon the selection of folklore items are both complex and profound. I will describe Polish-American folklore as it is experienced by the ethnic group in the following chapters, but it should be remembered that within the group there is great variation in the amount and type of folklore individuals use.

3

POLISH-AMERICAN EASTER CELEBRATIONS

> When a social group celebrates a particular event . . . it also cele-
> brates itself, what it conceives to be its essential life.
> —Victor Turner, *Celebration*

F or Polish-Americans, Easter (Wielkanoc) and Christmas (Boże Na-
rodzenie, or God's Nativity) are the two major calendar celebrations,
marking the beginning and ending of the annual agricultural cycle. As
Roger Abrahams has noted, such seasonal holidays generally happen
on "plateaus of the year" when nothing important is occurring, so they
must generate an excitement and energy all their own.[1]

To create this holiday excitement as well as a sense of ethnic identity, Polish-Americans manipulate carefully selected symbols and signs in
both their public celebrations of Easter and Christmas—the Dyngus
Day party and Kolędy Night, respectively—and their corresponding private festivities for group members only, the Easter święconka and the
Christmas *wigilia* (vigil meal). The święconka and wigilia meals are
shared either within families or at Polish-American social clubs. These
social club functions are not advertised to outsiders; I learned of them
accidentally during my fieldwork dealing with Dyngus Day and Kolędy
Night.

These Polish-American communal events are what Eric Hobsbawm has
called "invented traditions." He defines an invented tradition as a set
of practices, of a ritual or symbolic nature, which seeks to establish continuity with a suitable historic past.[2] Often, such traditions are invented during periods of rapid social change, which is the case with the
Polish-American traditions.

The urban Polish-Americans whom I studied share a cultural past that is agricultural and religious in nature. According to one man in his forties, Poland is "pretty much still a Catholic country. The one unique thing about growing up in a Polish neighborhood around a Polish church is that the church and all the things that connected with the church were like second nature to you. It was part of who you are. And so all the customs were connected to the church."[3]

Easter Customs

In Catholic communities, Easter and Christmas are preceded by Lent and Advent, respectively, periods of fasting, penance, prayer, and preparation. In peasant Poland, Lent, called *Wielki Post* (Great fast), was the time to eat fish rather than meat as well as a sour soup called *żur* made from fermented raw bread dough. By the end of Lent, peasants were so sick of the offensive żur that they buried the remaining soup and broke the pot.[4] In church, they attended Stations of the Cross and sang the Gorzkie Żale (Bitter Sorrows) hymn, the lamentations of the Passion of Christ and the sorrows of his mother, a Lenten observance that still continues in Polonia. They also continued a pagan springtime custom, the drowning of Marzanna, a figure representing Death that was braided from sheaves of grain into a human form. By drowning it in effigy, it was believed that Death would not visit the village that year.[5]

During the final week of Lent, Holy Week, Poles and Polish-Americans make preparations for Easter. Among them is a Good Friday tradition unique to Polish Catholic churches, a scene depicting the grave of Christ: "The people would bring their own flowers, the tulips, et cetera, around. It was like a wake, Friday after three o'clock through Saturday, until the Easter Mass of the Resurrection. So there were people there all the time, praying. You would have your guards there, altar servers, there would always be people on rotation there."[6] During Holy Week, Polish-American families often visit other churches to view the grave scenes there.[7]

People are also in church before Easter Sunday for another reason: the Holy Saturday custom of święconka—blessing Easter baskets filled with holiday food. This custom, with its origin in Poland, is still widely practiced in Polonia; in fact, since the 1980s it has spread to non-Polish parishes in western New York state.

The foods that are blessed include hard-boiled colored Easter eggs,

butter lambs, sausages, hams, coffee cakes and breads, and horseradish. Each item is of symbolic significance. The egg represents the renew-
al of life and the Resurrection. The lamb, of butter, cake, bread (or, in
Poland, roast lamb, sugar lambs, or molded plaster lambs), is the Pas-
chal lamb, the ancient sacrificial animal, and carries a red resurrection
banner symbolizing Jesus' victory over death. Sausages, hams, and other meats are emblems of prosperity; breads, coffee cakes, and sweets
represent the bread of the Eucharist; horseradish is a reminder of the
bitterness of Jesus' suffering; vinegar is symbolic of the gall given to him
on the cross; salt symbolizes hospitality and is a reminder that Catholics, as a result of baptism, are the salt of the earth; wine, represents the
blood of sacrifice; and newly sprouted greenery such as pussywillow,
flowers, boxwood and myrtle emerges from the death of winter just as
Jesus rose from the tomb.[8]

Families carry these items to church in wicker baskets covered with
white linen cloths, just as they did in the old country; children often
carry their own small baskets containing chocolate Easter candy, an
American variant. Depending on the parish, the priest may bless the
food either in the English or Polish language. First, he offers prayers
on the altar before coming down to sprinkle water on the baskets, either by walking down the aisles with the congregation remaining seated or by having parishioners line up to come forward for the blessing.
In most communities, the food is not eaten until after Resurrection Mass
the next morning.[9]

Easter Sunday is celebrated rather quietly. Families share a traditional meal and attend mass; fun, frolic, and visits with neighbors and friends
wait until the following day.[10] The Easter Sunday mass, known as Rezurekcja (the Mass of Resurrection), takes place at sunrise or, quite
commonly, on Holy Saturday evening. The church is filled with parishioners who participate in a procession, a hallmark of the Polish and
Polish-American Catholic faith: "All the little kids would have to be there
in their First Communion outfits. We'd all have to carry a lily and have
this big procession around the church with the statues, and the cross,
and the Blessed Sacrament, and go around and around, and be singing the Polish Easter hymns. They were really big for the processions.
And of course, everybody and his uncle would be in the procession
around the church, all the kids, and the ushers, and the sodalities, and
altar boys, and priests, the whole shebang."[11] Such processions also take
place in Poland on Palm Sunday, for First Communion, Corpus Christi

Sunday, and during the month of May, when the Virgin Mary, Poland's favorite saint, is honored.[12]

Traditional Easter hymns included "Wesoły nam dzień" (Christ the lord is risen), "Wstał Pan Chrystus" (Christ is risen), "Chrystus zmartwychwstan jest" (Christ the lord is risen), "Alleluja biją dzwony" (Alleluia rings triumphant), and "Zlóżcie troski" (Put aside your despair).[13] Unlike Polish Christmas carols, Easter hymns are sung primarily in church rather than at home. Fewer Polish-American church choirs perform them now, however, and the ones that do often sing them in English rather than Polish.

Following Rezurekcja, the family returns home to Easter morning breakfast, which features the blessed food.[14] In many families, the meal begins with the sign of the cross and a short prayer, such as the following, from the head of the household:

Panie Boże,
Błogosław nasze dary
Który będzemy spozwali
Przez Jezusce Chrystus
Amen.

(Dear God,
Bless our gifts
Which we are about to eat
Through Jesus Christ
Amen.)[15]

After the prayer, the patriarch or matriarch may share some of the blessed horseradish with each person because Jesus was given żółć (gall) when he was dying on the cross.[16] Alternatively, each family member shares a piece of the blessed hard-boiled egg while exchanging wishes for long life and happiness.

Of all the Easter foods, the egg is the most important to Polish-Americans, as it is in so many cultures around the world, as the symbol of renewed life. According to Venetia Newall, the egg figured prominently in early creation myths and in fertility cults from Christmas to the summer solstice.[17] She notes that egg games were played at Easter in Poland and were a part of courtship rituals until World War II.[18] Painted eggs were given as gifts in Central Europe; children would go out and ask for eggs, which Germans called *dingeier* (eggs that are owing).[19]

The Etymology of Dyngus Day

It is perhaps from the German word *dingeier*, or another German word *dingnis* (ransom), that the word *dyngus* is derived, although the etymology is obscure. A Polish-English dictionary suggests that "dyngus" is synonymous with *śmigus*, which means a dousing with water on Easter Monday.[20] Informants in the Buffalo area believe the word means "switch" or "a reed used in whipping."[21] A fine description of the event was offered at a Dyngus Day party in Buffalo by a middle-aged Syracuse, New York, man who was wearing a red and white hat adorned with pussywillow:

> Traditionally, Dyngus Day, better known as Dyngus Śmigus Day, is the Monday after Easter. According to ancient custom, the Monday after Easter, all the young men of a particular village would go around, they would take their pussywillows and swat the girls, and they would also either throw buckets of water or squirt perfume on the girls. I guess if you had a favorite girl and you would like to marry her, that is a sign of affection. Of course, then, the following day, the girls got their chance. They squirted water or perfume on the boys.[22]

Various theories explain the whipping and the dousing. Svatava Pirkova-Jakobson says one Slovakian informant in America told her the whipping was done "because we used to whip the Christ." Cezaria Jędrzejewicz offers an agricultural explanation for the dousing: It was necessary to ensure a good harvest.[23] I believe that the Dyngus whipping is related to a pagan Roman festival, the Lupercalia, a purification rite that took place on February 15, during the last month of the early Roman year. During the Feast of Lupercalia, men wearing only a loincloth ritually struck women with strips of skin from sacrificial goats, a ceremony thought to ensure fertility and an easy delivery.[24] Verification of any theory is extremely difficult; literacy did not emerge in Poland until well after the conversion to Christianity in 966 A.D.

Written sources trace the Dyngus switching custom back to the Middle Ages, women whipping husbands on Easter Monday and men lashing wives the next day, as a reminder of the prohibition on marital sex during the period of Easter communion.[25] Young people apparently carried things too far in fifteenth-century Poland, when the Bishop of Poznań issued a *"Dingus Prohibetur"* forbidding Poles to "pester or plague others in what is universally called *Dingus.* "[26] Despite the edict, the custom thrived among both peasants and nobility.

In some variants of the custom more recently, girls were obliged to give boys eggs in return. Slovakian boys received painted eggs after whipping girls.[27] In other versions, hard-boiled eggs, coffee cakes, or other Easter foodstuffs were offered to the boys.[28] One informant, a cofounder of Buffalo's Dyngus Day parties, noted that Dyngus was the day when Poles opened their homes to visitors and their tables were laden with food as a sign of hospitality.[29]

Young boys in particular visited neighboring homes in Poland and Polish-American towns in noisy processions known as *chodzenie po dyngusie* (going on the Dyngus).[30] Hauling a small, two-wheeled cart bearing a live rooster, the boys would proceed from cottage to cottage, crowing like roosters and singing songs that offered good wishes and requests for gifts and food. On Dyngus Day, some also dressed as bears, the animal believed by Poles to bring good crops and cure illnesses.[31]

The Easter whipping custom still exists in Central Europe; László Lukács cites variants in Poland, Hungary, and Germany.[32] Whipping and other Dyngus Day customs are seldom observed in the older Polish communities of the United States, some of which date from the 1880s. Water splashing, however, is still done as a joke in southern Ontario, where a more recent group of Polish immigrants has settled.[33]

There is, however, one striking exception: Chet Tarnowski, a county legislator in his seventies who dresses like a clown to carry on his late father's tradition of "whipping the girls." The Tarnowski family tradition, an example of what Richard Dorson calls the "private face" of ethnicity, used to be observed strictly in their Polish neighborhood in Dunkirk, New York, a small town fifty miles southwest of Buffalo.[34] Around 1965, however, when women began to work outside the home and Tarnowski took over his father's route alone, he modified it by going downtown to various banks, the newspaper, a nursing home, and city hall, conducting some business for the county legislature while garbed in a Harpo Marx costume. This was an update of his father's "immigrant" outfit that featured patched clothing and an old hat. Moving with lightning speed, at each stop he greets the woman with "Happy Dyngus Day, honey!" while lightly switching her lower leg with the pussywillow branch and occasionally stopping to chat. Afterward, Tarnowski heads for his brother's house, where a lunch featuring Polish Easter foods awaits him. His female victims, generally not of Polish descent, are amused but mystified by his tradition. Although he would like others to perpetuate it after he is gone, he admits that even his own adult sons will not accompany him on his Dyngus Day rounds.[35]

The Dyngus Day Party

Dyngus Day parties in Buffalo enjoy enormous popularity and attract several thousand people each year. True to Eric Hobsbawm's definition of "invented tradition," a party uses some ancient materials—pussywillow and folk costumes—to construct invented traditions for novel purposes.[36]

As with the British invented traditions cited by Hobsbawm, there was a break in continuity with respect to Buffalo's Dyngus Day observances. The old neighborhood whipping custom had died out by the time the Chopin's Singing Society party was created in 1962. The party's founders, Buffalo judge Ann Mikoll; her husband Ted, a lawyer; and his brother, James, decided that the society, a Polish cultural organization, needed to boost its declining membership. According to Ann Mikoll, her husband said, "Wouldn't it be great to bring back the spirit of fun and getting together the day after Easter, and have a grand old party?" So they began.

In the party's early years, the food, excluding drinks, was free. Businesses donated hams and sausages, and bakeries and singing society members baked breads. Later, as the event began to attract upward of three thousand, tickets were sold for the buffet meal. Other social clubs, churches, and taverns—some not run by Polish-Americans—soon followed Chopin's lead, selling tickets to what one major organizer calls in disgust merely a "moneymaker" by tavern-keepers unconcerned about the holiday's ethnic origins.[37] According to one estimate, there are twenty different parties in Buffalo and its suburbs on Dyngus Day, most starting early in the afternoon and lasting until the wee hours of the following morning.[38]

Chopin's Singing Society, which sets itself apart from later imitators by reminding all that it was the originator of the Dyngus Day party, presents a carefully crafted expression of Polish-American identity for the event, offering an opportunity for in-group bonding and a chance for outsiders, as Olivia Cadaval has noted in discussing Latino festivals, to experiment with another culture.[39]

Chopin's party features a number of elements, among them local dignitaries such as the Irish-American mayor and the Polish-American county executive, who officially sanction the event by giving short speeches.[40] During the lunch hour, many community leaders, judges, and aspiring politicians of all ethnic backgrounds find their way to Chopin's to socialize, a feature not found at the other Dyngus Day parties and a reflection of the leading role the society's membership plays in the community's political life. Not all politicians appear willingly, however; one retired Polish-American judge told me that his family considered the traditional Dyngus Day whipping barbaric and he appeared at the party only when he campaigned for office.[41]

Other elements of Chopin's party include the presence of a leading Polish-American priest who performs the święconka blessing in Polish before the food is consumed; spring flowers and pussywillow for sale at a flower stall reminiscent of those in Warsaw, another link to the old country; and young, costumed folk dancers, a reminder of the party's appeal to all ages. There are also Polish folk songs and American patriotic songs, ties to both America and Poland, performed by the Chopin Singers for both the crowd and the media. In common with all the other Dyngus Day parties, there is polka music and dancing, reflective of the Polish-*American* rather than the *Polish* heritage, as Charles Keil and several interviewees have pointed out.[42]

One organizer believes that the key to a successful Dyngus Day party is picking the right entertainment: polka bands that make people want to dance and lyrics sung in English rather than Polish.[43] That appeals to polka music's wide audience, which includes, according to the president of a polka booster club, those of not only Polish descent but also Italians, Germans, Irish, and others.[44]

Unlike a traditional neighborhood Dyngus Day of the 1940s, when Polish was spoken, party participants now converse in English, and nearly 60 percent of the polka lyrics are in English as well.[45] Both polka musicians and their audiences acknowledge a limited facility in the language, although those who are middle-aged or older may have studied Polish in parochial school and younger adults may have taken a formal Polish-language course in college. When songs at polka dances or Catholic masses are sung in Polish, most often they are sung phonetically.[46]

Another important element is the traditional food, a significant and emotional way of celebrating ethnicity and group identity. Festivals such as Dyngus Day and restaurants are two arenas in which Americans can taste food across cultural boundaries, thus experimenting with crossing those boundaries in a safe manner.[47] The singing society's party features a wide array of Polish Easter foods: ham, Polish sausage, hard-boiled eggs, lazy pierogi (a noodle-based casserole dish), breads and Polish coffee cakes, salads, cakes, and cheesecakes. Other parties offer either a more limited menu—Polish sausage is generally featured—or drinks only.

In addition to traditional foods, special clothing and other visual elements make a statement about ethnic identity. Party-goers often wear clothing in the Polish colors, red and white: Dyngus Day buttons and T-shirts, "Polka Maniac" headbands sold by various party sponsors, red and white bowties, and hats. Other visual elements include banners saying *witamy* (welcome); red and white balloons; Happy Dyngus Day signs in English; and the flags of Poland, America, Canada, or the sponsoring organization. All promote group identity. According to one organizer, "That's our logo: 'Polka Pals' with the eagle, the crown, and 'Buffalo, New York' on it. Anybody that sees that flag or the shirts that we wear, they know they're in for a good time."[48]

As in peasant Poland's *"po dyngusie"* (going on the Dyngus) celebration, contemporary American Dyngus Day revelers travel from party to party. Polka musicians who have the day off join local residents and busloads of tourists from other cities in the northeastern United States and Canada. Unlike the planners of the Chopin's party, who are intent on maintaining their heritage, tourists are seeking something else: "They're not looking at this as cultural anthropologists. They get on those buses, and the vodka's open by nine o'clock. I'm not saying they're rabble-rousers, but they party!"[49]

The immediate future of the Dyngus Day party "invented tradition" seems promising. Buffalo's major parties each draw upward of seven hundred people of all ages annually; Syracuse held its first party in 1993 with 650 people in attendance and has continued to match that figure in subsequent years; Chicago began a similar party in the early 1990s; and South Bend, Indiana, has held Dyngus Day parties similar to Chopin's for many years.[50] Since the 1990s, the news media in Buffalo have devoted increasing amounts of time or space to Dyngus Day; one year, a major AM radio station and the daily newspaper debated the merits of the various parties.[51]

Święconka Meals in Social Clubs

Media attention is absent from the private, communal side of the Polish-American Easter celebration, the social clubs' święconka. With its origin in the family święconka, a club event is for members only, often free of charge, and usually held on Holy Saturday afternoon or evening but occasionally at other times during the week before or after Easter. According to one man, there is a marked difference between this święconka and the Dyngus Day party: "The święconka is more of a holy ritual. You've been giving up everything for Lent. So come Easter Sunday, it's the Polish sausage, the pork, ham, the eggs. Everything is blessed. It's almost like the start of a new Christian year. It has a deeper meaning as far as your religion goes."[52]

The format of the święconka is more fluid than a Dyngus party. A priest may be present to bless the Easter food, but that is optional; recorded polka music may be playing softly in the background, but there is no band. Like the Dyngus party, drinks are sold at a bar and Polish Easter food is featured. Foods not normally served to outsiders may also be served: a creamy soup called *barszcz*, which includes cut-up sausage, ham, eggs, the water in which the sausage was cooked, and other ingredients from the Easter meal, and *czarnina*, a soup made of duck's blood, duck meat, noodles, and prunes.[53]

Polish-American social clubs have held these święconkas for many years as an occasion for expressing group solidarity, but since the 1970s there has been an additional reason: changes in the American family.

GERALDINE ZIEGLER: See, a lot of these men don't have families [in town], so they'll do the święconka here.

SILVERMAN: That's interesting. In the old days they all had their families around them, the kids stayed in town, so it was different in that way.

ZIEGLER: Right, like me. My family is, they're all out of town, so there's nobody. I have one daughter here with grandchildren, but other than that we don't even have the święconka. They all go their own ways once they're married.[54]

Rather than abandon the święconka tradition, the older adults continue it in the group setting. This phenomenon is reminiscent of the elderly East European Jews in California who re-created parts of their shtetl lifestyle in their Jewish Center.[55]

4

THE CHRISTMAS CYCLE AND
MINOR HOLIDAYS

Gdy się Chrystus rodzi,
I na świat przychodzi.

(Christ the king is born,
On an early morn.)
—"Gdy Się Chrystus Rodzi," a Polish Christmas carol

A Polish-American social club swięconka is similar in function to another social club event held at Christmas, the wigilia. Like the Easter swięconka, the wigilia originated in Poland as a family gathering, a meatless evening meal as required by the Catholic Church on Christmas Eve, a day of fasting and abstinence.

The wigilia in Poland would begin when the first star was sighted in the sky, an event calculated to keep the children busy looking outside and out of mother's way.[1] A Polish-American priest noted that it resembled a Passover meal in some respects because there would be an empty place at the table for a guest: "You always welcomed someone to the table. You know, a guest in the house is Christ in the house, and so the idea was, if a guest came, you invited Christ to the table."[2]

Often a place would be set at the table for a recently deceased family member, or, because this was a time when the dead returned to earth, food would be left out all night.[3] It was important to set the table for an even number of people, otherwise a guest would die during the coming year.[4] A Polish woman who emigrated to the United States in 1976 at age seventeen recalled her family's wigilia:

GABRIELLE MERTA: What we did is, we put the tablecloth on. Under the tablecloth there was straw, and there was money.

SILVERMAN: Money!

MERTA: The straw was for a good harvest and the money for a prosperous year. Then we made the food. We had kasha with mushrooms, we had mushroom soup, the dark mushroom soup, we had fish, you had your *opłatki* [communion-like wafers].[5] The opłatki, everyone had a piece and we started out from the oldest person in the family to the youngest person. You had your pierogi, you had your *kopitka*.

SILVERMAN: What's kopitka?

MERTA: Kopitka is, you take your mashed potatoes, you add some flour to it, eggs, and you make like a roll, you roll them out, and you cut small pieces and you boil it. That's kopitka. You can add filling to it if you want. We didn't. What else did we have? Let's see. You had your bread.

SILVERMAN: Did you have a certain number of foods?

MERTA: Twelve.

SILVERMAN: Was there a reason for that number?

MERTA: For the twelve apostles, we had the twelve foods, because according to the Bible, they did bring the food to the table. Everyone brought the food to the table.[6]

According to most other interviewees, straw or hay would be placed under the tablecloth because Jesus was born in a manger.[7] In some homes, a garlic bulb, good for curing a headache or cough, was placed within the hay.[8]

Central to the meal was the opłatek, the communion-like wafer blessed by the parish priest and sold by the church organist. The head of the household, moving around the table from eldest to youngest, would offer a greeting to each, such as "a życzię cię, szczęście zdrowia" (wishing you good luck and good health), while breaking off a piece of the wafer. The person then ate the wafer while blessing himself or herself, the same as receiving communion in church.

The number of dishes at the wigilia would vary depending on how many items a family could afford to prepare, but the food represented a harvest of fields, orchards, vegetable gardens, forests, and streams.[9] Although Gabrielle Merta's family served twelve kinds of food, most households prepared an odd number; seven, nine, or eleven dishes were the most common, based on the belief that an odd number allowed for the possibility of increase.[10]

The pierogi at an old country wigilia were filled with cheese, cheese and mashed potatoes, sauerkraut, prunes, or blueberries and cherries; the fish was generally herring (*śledzie*), pickled either in a wine or cream sauce. Occasionally, boiled, baked, or creamed pike or trout would be served. There also might be sweet and sour cabbage, *kapusta* (sauerkraut, mushroom, and kasha soup), barszcz (beet soup), mushrooms in butter, sauerkraut with dried peas, and other vegetables topped with browned buttered bread crumbs; various desserts such as cheesecakes, coffee cakes (especially poppyseed coffee cake, *strucel z makiem*), and *nalesniki* (filled pancakes) completed the meal.[11]

Christmas Eve in the old country is recalled as a magical evening, an auspicious time to ensure fertility on the farm.[12] None of the special holiday foods were wasted:

> STEPHANIE ROZEN: After we finish, whatever is left over, we go to the barn and give to each cow a little eat, whatever to finish. The cows never go to sleep until they finish our food, like what's left over.
>
> SILVERMAN: What do they usually have? Pierogi?
>
> ROZEN: Yeah, same like I do.
>
> SILVERMAN: Is there anything they would like more than other foods?
>
> ROZEN: Yeah, they got what they call *kasza*, I don't know how you say it. . .
>
> SILVERMAN: Is that like buckwheat?
>
> ROZEN: Yeah, they got those, and cabbage, and all kinds, different stuff than we got because we can't find that over here.
>
> SILVERMAN: Did you feed the opłatek to the animals, too?
>
> ROZEN: Yeah! We give a piece of opłatek, and what's left over at every plate, we put on one big plate and we go from cow to cow. Each cow got a little bit. They don't go to sleep, they stay and they wait for the opłatek and they take it and then they lay down and they sleep after that! And on the next day [after] Christmas, they call it Święty Stefan [St. Stephen's Day, December 26], then we give the horse the opłatek. We go to the barn, we bring in the horse into the house, and we give it the opłatek, and he's going around, and that mean we are supposed to be healthy like the horse. And early in the morning, everybody wash their face with a silver dollar, I mean *złoty*, so you got a face, complexion, you got no pimple.[13]

Rivers and lakes were believed to possess healing properties on Christmas Eve; it was thought that dipping an affected body part into the water while the bells pealed for midnight mass would induce a cure.[14] There also were other special procedures to be followed on Christmas Eve:

> STEPHANIE ROZEN: After we eat supper in Poland, we go outside, and we go knock every tree with a baseball [bat], and we say, "Are you gonna have fruit enough? Or we gonna cut you up?" There were so many things. We go to

a pig in Poland, we knock it with a baseball, if the pig's head bounces on it, that means the boyfriend's gonna come, you're gonna get married.

SILVERMAN: Okay, go on with that. What do the young girls believe about boyfriends at Christmas?

ROZEN: They bring in wood in the house, and they say, "Pair and a pair." If there's one [stick of wood] left, she's gonna be an old lady [old maid].[15]

Another woman, who emigrated to America in 1914 at age thirteen after working on farms in Germany and Denmark, recalled that after the "pair and a pair" custom, girls in Poland would go outside to listen to barking dogs. The sound would indicate the direction from which a future beau would come. The entire family also would try to predict the coming year's harvest by tossing rye behind the beams in the house; if a lot of the rye remained there it would be a good year.[16]

Afterward, Polish Christmas carols called *kolędy* would be sung before the family went to Pasterka (Shepherds' Mass), the midnight mass attended by all except the youngest children, the infirm, and the elderly. Even now in Poland, midnight mass, like the Easter Resurrection Mass, is a lengthy service accompanied by the blowing of trumpets, fire sirens, and church bells to welcome the birth of Christ. Like Easter Sunday, Christmas Day itself is a time to be spent quietly with the family, but in the following days costumed entertainers would visit homes. According to Gabrielle Merta, "When I was growing up, we had people going door to door during Christmas. Guys dressed up in all kinds of funny costumes and they were going door to door, especially where there were girls. They were kissing the girls, getting them all dirty. And of course you had to put the vodka on the table and some food and stuff. And they were celebrating, singing Christmas carols. It was beautiful." The custom died out after Poland's riots of 1974 "because there was a lot of drinking, and a lot of guys just fell asleep with the cold weather, and they didn't make it [to the caroling]."[17]

Adaptation and Change in Polonia's Christmas Celebrations

Polish-American families still hold Christmas Eve wigilias; in fact, the wigilia and the Easter swięconka continue to be the most popular traditions. As could be expected, however, there have been many adaptations in response to the urban New World environment. Gone are the fortune-telling among the young girls and the post-wigilia visits to the orchard and barn to invoke fertility. The table is still set for an even number of guests, but with a modern twist:

> EMILY BORUSZEWSKI: One year there was only eleven of us after my husband died, and I said to my daughter Sandy, "Maybe I'm superstitious." She had a blow[-up] doll, she blew that up and put it on the chair . . .
>
> SILVERMAN: To make it the extra person so you'd have an even number? [Laughs.]
>
> BORUSZEWSKI: Right! [Laughs.] I don't know if that makes any sense. I don't think anyone has done what my daughter did, blowing up a doll! But that's what she did to make me feel like I shouldn't worry about the following year.[18]

Straw or hay is still frequently placed under the tablecloth in Polonia, but a few wisps may be taken from the church's manger scene: "As a matter of fact, what we were doing in some cases was actually tying up some of the straw with ribbons, because people were ripping it right out of the church crib," recalls Robert Hora.[19]

The opłatek is still sold by Polish-American churches, but by nuns rather than the organist as well as by Polish-American markets such as Buffalo's Broadway Market and by mail from Polish-American newspapers. The wafer is commonly mailed to relatives who will be absent from the wigilia table, a custom that became widespread after the period of mass migration from Poland.[20] The greeting usually is in English now, unless the head of the household is a Polish immigrant whose family speaks Polish.

Families still serve the traditional foods, but they make shortcuts in food preparation, a response to the large number of women working outside the home. According to one Buffalo woman in her late fifties, "I hear from some of my friends, what they do is they'll order their fish ready-made. See, I still buy it and bread it and fry it. But they'll go to Long John Silver, and when it's ready to eat, just come home with a batch of fish."[21]

Other women purchase their breads and coffee cakes at a Polish-American bakery and pierogi at a supermarket or an ethnic market such as the Broadway Market. They may also substitute quicker-to-prepare ingredients such as canned poppyseed filling for the time-consuming homemade mixture used in poppyseed coffee cake. A number of families I interviewed have dropped herring and other fish dishes from the menu in response to individual family preferences, but the meal remains meatless.

New items also are making a debut on a "hybridized" wigilia menu. An Italian-American daughter-in-law, for example, may bring a vegetable casserole that still fulfills the meatless requirement, or an American-style macaroni salad or potato casserole may be served. Many varieties of Christmas cookies, an American addition to the Yuletide season by way of Western Europe, appear alongside or in place of Polish coffee cakes and pancakes.

For those whose families live far away, a social club wigilia for members only is a comfortable substitute which, like the club święconka, emphasizes identification with the ethnic group. The menu, however, may depart from the traditional meatless meal by offering ham, sausage, and czarnina soup in response to the membership's food preferences.[22] Club wigilias are generally held early on Christmas Eve afternoon so as not to interfere with club members' other holiday plans with friends or neighbors.

Kolędy Night

The public counterpart to a club wigilia is a relatively new "invented tradition," the Kolędy Night, which like the Dyngus Day party is another carefully crafted public expression of ethnicity. It is an evening featuring the singing of Christmas kolędy. In Poland as in other countries, caroling door to door was very popular throughout the Christmas season; costumed actors often presented plays in tandem with the caroling as they were *chodzenie po kolędzie* (going caroling), a continuation of the old caroling tradition of pagan times.[23]

In Polish-American communities earlier in the twentieth century, kolędy were sung in homes, social clubs, and churches. According to a forty-five-year-old accordion player, "Everyone grew up knowing the Polish kolędy. You learned them from the nuns, the schools and church. Maybe you didn't know what you were singing, but you knew what the carol was about and how to pronounce the words and sing it."[24]

In Poland today, an estimated four hundred carols exist, but only seventy-six of them are still in circulation.[25] The carols originated from two sources in sixteenth-century Poland: *pieśni* (religious songs about Jesus' birth), which were sung on Christmas Day, and secular "greeting" songs sung on New Year's Day and called "kolędy" from the Latin word *calendae* (time, especially the first day of the month).[26] Eventually, that distinction disappeared, and both types of songs were sung during the Christmas season. A folk-Christian carol repertoire evolved featuring pastorales, products of the Church that were popular throughout Polish society, and folk carols derived from oral tradition. The emphasis in these carols is not on a return to the chaos of the mystical beginning of the universe but on a new, cosmic harmony.[27]

Both Polish and Polish-American choral and instrumental groups have recorded many albums featuring popular kolędy. Whenever I asked informants to sing their favorite Polish carols, those who felt comfortable performing generally sang a verse before pausing to find an album or sheet music to bolster their memory.[28] These cherished books and other artifacts of tradition are, as Richard Dorson has noted with respect to the urban folklore of Gary, Indiana, items of "talismanic character" in ethnic homes, bridging the gap between old country and new.[29]

Among the most popular kolędy in Polonia are "Bóg Się Rodzi" (The lord is born), "Wśród Nocnej Ciszy" (In the stillness of the night), "Dzisiaj w Betlejem" (Today in Bethlehem), "Gdy Się Chrystus Rodzi" (When Christ is born), "Lulajże Jezuniu" (Hush, little Jesus), and "Pójdźmy Wszyscy Do Stajenki" (Let's all go to the stable). These carols were cited repeatedly by informants and appear most often on recordings, song sheets distributed at Christmas gatherings in Polonia, and in Polish-American newspapers such as the *Polish American Journal,* which annually urges readers to learn the Polish lyrics as a means of preserving their heritage.[30]

These kolędy and others also were sung in Polish-American taverns until the late 1980s. The taverns would hire a polka band and then break for the singing of kolędy in Polish and American carols in English. To jog people's memories, the Polish lyrics would be handwritten on big placards and the violin player would use his bow to point to the words to encourage the crowd to sing.[31]

Kolędy Night, re-created in Buffalo in 1991 by a polka band leader and polka booster group, was an effort to fill the void left by the demise of the old tavern tradition. "You can hear all the kolędy you want now on the radio," says the band's leader, "but it's a real community thing for everybody to get together and sing them. I think that's why people come out."[32] A polka booster group in New York state's Mohawk Valley hosts a similar event.[33]

Like the Dyngus Day party, Buffalo's Kolędy Night has distinctive elements: the singing of both kolędy in Polish and American carols in English, with polka music before and after; a Polish-American priest who blesses the opłatki, which are then shared by the crowd; a *szopka* (manger scene), set up in the corner, reminiscent of the szopka carried door to door in the *Jaselka* (Nativity) plays performed by groups at Christmas in Poland; colorful costumed entertainers dressed as a Christmas tree or Santa Claus, who, unlike their Polish counterparts, do not perform a play; a wandering band, including a violin, concertina, accordion, trumpet, and clarinet, which strolls through the party performing kolędy, much like the roving bands of old Poland; the donation of food for the poor; and small gifts on the Christmas tree for the children in attendance. Unlike the wigilia, no Christmas Eve foods are served; there are drinks and snacks only.

Because there are so few Kolędy Night events and the practice is of recent origin, it is too early to predict whether they will become as firmly entrenched as Dyngus Day parties, but the first several events averaged five hundred people each, which has encouraged organizers to continue.

Minor Holidays in Polonia

The Christmas season in Poland would officially continue for several more weeks with celebrations of lesser importance. January 6, for example, was called Trzech Króli (Three Kings' Day). In peasant Poland and in America's immigrant communities as well, it was a day for baking: "They make like a bread, and they make like a horseshoe. Yeah, they make like a horseshoe. And the kids go and collect those. They call them *szczodraki.*"[34] The practice no longer exists in Polonia.

Another custom was the inscription of the three kings' initials over a doorway. In Poland, the parish priest comes to the house with blessed chalk to inscribe the new date and "K+M+B" (Kaspar, Melchior, and Balthazar) over the door:

GABRIELLE MERTA: He had incense, but that was years ago. But now, he just brings holy water. At first the boys come and they ring the bell, that the priest is coming. And they stand by your house, that this is the next house. And then the priest comes in with the organist from the church.

SILVERMAN: The priest and the organist. And so they come in with the holy water and the chalk?

MERTA: Yup. And if you want, you say a couple of prayers, you say your "Our Father" and "Hail Mary," and he blesses your house, he blesses you, and then you give him the money and he goes.[35]

In Polish-American communities, homeowners themselves would inscribe the initials over the door with chalk that had been blessed in church "so the evil spirits wouldn't go near you."[36] Eventually, however, both the informant and her parents discontinued the practice in America: "I didn't believe in that, really. I thought if you were a Christian and you believed in the Lord, you didn't put all those spooks and stuff up there over the doors." It is a practice that has virtually disappeared, although a Polish-American folk artist who travels to various ethnic festivals sells Three Kings' Day kits intended to spur interest in Polish heritage and complete with bits of gold, myrrh, and incense (the kings' gifts to Jesus), chalk, charcoal, and a brief history of the custom.[37]

The final celebration during the Christmas season occurs on February 2, known in Polish as Matka Boska Gromniczna (Mother of God of the Blessed Thunder Candle). As in other European countries, that day, Candlemas Day, was traditionally devoted to the blessing of candles in church, a practice dating to the eleventh century in the Catholic faith.[38] On that day, Poles brought candles decorated with ribbons or liturgical symbols to church to be blessed by the priest. Afterward, these *gromnice* (from *grom*, meaning "thunder") were used in homes to protect a dying person from Satan or as an aid in the ritual "cleansing" of a new mother forty days after the birth of her child. The candle's most important function, however, as suggested by its name, was to protect a house from lightning and thunder; nineteenth-century prayer books contained special prayers used during thunderstorms.[39]

As in America, the day also was a time for predicting the weather via such proverbs as "gdy na Gromniczną mróz, szykuj chłopie wóz; a jak lanie to sanie" (if there's frost on Candlemas, prepare the wagon; if rain, the sleigh). Rather than the groundhog, Poles of the Tarnów-Rzeszow region watched the bear on February 2. If he came out of his lair and found frost, he would tear it apart because winter would be ending soon. If the day were damp, he would come out and "mend" it because winter would linger.[40]

The belief in the effectiveness of gromnice persisted for many years in Polonia, particularly among immigrants and their children who continued to keep the candles in their homes. More important, Matka Boska Gromniczna officially ended the Christmas season, and Polish-Americans turned to the pre-Lenten gaiety of *karnawal* (carnival time), also known as *zapusty* (the empty days), when many marriages were celebrated. While the Polish nobility indulged in *kulig* (a sleigh-ride party) during this period, young peasant men continued to sport the animal costumes seen during the Christmas season, with the goat, bear, horse, and stork figuring as prominent fertility symbols.[41] This activity culminated on Shrove Tuesday, when costumed masqueraders dressed as old men and women, Jews, chimney sweeps, gypsies, and policemen formed processions through villages. "Accompanied by music, the procession was led by an individual cleverly disguised on a wooden horse. It was he who asked the homeowner if the group could enter. If the head of the house agreed, everyone entered. The musicians began to play a tune and the head of the house was required to dance with the masqueraders."[42]

After the peasant landowners provided food and drink, revelers would proceed to the next home. Late that evening, the group would continue on to a tavern or home for *podkoziołek*, a dance between single men and women that was a remnant of the ancient custom of buying the bride. Marriageable young men and women who had failed to choose a mate during the preceding courtship season were punished by having token logs, chicken feet, or herring bones pinned on their clothing.[43]

Large quantities of doughnuts also were eaten on Shrove Tuesday in Poland because they and other sweets would be taboo during Lent.[44] It is from this custom, the consumption of *pączki* (doughnuts), that the Polish-American holiday derives its name: "It's a doughnut, sure. You put milk, and flour, and yeast, and raise [it]. And after you make the dough, put the pieces, and when they grow, just throw them in the grease. I used to make them for the kids when they were small," Kate Moch remembered.[45] Both the doughnut-making and Pączki Day dances sponsored by clubs continue to thrive in Polonia.

In late spring, Poles observe the Catholic feast of Corpus Christi (Boże Ciało), which commemorates the Holy Eucharist, with a special procession.[46] In a custom widely practiced in Polish-American parishes until the 1950s but now rare, four portable altars, one for each of the four Gospels (Matthew, Mark, Luke, and John), are constructed. The altars are decorated with greenery, fresh flowers, and small herbal wreaths containing the first words of each Gospel reading. As at Easter, the entire community joins the priest in a celebration honoring the Eucharist, walking and singing as they move from altar to altar. At each location, the priest, bearing the monstrance, stops to give a Gospel reading that is followed by a special prayer for the intentions of parishioners. Incense also is dispensed. Then the group continues in similar fashion to the next altar before returning to the church.

Other Polish holidays have either been revived in Polonia or continue in attenuated form. In the mid–1980s, for example, Buffalo's Chopin's Singing Society reenacted a St. John's Eve (Świętojanki) celebration on the night of the summer solstice, June 23. In Poland, the holiday was derived from a Slavic pagan celebration honoring Kupala, the god of light, and featured dancing by young people around huge bonfires and *rzucanie Wianków*—young women throwing wreaths into a river to make predictions about their future marriages.[47]

In similar fashion, harvest festivals (*dożynki*) are re-created during August in farming communities such as in Florida, New York, known for its onion harvest and a harvest festival first presented in 1939. On August 15, the Feast of the Assumption (also known as Matka Boska Zielna, Our Lady of the Herbs), Poles and early Polish-Americans would carry a harvest wreath and various herbs and flowers to church to be blessed.[48] The custom is, however, no longer widespread among Polish-American parishes.

St. Andrew's Day (Świętego Andrzeja), on November 30, falls during Advent and is a fortune-telling holiday popular among young Polish girls and immigrants in Polonia.[49] "When I work in Pennsylvania," Kate Moch told me, "and there was fourteen girls work in the shop, all the girls, one girl took the shoe off, and they put them in a pile, and take one girl and tied her eyes [blindfolded her], and whose shoe got picked up first, she gonna get married first. I didn't believe it, but there was fourteen girls and they pick my shoe and, by God, I was married first!"[50]

In Poland, girls made predictions about future spouses from the shapes formed by pouring spoonfuls of melted wax on cold water or by preparing food for a dog. The girl whose morsel was first eaten would be first to marry.[51] Such fortune-telling methods, no longer practiced in Polonia, are being recalled in yet another kit that includes a sheet explaining the history of St. Andrew's Eve fortune-telling customs; wax hearts, a candle, a key, and foil for pouring wax; a walnut-shell game that predicts whether a player will enter religious life, remain single, or get married; and a walnut-shell "boat" with a small candle, which predicts whether the player will receive a marriage proposal from a particular individual during the coming year.[52]

Julianna Miga, a Polish immigrant, and her three daughters outside their home in the Polonia of Dunkirk, New York, in 1895. (Courtesy of Adriana Anders)

Święconka blessing, 1995. The Rev. P. Janaczek, pastor of St Hedwig's
Church in Dunkirk, New York, blesses food for the święconka at the
neighborhood's Polish-American club, the Kosciuszko Club.

Standing in front of his yard, Chet Tarnowski, of Dunkirk, N.Y., models his 1995 Dyngus Day costume.

Erie County, N.Y., executive Dennis Gorski, flanked by the Rev. David Bialkowski (at left) and members of Chopin's Singing Society, addresses Chopin's 1995 Dyngus Day gathering.

Clara Andrzejewski of Dunkirk,
N.Y., and the Three Kings' Day
inscription over her doorway, 1991.

A Corpus Christi procession in 1949 in the neighborhood of St. Hyacinth's Church
in Dunkirk, N.Y. (Courtesy of Monica Sekula)

First Communion, circa 1900. Photographs such as this of Valentine Gestwicki of Dunkirk, N.Y. (at left) and an unidentified relative were important in Polish-American First Communion rituals, even in families of modest means. (Courtesy of Clara Andrzejewski)

Parental wedding blessing for Daniel and Alice Kij (both kneeling) of Buffalo, N.Y., July 17, 1954. Alice Kij's parents, Apolonia and Frank Lasota, are at left; standing next to them are Daniel Kij's parents, Melanie and Joseph F. Kij, Sr. (Courtesy of Daniel Kij)

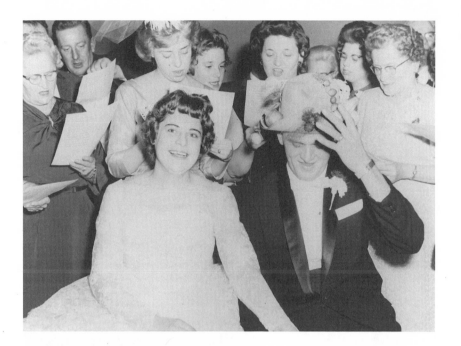

(Above) The oczepiny ceremony, including the placement of a vegetable hat on the groom, was performed at the 1963 wedding of Carol and Gerald Kozlowski of Dunkirk, N.Y. (Courtesy of Carol Kozlowski)

(Left) Florence Ruszaj of Forest-ville, N.Y., next to her yard shrine, which houses a statue of the Virgin Mary, in 1991. The shrine was created by her late husband, Alexander, during the 1940s. Fresh flowers and greens in the vases next to the statue are complemented by lilac bushes behind the shrine.

A picture of Our Lady of Częstochowa by Buffalo, N.Y. folk artist Joseph Mazur.

Lillian Halasinski and daughter Geraldine at home in 1996 with a photo album of their 1993 trip to Rome for the beatification of Mother Angela Truszkowska. The Vatican has certified that Lillian was miraculously cured of diabetic neuropathy by praying to Mother Truszkowska. As a result, Mother Truszkowska was beatified, the first step toward sainthood in the Roman Catholic faith.

5

RITES OF PASSAGE:
BIRTHS AND DEATHS IN
POLISH-AMERICAN COMMUNITIES

Jakie życie, taka śmierć.

(As life, so death.)
—Zand, *Polish Proverbs*

Births, marriages, and deaths are occasions for demonstrating kinship ties and ethnic group solidarity. Among Orthodox and Conservative Jews, for example, brides and grooms take their vows under a canopy (chuppah) traditionally made of white silk or satin and symbolic of the new husband's home.[1] Among Mexican-American families, an important rite of passage is the *quinceañera*, a celebration of a girl's fifteenth birthday that marks her entrance into adulthood and, similar to a wedding, often features a dinner, dance, and reception for many people.[2] Earlier in the twentieth century before the use of funeral homes became commonplace, friends and relatives would fill Italian-American homes where a death had occurred for a wake lasting two or three days; the body would be surrounded by mourners singing lamentations.[3] Food, known as *recuonzolo* (consolation), would be brought to the mourning family.[4]

Quite often these events also pose crises of identity, and for that reason they are intrinsically emotional, unlike seasonal festivals where the participants' energy levels must be raised.[5] Because they are moments of great anxiety, births, weddings, and deaths provide perfect opportunities for a folk community to educate an initiate, often through special rituals filled with songs, proverbs, and other narrative forms.[6] These social occasions, best described by Arnold van Gennep's 1907 term *rites of passage,* follow his tripartite form: separation, liminality, and reincorporation in the community. That structure is especially apparent in the Polish wedding tradition of the *oczepiny* (unveiling ceremony), which will be discussed in chapter 6.

"Each Year, a Prophet": Births in the Polish Family

Children, especially boys, were highly desired by peasant Polish parents. No matter how large the family, they trusted that the Almighty would provide: "Da Pan Bóg dzieci, da i na dzieci" (God gives children, he will give also for children).[7]

Given that perspective, it is no surprise that Poles in the old country held a complex web of beliefs regarding fertility. Nature provided signs of such good fortune. For example, if a spider plant (a houseplant) had white flowers on it, there would be either a wedding in the family or a baby would be born; there would also be a new baby soon if a stork flew over the house or the cherry tree blossomed.[8]

In an effort to conceive, a childless couple would try prayer, fasting, votive offerings, pilgrimages to holy places, or magic.[9] Various folk medicines also were employed, such as the herb *bylica* (mugwort, *Artemisia vulgaris*). If it was picked from the borders of nine different fields, it increased a woman's fertility.[10]

Many of these Polish folk beliefs persisted in American immigrant communities, although fewer women believed in them. One Polish-American woman, Martha Steffan, the daughter of immigrants, laughingly recalled the advice she had received more than sixty years earlier during her pregnancy:

> I was in the back shed, sitting on the steps, and I was cleaning my shoes. Up comes my neighbor, she takes my shoes away, and says, "You're not supposed to shine your shoes because the kid will be born without any legs!" So she took my shoes and she shined them. Then another time, I was sitting and I was tying my shoelaces, and she says, "You're not supposed to tie your shoelaces because you're going to tie your baby's tongue!"
> SILVERMAN: Don't tie your shoelaces. [Martha Steffan laughs.]
> STEFFAN: Oh, those superstitions were just terrible. You didn't dare move. And don't ever cross a fence. If you cross a fence, your kid will be born with a cord around its neck. [She laughs again.] I did all those things, and my daughter was born perfect.[11]

Many beliefs reflected great fear that a child would be born with birthmarks or other deformities. It was thought in Polonia that if a pregnant woman looked at an ugly baby her own child would be born ugly; if she looked at someone she disliked, the child would resemble that person; if another pregnant woman touched her, the child would be born with a birthmark shaped like a hand; and if water splashed on a mother-to-be, her baby would have a birthmark at the same spot on its body. In addition, pregnant women frightened by snakes would have children bearing birthmarks resembling a snake; if a woman were frightened by a fire and put her hand to her face, the baby would have a red birthmark on its face; and if a mother-to-be fell, her child would be born with a birthmark. Pregnant women should look at pictures of handsome or beautiful movie stars to ensure that their children will be equally attractive. Others were warned that sewing their own clothes or crossing their legs when seated would cause a difficult labor.[12]

Still other beliefs guarded against the death of the infant. It was considered bad luck to name a son after the father, because the infant would die. If a pregnant woman became a godparent her own child would be stillborn. The same thing would happen if she looked at a dead person. In addition, the baby should be kept at home until after the christening; otherwise it would die of some illness contracted outside the home.[13]

In Polonia's early days, midwives rather than doctors were used, both because they were less expensive and because they more closely resembled the Old World *baba,* an older woman who would attend the mother during delivery and for a few days afterward, serving as midwife, nurse, and housekeeper and later as a prominent participant at the baby's christening.[14] Some hardy Polish-American women eschewed all assistance during childbirth:

MARTHA STEFFAN: My mother always had guts, I'll tell you. We come home one day and there was a baby layin' on the bed.

My brother says, "Where the hell did that kid come from?"

I said to him, "How should *I* know?"

With that, my mother walks in with Doctor Sullivan, and he says, "Mary, Mary, what the hell's the matter with you, having a baby at your age! You ought to be ashamed of yourself!"

My mother had my brother Albert all by herself. She had tied the cord, took the afterbirth, buried it, she washed herself, washed the baby, changed the baby, walked to the corner, and got the doctor. And then on top of it all, eight days later the neighbor's wife had a baby, and she died. My mother used to go over there for two years and nurse that baby and nurse my brother.[15]

The infant generally was named after the Catholic saint whose feast day was being celebrated on the day of birth. In Poland and early Polonia, children celebrated their nameday (*imieniny*) rather than their birthday (*urodziny*).[16]

A christening was a festive, joyful occasion. In Poland, it used to be a large, lavish feast attended by the entire village and lasting several days, but since the World War II era it has been limited to one day, with only godparents, close relatives, and friends in attendance.[17] Polish-American christenings have likewise become smaller in scale, and godparents no longer are expected to serve as the child's patrons and protectors.[18]

The new mother in Polonia, like the initiates described by Arnold van Gennep, participated in rites of passage involving three phases. In the first phase, separation, she was physically separated from the community during childbirth, with the baba, and other women as her guides. The second phase, liminality, began with the birth of her infant and lasted until the christening. The next day, the final phase, reincorporation into the community, occurred through a Catholic rite called *do wywódu* (churching). This rite originated in the pagan past but was preserved by the Church in the Feast of the Purification of the Virgin Mary, forty days after Christmas.[19] One Polish-American couple recalled the practice:

DELPHINE JACOBS: The babies were always baptized on Sunday. Then the mother would go to church Monday morning, and when I was going to school, the mother would be in the back of the church in the last seat. And after mass, would the priest come, or just the altar boys? [Looks at her husband.]

FELIX JACOBS: The priest and one or two altar boys would walk with a candle and the holy water down the middle aisle after mass and go to that lady. And the priest would pray over her, well, he'd give her a candle . . .

DELPHINE: No, they escorted her down to the front.

FELIX: No, no. When I was going to St. Hyacinth's School, I had to go to church every morning. And the priest, after mass, would go into the sacristy and change, just have the surplice and the white smock. Then he'd walk down and he'd have the prayer book, and one altar boy would have the sprinkler, and the other altar boy would have the candle. Then they'd walk down, and they'd give her the candle . . .

DELPHINE: To the altar?

FELIX: No sir. After he sprinkled her and said some prayers, then she could come down to the front. She could not come down to the front of the church until she was cleansed. Then she walked down with the candle to the front seat.

SILVERMAN: Was this done to cleanse her from having a baby?

FELIX: Yes, because it was a sin to have intercourse.[20]

Once this purification was completed, the new mother was allowed to resume her normal activities within the community, having thus safely completed passage through the perils of childbirth. Now, the practice has largely been abandoned in Polonia.

First Communion

Although not celebrated with quite as much pomp by Poles and Polish-Americans, a child's First Communion is another rite of passage, this one a springtime event marking the entrance into the community of practicing Catholics as a communicant. As such, it is an occasion for religious ritual, elaborate costumes and photographs, and a celebratory meal second in importance only to baptism in a child's life. An immigrant recalled her First Communion in Poland in 1970, when she was in the fourth grade:

GABRIELLE MERTA: At six o'clock in the morning, the hairdresser comes in your house and does your hair, the mother's hair and the daughter's hair. Then you go to church for, say, eight o'clock in the morning. You walk to the church. You go to the church, and we all gather outside. And the priest that was our teacher gathered everybody outside to make sure everybody was there, and then *everybody* else got in church, the people. The children were still outside. And then everybody stood up, and the children walked in, through the middle of the church. And they all sat in the first few pews in front. Then we all got our First Communion, ourselves first, then the parents, then the rest of the church. Then you could go home. But in the afternoon you had to come back to take pictures.

SILVERMAN: That's different. Usually here they do it all at once.

MERTA: Oh, no. You had to come back in the afternoon. The photographer was there, and you could take pictures with everybody and the priest. I've got a picture with the pope that my mother once sent me.

SILVERMAN: That's nice! So did you have a party then?

MERTA: Oh, yeah, we had a big party. The godparents get together, the godmother always gives you the earrings, and the godfather gives you the watch. The rest of the family gives you money.[21]

In Polish-American families, the ritual has remained much the same for more than a century. The First Communion class walks in procession to the church for the mass, followed by a group photograph with the priest. Later in the day, a family party is held at the home and the child receives gifts of money.

"Old Age Is Not Joy, Death Is Not a Wedding": Funeral Customs in Polonia

Polish peasants approached old age and death with a measure of stoic resignation. They realized that this final, sometimes painful, phase of life was in accordance with God's will, as exemplified by a proverb: "Starość nie radość, śmierć nie wesele" (old age is not joy, death is not a wedding).[22] Ironically, although children were taught to respect old people, most elderly peasants depended upon their grown children for financial support because they had given all their property to their sons upon their marriages. *Dziad* (old man or grandfather) also is the word for beggar.[23]

Fear intermingled with respect for deceased ancestors permeated the Polish peasant's belief system, as noted in the discussion of the Christmas Eve custom of setting a place at the table for a dead relative (chapter 4). "They did believe in an awful lot of ghosts," remarked one immigrant in her eighties. "They believed that people presented themselves to them after they died, and they could see people, and they believed in that. But I never did. They had us scared."[24]

Despite their fears of poverty and the dead, aging Catholic peasants believed a normal death in the fullness of years was part of the life-cycle and, as their religion taught them, the gateway to a better world.[25] A number of beliefs and rituals aided in this transition. For example, Death (called Baśka in the Mazowsze region, Jagusia or Zośka in Kraków) was envisioned as a tall, thin woman draped in white, not malevolent and capable of being outwitted.[26] Her approach could be foretold. According to many Polish-Americans, if a dog howls, there will be a death in the neighborhood; if a bird hits your window or flies in, you will hear of a death; deaths occur in groups of three; if someone is laid out over a Sunday, two more deaths will follow; and if a window or mirror cracks, a death will occur.[27] If a picture falls off the wall, there will be a death in the home.[28] One recent immigrant recalled that belief in connection with her uncle's death: "My mother and I were sitting at home [in Poland], this was in '73, and a picture fell off the wall. It just fell off for no reason at all. I went to school the next day, and the mailman gave the kids the mail, always, at school, and we had a telegram. At that hour, this was at 3 o'clock in the afternoon, they had found my uncle. He hung himself. So I do believe in that stuff. I'm not superstitious, but I believe there's something that tells you when something's going to happen."[29]

If someone who is seriously ill hears knocking on a window, it is a sign of the person's impending death. That belief is reflected in another family narrative also told by Gabrielle Merta: "When my uncle was dying—my grandfather had died in Auschwitz—my grandmother was holding him on her lap, his head, and he says that Dad came. And he heard a knocking on the window. My grandmother heard the knocking on the window, but she didn't see nobody. And my uncle was telling her, 'Mother, it's Dad. He's telling me that I'm going to die. Something's going to happen with the number three.' He did die at 3 o'clock, March third."

Many Poles and Polish-Americans believe that a person who has just died will bid farewell to friends and relatives through various means. If, for example, you hear a knock at your door but no one is there, a family member or acquaintance has died and is saying goodbye.[30] A variant is that a door will swing open on its own: "I was sitting there and reading all by myself, and the door swung open like somebody shoved it open, and I had this weirdest sensation of my Aunt Marie being present, and it had nothing to do with the way it smelled or the way it felt. It was like, holy mackerel, Aunt Marie, what are you doing here? It was like, so overwhelming that she was present—and she was not close to me at all. And then it left, and we got a call that she had died. And that's a true story."[31]

Of greater concern to the dying person's immediate family were measures to ensure a comfortable departure from this world. In the old country, prayers were said so God would change the course of events or grant a speedy death; if there was a prolonged struggle with death, the family would pay to have the church bells rung, bells called *dzwonki za konajacych*. The pillow might be removed from under the head of a dying person, who might be placed on the ground to assist the soul in going underground.[32] A dying infant would be taken in its crib and placed with its head halfway out the door to start it on its way.[33]

These customs did not survive the journey to the New World, but others remain prevalent here. Polish-American families call the priest to the dying person to hear the final confession or administer the sacrament of extreme unction. The *gromniczna,* the candle blessed on February 2, is placed in the hand of the dying person to ease his or her agony, and the person's children and other relatives are at the bedside to bid farewell.[34]

At the moment of death, clocks are stopped so the soul can leave comfortably; mirrors are covered, because someone looking at one might see the dead person and thus cause another death; window shades are drawn and the picture of the deceased draped with black crepe.[35] To mark the home of the deceased in Poland, a black cloth or mourning banner was nailed to the front of the house. In early Polonia, however, a wreath of flowers called *gaza* was placed on the front door.[36]

In both Poland and the United States until the 1950s, the deceased was bathed and embalmed at home because there were no funeral parlors. The body would be laid out in a fine coffin, with a rosary and prayerbook or a crucifix placed in the folded hands. Generally, there would be a three-day lapse between the death and the funeral, perhaps because Jesus was laid out in a tomb for three days before his resurrection.[37] In other cases, however, the three-day rule would be suspended. "The art of embalming wasn't too good in those days, so you couldn't afford it. If the person died of some disease, you didn't hold him any too long," one Polish-American man recalled of funerals here when he was young.[38]

Generally, the body would be laid out at home until the funeral. A wake, or *pusta noc* (empty night), would be observed.[39] "The last night, everybody stayed up to watch the person, the last day," Alton Nowak recalled. "Everybody stayed awake. See, they didn't leave the body in the funeral parlor, nobody wanted to leave the body in the front room of the house alone, so the company just sat there and drank and talked or played cards or something. You stayed there all night long until the priest came over in the morning."[40]

If the deceased person were a man, men kept the wake; if a woman or child, women or men kept it.[41] In Poland, but not in Polonia, photographs were taken of the deceased person in the casket, a custom described by one Polish-American as "gruesome": "I mean, here my mother gets a big thick letter from Poland, she gets all excited and opens it up, and finds out that there's all these pictures in there of her father laying in a casket. That's got to be a shocker. But she says that they do that."[42]

In both Old World and New, however, a formal leave-taking would occur on the morning of the funeral. All the mourners would gather at the home to bid a final farewell to the deceased before the coffin was closed. Starting with friends and distant relatives, they would go up one by one to offer a parting word or touch a hand. Brothers or sisters would be next, followed by the children and, finally, the spouse.[43] The custom still continues in Polonia, but at funeral homes.

Afterward, a funeral procession forms to take the body to church for a Requiem Mass, on foot if the church is nearby or by wagon (in earlier times) or automobile today. In peasant Poland only, as soon as the coffin was on the wagon, all the doors and windows of the home were flung open to give the dead a last chance to view the home and ensure the soul was not shut in. All would be closed again as soon as the funeral cortege started so the soul would not come back, allowing the surviving spouse to marry again.[44]

Both in the old country and in early Polonia mourners wore white, as one Polish-American woman recalled: "When my father died, I was eight years old. Four of us children—I was the second-born—we were all dressed in white dresses and walked in the funeral procession from our street to the church to the cemetery. We wore white, not black."[45]

The Requiem Mass would be sung if the family could afford it; otherwise there would be silence followed by the procession to the cemetery. In Poland the procession featured a pause at a wayside shrine or the crossroads leading out of the village for the *odpraszanie* or *przemowa pożegalna* (goodbye or forgiveness speech). It was given by a respected individual on behalf of the deceased, asking for forgiveness of any transgressions that person may have committed.[46] In Polish-American communities, the speech was replaced by the priest's final prayers over the deceased at the cemetery chapel before burial.

Until recently in Polonia, the body was lowered into the prepared grave while mourners wept and sang the funeral hymn "Witaj, Królowo Nieba" (Hail, queen of heaven). Then the priest would sprinkle a little soil over the grave, saying, "Niech mu ziemia bedzie lekka" (may the earth bear lightly on him). Friends and, in some regions, the immediate family follow suit.[47] Afterward, all would depart, saying, "Zostancie z Bogiem" (remain with God).[48] Today, the final leave-taking occurs either at the mass or at the cemetery chapel.

For the immigrant families, burial in the United States was considered to be in alien soil; even now there are accounts of relatives bringing Polish soil back to be sprinkled over the graves of immigrants.[49] For that reason, the *stypa* (funeral meal) that followed the burial was rather brief and somber in early Polonia, not filled with music, singing, and even dancing as in peasant Poland.[50] As Helen Stankiewicz Zand has observed, "Bereavement was more real here [in America], the widowed wife or husband had not the clan, the community and the land to count on as in Europe; death of the provider or of the mother was often prelude to tragedy and felt as such."[51]

Still, the stypa is a ritual meal that is as elaborate as a family can afford as a sign of respect and honor to the dead. In peasant Poland, it was a feast featuring a freshly killed pig, calf, or geese along with the traditional foods served at funeral feasts and the Feast of All Souls: peas (*pecak*) and noodles prepared with poppy seeds and honey (*lazanki*).[52] There also might be *kasza,* a porridge of rye or barley, with honey poured over it. Vodka with honey would be passed around while people uttered "may he rest in peace."[53] In Polish-American communities, various luncheon foods such as sausage, ham, scalloped potatoes or other hot potato casseroles, tossed salads, cakes, pastries, and coffee are served buffet-style, either at the home of the deceased or, more commonly, at a restaurant. As the mourners eat, they speak of the person who has died, always in positive terms, such as "a good man, may God give him rest."[54]

The period of mourning in Polonia, as in Poland, is generally a year; after that a widow or widower may marry without criticism from the community. Exceptions to that rule are made, however, in the case of a widower with young children. The deceased person is remembered often in conversation and through prayers; in church, candles are lit for them and special masses said for the repose of their souls; and their graves are well tended by relatives.[55] Through these means, the individual remains a part of the family circle.

6

FAITH, LOVE, AND COMMUNITY:
THE WEDDING IN POLONIA

Już dziś ostatnią nockę
U dziadunia spała,
A jutro gospodarstwo
Będzie swoje miała.

(This is the last night she'll spend
In grandfather's old place,
And on the early morrow
Her own fair home she'll grace.)
—"Już Dziś Ostatnią Nockę," in *Treasured Polish Songs*

Among Polish peasants, love and courtship were of great interest to the entire family. One's prestige in the community was intrinsically linked to the marriage partners one could secure for a son or daughter. Their wedding (*wesele*) was regarded as a prophecy for their future life, as reflected in the proverb "jakie wesele, takie życie" (as the wedding, so life).[1]

In the old country in the years preceding the mass migration, a marriage ceremony was a drama containing eight acts over a period of months: *wywiady*, the young man's inquiry and proposal with the assistance of the *swat* or matchmaker; *zareczyny* or *zrekowiny*, the betrothal; *dziewiczy wieczor*, the maiden evening, when the unbraiding of the bride's hair took place; *korowaj*, the baking of the wedding bread by the women of the village; *wesele*, the marriage ceremony itself; *pokladziny*, the putting to bed of the bridal couple; *oczepiny*, the capping of the bride; and *przenosiny*, removal to the groom's home.[2] A wedding celebration often lasted several days.

Although the cast of characters selected by the family to participate in this drama was determined partially by kinship and friendship ties, certain critical roles were filled by those who were witty, eloquent, and knowledgeable about local traditions.[3] A central role was that of the swat and his wife, the *swatka* or *staroscina,* who directed the ceremonies leading up to and including the wedding.[4] Once the immigrants arrived on-American shores, however, the institution of the swat, or go-between, vanished. Young adults chose their own mates without parental approval.[5]

There were other changes in wedding customs in early Polonia, including the *wybieranki* (choosing party), an institution unknown in Poland, when bridesmaids and ushers selected their partners based on personality, appearance, social standing, and wealth. These were important considerations because the entire bridal party would be photographed. Photos of individual couples in the bridal party were paid for by the man; no one wanted to be immortalized with a distasteful partner.[6] Wybierankis are no longer held.

The dowry continued to be an important consideration for a time in Polish-American communities, as it had in Poland. "In the old country, if you didn't have a dowry, forget it! You wouldn't get married," according to one woman.[7] In Poland, a girl's parents would furnish such items as bedding, pillows, a feather tick called the "pierszyna," other household goods, money, clothing, and perhaps a heifer and some land.[8] Later, some families continued to supply a dowry consisting of bedding and household items, but the dowry as an institution eventually was replaced by the American bridal shower.

A Polish groom usually received his inheritance of land from his father as a wedding present, a custom that did not continue in the New World. Because the young man did not inherit property in the United States, newlyweds no longer went to live with the husband's family as they had done in the Old World; instead, they lived with the bride's parents or on their own.[9] The new arrangement gave Polish-American wives additional power in their homes.

The Wesele

Despite such changes, many Old World wedding customs and superstitions thrived in Polonia, such as the beliefs that rain on the wedding day meant bad luck, the bride should borrow an item from the groom for good luck, and a pregnant bridesmaid would bring bad luck to the newlyweds.[10] This concern for the proper protocol was especially important on the wedding day, formerly a weekday but in more recent times on Saturday. The day traditionally began at the *dom weselny* (wedding home, generally the bride's home), where the young couple asked for their parents' blessing:

> CELIA PUROL: They would say "Błogosław i was Pan błogosław i matka na świę-ty," you know, it's always God's words. And then they'd have the holy water and bless them with the holy water. My mother had one of those—I don't know, have you seen that old-fashioned one with the little brush on the end? Before, in church, they used to have what looked like a little broom, really, and the priest would dip it in [the holy water] and he really sprinkled you! But now they have just a little ball. But this one we had wasn't like that. And so the parents would bless you.
>
> SILVERMAN: Was that for a good marriage?
>
> PUROL: Well, naturally. Of course, nowadays they don't believe in the parents blessing the children, but I think it's a nice custom.[11]

With that, the group, serenaded by musicians, would form a procession to church, either on foot or by wagon or automobile. Occasionally, as a joke friends would create impediments to the impending marriage, as Gabrielle Merta recalled of her cousin's wedding in Poland during the early 1970s:

> We put the groom in the first car. The bride goes in the last car. The guests go in between. And we're going to church. In the meantime, you have roadblocks, people, neighbors do that. You have to have either money or liquor to bail yourself out, otherwise they won't let you through.
>
> SILVERMAN: Now, who pays that to the neighbors along the way? Is that the groom who does that, or the bride?
>
> MERTA: The groom, if he wants to get through, so that's why he's in the first car. They have a pretend pregnant lady saying that's his child, and he has to pay up, otherwise she's going to go to the bride and tell her!

Wedding processions to church without the pranks were common in America's Polish communities as recently as the 1950s.[12] Upon arrival at the church, the priest marries the couple during a nuptial mass, thus completing the formal religious ceremony uniting the couple. The community, however, also endorses the union by means of various rituals beginning after the church ceremony.

In some communities in Poland and southern Ontario, wedding guests throw money at the newlyweds as they are leaving the church so they will have a prosperous marriage.[13] Concern for prosperity also accounts for a more widespread practice both in Poland and Polish-American communities: the bride's parents greet the young couple with bread and salt upon their return to the parental home after the church service. According to most interviewees, the bread and salt ensures that there will always be food on the newlyweds' table. One woman, however, reported that the bread was for the sweet things in life and the salt was for the bitter; if the portion of bread was larger than the salt, it would protect the couple from the bitterness of life.[14]

Another tradition reported among Chicago's Polish-Americans of the 1920s was the shivaree (*Kocia Muzyka*), a transplanted European tradition in which merrymakers blew horns, beat drums, and followed the wedding party down the neighborhood's streets, sometimes presenting the bride with a baby carriage.[15]

Some families in early Polonia remained at the home of the bride's parents for the wedding reception if there were not too many guests, but others rented space at local saloons or halls owned by social clubs in order to accommodate larger crowds, a trend that still continues.[16]

Meals served to guests also have changed over time. Originally in Poland and the immigrant communities, many families could afford to offer three meals. One elderly immigrant recalled her aunt's wedding reception at the turn of the century in Poland: "I remember my grandmother was baking all those pierogi from the *jagwie* and that, that buckwheat, and they make another kind of pierogi. You take millseeds and you grind that, and they make like a poundcake. That I like, but the rest I didn't care for. Who wants rice and kasha and all that stuff?"[17] The menu also featured dessert pierogi but no wedding cake.

Seventy years later, another immigrant who had attended a wedding in Poland before coming to the United States remembered that the family had killed three cows and two or three pigs. They and neighbors prepared all the food, which included chicken soup or beef soup, pork chops, sausage, *bigos* (sweet and sour cabbage with ribs), mashed potatoes and gravy, and cakes and coffee. Later in the evening, snack foods including pickles, herring, rye bread, and *kanapki* (slices of rye bread topped with slices of kielbasa, hard-boiled eggs, tomatoes, and pickles) were served with coffee and liquors.[18] At Polish-American weddings earlier in the twentieth century there would be sausage and ham for breakfast; the dinner menu would include chicken soup; and potatoes and different kinds of meats such as veal or roast pork would be served for supper. Because such an extensive menu became too expensive, the practice of serving three meals eventually was discontinued.

Music is a central element in Polish and Polish-American weddings. Alton Nowak, whose band earned about $14 a day playing for many Polish-American weddings during the 1920s, recalled:

> The orchestra would be hired from eight o'clock in the morning until two o'clock on the following morning. I can remember one wedding on Townsend Street. We paraded all the way up in the rain, up to St. Hedwig's Church, with a whole bunch of people, everybody, the bride, walking in this rain. Then we played in church for them, then we paraded them all the way back down to this place, and they just danced all day, continuously. In fact, one of the things was a marathon dance, to see how long somebody could dance. In one particular case, I think it was about an hour and forty-five minutes.[19]

For weddings, orchestras played a variety of Polish pieces, including *obereks, mazureks,* and *krakowiaks* (chapter 12). Musicians had to be prepared to perform many requests. "Somebody would come along with some old-time song that he remembered from way back in the boondocks of Poland," Alton Nowak said. "He'd start singing, and pretty soon you'd discover that everybody else knew the song. And in fact, the orchestra improvised the melody to try to keep going with it."

Whenever new guests arrived, the band would greet them with a march, a wedding custom in early Polonia that continues to thrive in Poland.[20] From the musicians' viewpoint, the march offered financial gains. "Whenever some stranger came in—let's say, at the beginning of the wedding," Alton Nowak recalled, "it was just the immediate family there. But as the day progressed, up comes some uncle who hasn't been around. Well, right away somebody went over. So we'd go over and play a tune for him. Well, naturally, he'd toss a silver dollar or something down. We picked up quite a few bucks extra, serenading those guys when they came to the wedding."[21]

Silver dollars were also part of another musical custom, the dollar dance with the bride. "One man would sit there with an apron and a big dish, regular dishes that they ate dinner with," Alton Nowak explained. "You'd have the privilege to dance with the girl if you threw the silver dollar on the dish and broke it, see? That's where she built up the big bunch of money for her wedding present." Men formed a continuous line to dance with the bride, each dance costing a silver dollar.[22] In

Chicago's Polish-American neighborhoods, there was a slight variation: If a man broke the dish with the silver dollar, he could retrieve his coin and dance with the bride for free.[23] Although no longer common among Buffalo's Polish-Americans, the silver dollar dance still is performed in Syracuse with paper dollars and has been revised so women can offer a dollar to dance with the groom.[24] According to a polka musician from Buffalo, only one in ten Polish-American brides now asks for the dollar dance, which his band performs as the polka "Dzisiaj Dusze Wesele" (Today there is a big wedding). At one wedding in 1995 the bride did not know how to dance the polka, and the band performed a medley of contemporary mainstream American "slow songs" while she did the "dollar dance" with all the men. The payment is no longer a dollar but whatever a man can afford.[25]

In their eagerness to establish a nest egg for the newlyweds in this manner, some families would go beyond the bounds of propriety. One woman remembered her cousin's parsimonious behavior: "His son was getting married, so he was sitting there as you enter with a basket. Well, most people didn't give him nothing. Then he'd go outside, he'd collect for the bride's shoes. Collect for the bride's veil. Collect for the bride's this-and-that, and finally he says, 'Now, if you people want to drink, you can go downstairs and get it at the bar, but you have to pay for it.' What do you call that?"[26]

Often wedding guests would sleep in six-hour shifts at the house so the merriment could continue all night, as Gabrielle Merta remembered:

> Our guests took a walk with the band and the whole thing through the village. They went seven miles to the bakery. They wanted to embarrass our cook. They said that she didn't bake fresh rolls, so they went and got the fresh rolls from the bakery. They went across the whole village at five in the morning, the band and all, playing through the village. So when they came back, instead of putting the dinner on the table, she put all the bones from the pig and other carcasses and said, "You don't like my food? Here it is!" A lot of joking around.[27]

The Oczepiny

The wedding evening comes to a climax with a custom unique to Poles and Polish-Americans: the czerpiny or oczepiny (the unveiling or capping ceremony).[28] The words are derived from *czepek*, a matron's cap or bonnet placed on a bride's head after her veil is removed, thus signifying, as do removing the garter and tossing the bridal bouquet, that she has joined the community of married women. In Poland the ceremony was held late at night at the height of the festivities; only afterward could the groom exercise his marital privileges.[29]

The oczepiny is the vestige of a series of ancient customs illustrating Arnold van Gennep's concept of "rites of passage," in this case the transition from maiden to married woman. The first phase, separation from the maidens, included the prenuptial festivities: the symbolic removal of the hair wreath worn by the bride that represented her virginity and the unbraiding and cutting of her long hair.[30] The second phase, liminality, was the wedding day. The bridal couple could be described as liminal individuals: "Liminal entities are neither here nor there; they are betwixt and between the positions assigned and arrayed by law, custom, convention, and ceremonial. . . . thus, liminality is frequently likened to death, to being in the womb."[31]

On her wedding day in Poland, a girl would want to wear the most ambitious headdress of her life, a wreath or crown streaming with colored ribbons, flowers, feathers, or beads, because thereafter, as a married woman, her hairstyle and headdresses would be much simpler.[32]

Symbolic of van Gennep's final phase, reincorporation in the community, was the czepek, the bride's marriage cap. It was given as a gift from the bride's godmother or made by the bride herself and was to be worn only for special occasions such as church, folk festivals, and, finally, burial. Many songs were sung by the women during the oczepiny, the period when liminality ended and reincorporation was achieved. In the Czersk region of Poland, bridesmaids would unplait the girl's hair while singing:

Oj warkoczku, warkoczku!
Oj drobnem cię splatała
O jak mi cię ustrzyg̨a
O będę cię płakała.

(Oh braids, braids!
I plaited you so fine
When they cut you off
I will cry for you.)[33]

Bridesmaids and matrons would sing in opposition throughout the ceremony, the maids mourning the loss of their companion and the married women welcoming the bride to their ranks. The first and final stanzas of one such "mourning" song are as follows:

Dear young woman, you will have to change your life
Now you will be a pretty housewife
You will have the keys in your hand
And you will take care of everything, day and night.

No more will you dance with us
Neither at spinning evenings nor at harvest time
You will have to look after your household
And take care of the babies.[34]

Although the bride and her friends shed genuine tears over her change in status to the difficult role of a married woman who would, in Poland, go to live with her husband's family, it must be remembered that Polish young men and women were expected to get married. Those who did not were ostracized. Ethnographer Sula Benet notes that to a certain extent, male dominance in Poland is more formal than functional. Wives are revered and referred to as "mother" by husbands with a degree of the veneration accorded to the Virgin Mary.[35]

The oczepiny underwent some revisions in Polish-American communities. The sharp opposition between single and married women was modified, replaced by a community of women who functioned as a chorus during the ceremony. It is still an emotional occasion, however:

CELIA PUROL: There would be a couple of women that knew the songs, you know, and they would sing while they were taking the bride's veil off. But first the orchestra would play "Serdeczna Matka" [Soft-hearted mother], and that makes you cry because it was so sad, the melody.

SILVERMAN: Someone told me that those songs that they used to do during the czerpiny were very sad.

PUROL: Well some of it would be sad, but otherwise it wouldn't be too bad. They would take the veil off and then they put a little—out of nylon, you know, the net—just a little bow, that she was married.[36]

Melania Rucinski described a czepek as made of lace, about six inches across, and resembling the yarmulke, the skullcap worn by Jewish males. Other songs performed by the Polish-American women gathered around the bride included "Rośnie Trawka" (Grass grows), "Dwanaście Aniołów" (The twelve angels), "Spadła z Wiśni" (She fell from the cherry tree), and "Jak Szybko Mijają Chwile" (How quickly time flies).[37] The texts of selected wedding songs will be analyzed in chapter 10.

In Polonia, the oczepiny also includes the placing of a vegetable hat on the groom's head when the czepek is placed on the bride's. "Sometimes they have fruit and sometimes they just have any old thing, just an old hat—meaning that he's an old man, not a single guy any more," Melania Rucinski explains.[38] The vegetable hat, which may be laden with carrots or grapes, eggs, and other items, is intended as a humorous counterpoint to the bride's capping.

Although the popularity of the oczepiny waned for a time in the mid–1900s, it is a resilient wedding custom. There is renewed interest today, even among those not of Polish descent, according to one elderly Polish-American woman: "I was to a wedding about a month ago. The parents of the bride and groom weren't Polish at all. One of the ladies was Polish, and she wanted them to have the oczepiny, and then nobody knew it. So she asked me to sing and kind of explain it. They all enjoyed it. Then I had to tell them when to take the veil off the bride and put the flowers in and when to put the man's hat on, and to explain it to them, because they never sang anything like that."[39] Other older women have recounted similar experiences but have hesitated to lead the singing because they are not performers.

In a number of interethnic marriages, the oczepiny ceremony has been popular for decades; a former mayor of Buffalo, an Irish-American, said that during the 1950s his brother wore a vegetable hat as part of the oczepiny at his wedding to a Polish-American.[40] Several Polish-American informants said that their daughters had requested the oczepiny for their weddings in the 1980s to non-Poles. On another occasion, a country-western band hired by a Polish-American mother performed a series of oczepiny songs for the daughter's wedding to a Polish-American in Niagara Falls, New York, in 1983.[41]

The oczepiny also is making an appearance, in revised form, as part of fiftieth wedding anniversary rites. One woman recalled her golden anniversary party in 1991:

BELLE GRAMINSKI: We didn't have a big wedding, so what they did, I don't know if you ever heard of that Polish custom where they sing over the bride about the angels ["Dwanaście Aniołow"]? So would you believe, they brought my veil from when I was married, and they sang that song over me! I sat there like a blushing bride!

SILVERMAN: Did your husband have the vegetable hat, too?
GRAMINSKI: No, they didn't have a hat, so they put vegetables on his head! [Looks at her husband Ed and both laugh.] He had a carrot, celery, piece of broccoli, and he stood there.[42]

Other Polish-American families are displaying "creative ethnicity" by altering the lyrics of the oczepiny song to include the names or occupations of the bridal couple. One father, for example, altered the lyrics of two songs, "Spadła z Wiśni" and "Rośnie Trawka," for his daughter's 1982 wedding to refer to the bridal couple by name and to their occupations. He then printed a sheet containing the original Polish lyrics to both melodies, followed by his customized version in English. Although the bridegroom was not of Polish descent, the songsheet that resulted was well received by the wedding guests, as could be seen from their reactions in the videotape of the wedding.[43]

Although there is interest in the oczepiny, there is also a lack of knowledge about the custom and the songs' lyrics. Songsheets, typed or printed out on home computers and often in both Polish and English (fig. 2), are becoming increasingly popular. The American standards "Let Me Call You Sweetheart" and "I Love You Truly" have become part of the Polish-American wedding repertoire.[44] Polish-American community organizations also print the lyrics to Christmas kolędy for distribution at holiday events.

The *Poprawiny*

The wedding celebration continues at a *poprawiny*, a smaller party held on either the Sunday or Monday following the wedding. In the days before honeymoon vacations were common, the newlyweds attended the poprawiny along with the bridal party, the families, and close friends, but now in both Poland and Polonia the bridal couple is generally absent. According to one musician, "We had to come back the next morning at 10 o'clock, and there were those diehards, about half-asleep, and some of those people came back again to start the second day of this wedding ceremony. The bride and groom, naturally, were gone, but the people just continued on."[45]

The poprawiny remains popular, even at second weddings. As one middle-aged Polish-American woman recalled, "I've been married a year now, and I had a Polish wedding, a Polish 'traditional' wedding. We had

UNVEILING CEREMONY (OCZEPINY)

IT HAS BEEN TRADITIONAL AMONG BRIDES TO HAVE THE UNVEILING ACCOMPANIED BY THIS CEREMONIAL SONG. IT CULMINATES THE GREATEST DAY OF A COUPLE'S LIFE, THE RECEPTION OF THE HOLY SACRAMENT OF MATRIMONY. THE DAY BEGINS WITH THE PARENTAL BLESSING. AFTER THE EXCHANGE OF WEDDING VOWS, THE FIRST THING A COUPLE PARTAKES ON ARRIVAL AT THE RECEPTION IS SALT AND BREAD. THIS IS A WISH THAT THEY WILL NEVER KNOW POVERTY AND THAT THEY WILL ALWAYS HAVE PLENTY TO EAT. THE BRIDE'S VEIL IS REMOVED AFTER THE MAIN DISCOURSE. THE BRIDE AND GROOM MEDITATE ON WHAT HAS TRANSPIRED THROUGHOUT THE DAY AND WHAT THEY VOWED TO EACH OTHER. IT SYMBOL-IZES MARRIAGE AS AN EVERLASTING VENTURE, DEVOID OF ANY INTERFERENCE FROM ANYONE. THE FINAL WISH IS THAT THE FUTURE WILL BRING FORTH CHILD-REN TO CARRY ON THE NAME AND TRADITIONS OF BOTH PARENTS.

1

As lovely green grass grows, throughout the promised land,
Before the main altar, you've given him your hand.
You've given him your hand, he gave a golden band,
Your eyes swelled up with tears, before your friends on hand.
Twelve lovely white petals, attached to this white rose,
Twelve heavenly angels serve, the young bride they had chose.

The first angel has brought a white candle's brilliance,
The second angel brought a lily's full fragrance.
The third angel has brought, a lovely bouquet to hold.
The fourth angel has brought, your wedding band of gold.
The fifth angel has come, with blessings from the Lord.
The sixth angel has come, with marital accord.
Six angels that remain, come with a crown so keen.
They'll place it on your head, as if upon a queen.
You promised to be true, love, honor and obey,
In all your days ahead, uphold vows made today.
So now you'll be true, your right hand on the cross.
You've pledged your life to him, who now will be the boss.
Remember to be good, and live a life-of-prayer
And in a year or two, present him with an heir.

2

LET ME CALL YOU SWEETHEART

Let me call you sweetheart
I'm in love with you
Let me hear you whisper
That you love me too.
Keep the lovelight glowing
In your eyes so true,
Let me call you sweetheart,
I'm in love with you.

5

I LOVE YOU TRULY

I love you truly, truly dear
Life with its sorrow
Life with its tears,
Fades into dreams
When I feel you are near
Cause I love you truly,
Truly, dear.

3 JAK SZYBKO MIJAJA CHWILE

JAK SZYBKO MIJAJA CHWILE,
JAK SZYBKO PLYNIE CZAS
        (REPEAT)
ZA ROK ZA DZIEN ZA CHWILE,
RAZEM NIE BEDZIE NAS,
        (REPEAT)
A KIEDY MLODE LATA,
POPLYNA SZYBKO W DAL.
        (REPEAT)
A W SERCU POZOSTANIE,
TESKNOTA, SMUTEK, ZAL.
        (REPEAT)

6

SERDECZNA MATKO

SERDECZNA MATKO, OPIEKUNKO LUDZI
NIECH CIE PLACZ SIEROT DO LITOSCI WZBUDZI
WYGNANCY EWY DO CIEBIE WOLAMY:
ZMILUJ SIC ZMILUJ NIECH SIE NIE TULAMY
DO KOGOZ MAMY WZDYCHAC NEDZNE DZIATKO?
TYLKO DO CIEBIE, UKOCHANEJ MATKI:
U KTOREJ SERCE OTWARTE KAZDEMU,
A OSOBLIWIE NEDZA STRAPIONEMU.
ZASLUZYLISMY, TO PRAWDA, PRZES ZLOSCI,
BY NAS BOG KARAL ROZGA SUROWOSCI:
LECZ KIEDY OJCIEC ROZGNIEWANY SIECZE,
SZCZESLIWY KTO SIE DO MATKI UCIECZE.

4

SERDECZNO MATKO

SERDECZNO MATKO
OPIEKUNKO KUDZI
NIECH CIE PLACZ SIERUT
DO LITOSCI WZBUDZI
WYGNANCY EWY
DO CIEBIE WOLZMY
ZMILUJ SIE ZMILUJ
NIECH SIE NIE TULAMY

7

WIWAT WIWAT

WIWAT, WIWAT, NIECH DLUGO ZYJA NAM,
WIWAT, WIWAT, NIECH DLUGO ZYJA NAM,
NIECH DLUGIE LATA, SZCZESCIE IM PRZEPLATA,

NIECHAJ ZYJA NAM

Figure 2. An explanation of oczepiny precedes the lyrics on this songsheet from a 1983 Polish-American wedding in Niagara Falls, New York. A country-western band performed the lyrics with assistance from the bride's mother. (Courtesy of Edward Silverman)

what they call a poprawiny three days later, you know, you have a party. Everything. The kielbasa, the pierogi, the gołąbki, everything."[46]

In Poland, wedding festivities continue one final time. "A year later, some people come back on a wagon, a dressed-up wagon, and if the girl's not pregnant yet they pick on her. And then they party again for the first wedding anniversary."[47] That custom is not observed in Polish-American communities.

The conclusion of the poprawiny brings the formal wedding celebration to a close. The newlywed couple is now recognized as a new family unit, tied closely to the extended family and friends in Polonia and yet independent.

7

SPINNING TALES, WEAVING THE FABRIC
OF IDENTITY: POLISH-AMERICAN NARRATIVES

Different forms of storytelling are a way of expressing a regional,
a family and a personal identity.
—Steven Zeitlin, *Celebration of American Family Folklore*

Until the advent of radio and television, long autumn or winter evenings in rural Poland were spent by the fireside at spinning or har-
vesting parties. Like similar social occasions among other European cultures and Native American societies, these evenings had a second purpose:
storytelling, which provided an education in the ethnic group's lore:

> There is always some one outstanding for ability to tell tales of heroes,
> devils, saints and spirits—often an older person, perhaps a wandering beg-
> gar who has picked up wondrous facts and fancies on his travels. To delight
> or terrify an assembled company with songs and stories during winter nights
> is a recognized function of the beggars, and their repertoire of folklore and
> anecdote provides one of their claims to a place in the social sun. Younger
> people also add their share to the narratives, and sometimes they contin-
> ue the entertainment all night, "cursing the cock's crow that calls them to
> work in the morning."[1]

Folktales, legends, and myths abounded at such gatherings.[2] There
were legends about the origin of amber and *pisanki* (decorated Easter
eggs); legends about holy figures such as the Black Madonna of Częstochowa, the martyrs Św. Stanisław (St. Stanislaus) and Bishop Adalbert
and Św. Jerzy (St. George), slayer of a dragon; legends about the Polish
magician Pan Twardowski, the scientist Copernicus, the sailor-adventurer
Jan Scolnus who discovered Labrador, and the Trumpeter of Kraków who

was murdered by invading Tartars while sounding the alarm; and folktales about such colorful characters as Janosik, the Polish Robin Hood who was robber-chieftain of the Tatra Mountains.[3] Many of these folk narratives developed in conjunction with the Polish nation between the years 963 and 1772, when the first partition of Poland occurred. They continued in popularity among peasants after the final partition and initially among some immigrants to the New World.

The pages of the journal *Polish Folklore,* published during the 1950s and 1960s by Alliance College of Cambridge Springs, Pennsylvania, are filled with such immigrants' stories. In most cases, the folklorists who collected these narratives in piecemeal form reconstructed the stories before publishing them in a polished, literary English translation (the original Polish versions are not given). Among them is the following tale, collected in the 1950s from a seventy-four-year-old Polish woman who emigrated to Pennsylvania. It focuses on a saint's visit to a Polish graveyard on a Catholic holiday honoring the dead, All Souls' Day:

How St. Roch Came to *Lubotyń*

In the village of *Lubotyń,* in the lake-studded *Łomża* region of Mazovia, near the River *Ruź,* All Souls' Day dawned bright and crisp. . . .

Since daybreak the roads had been crowded with people, coming and going, setting out for church, going home after church. In *Lubotyń* itself there was no church—no church, but what a graveyard! Ancient and mysterious, with a personality of its own, and on this one day of the year, as important in the people's worship as the church itself, which was in a neighboring village. . . .

And on every grave a candle, specially lighted for this day of remembrance. For this was the Feast Day of the Ancestors—what Adam Mickiewicz calls *Dziady*—and besides the many candles twinkling in the vari-colored bowls, there were plates of food set out so that those being remembered should not, on this night when they were expected to return, want for sustenance.

The day was nearly over, and it was beginning to grow dusky. Beside every grave was someone kneeling in reverent worship, communing with his departed loved ones. There was no sound, save for a murmured prayer now and then, and no movement in the air.

Then in a twinkling all was changed. A shrill screeching sound shattered the solemn stillness. The air swished as if a giant fan had been turned on.

The worshippers raised their heads, fearing what they might see, and in the air beheld a vast swarm of parrots. Parrots. Hundreds and hundreds of these, brilliantly green, with touches of crimson and yellow and white.

"Roch, Roch, Roch, Roch!" the birds seemed to be crying. "Roch, Roch, Roch!"

"What is it?" an old man asked, cupping his hand to one ear and straining to understand. . . .

No one really knew, and the worshippers, interrupted in their devotions, strangely upset, rose from the twinkling graves and crowded together.

As for the parrots, well, there was a mammoth chestnut tree in the graveyard, larger than all the other great chestnuts . . .

And so it was to this tree the parrots sped, and the villagers, hardly knowing what to do, followed in their wake. . . . when . . .

"What is it?" someone cried, "that moaning, that sobbing?"

For through the graveyard now began to be wafted yet another sound. "Dla Boga! Dla Boga!" it seemed to be crying, "For God! For God!"

The people were stricken dumb. They fell to the ground, some kneeling, others prostrating themselves before the divine revelation. For revelation it was, as became quickly apparent.

"Look! Look!" someone cried, and as all lifted their eyes, there under the spreading branches of the great chestnut tree, revealed in a dim, candle-like light, was seen the figure of a man. A tall, saintly figure it was, and in his right hand he carried a stout walking stick, shoulder high, while at his left side was a little dog.

The little dog gave the secret away.

"Roch! Roch!" the people cried. "It was St. Roch the parrots were heralding!" . . .

It was a wonderful gift, all agreed, from God Himself. As the living remembered the dead on this holiest of days, so, God was saying, were the dead not unmindful, on their part, of the living, and one of the most holy of their number had returned to tell the people this. . . .

And in Roch's name miracles were performed. The blind were made to see, cripples were released from their bondage. A chapel was built in the graveyard, but it was not this which was held in the most reverent regard— it was the chestnut tree.

Eventually a church was built in *Lubotyń*, at a little distance from the old graveyard, and to this, as soon as the belfry was finished, the parrots of St. Roch migrated, from its sacred height to continue their everlasting proclamation, "Roch, Roch, Roch." You can hear them there still, if you listen.[4]

More recently, I collected the following narrative from a young Polish-Canadian woman visiting Buffalo, New York, for Dyngus Day. It is a version of "Krak and the Dragon," which concerns Krak, the man who killed a dragon and founded the city of Kraków: "Now, there was this dragon that lived in the castle underneath where the Wawel is, that's this great big castle. And they wanted to get rid of the dragon, and nobody knew how to get rid of it until this one shepherd boy came, and he put this, he made this lamb full of poisons and stuff, and he put the lamb in front. Whoever was to kill this dragon was to marry the princess, so he put this lamb out in front, and the dragon ate it, and he died, and he married the princess."[5]

From Folktale to Memorate

The attenuated legend of Krak is one of the very few I was able to collect. Because many Polish immigrants switched from agricultural to industrial occupations after their arrival in the United States, much agricultural lore disappeared, as did accounts of magical castles, dragons, handsome princes, and beautiful princesses. The castles of the European landscape were replaced by the smokestacks of industrial America.

Among ethnic groups in the New World, longer, more complex narratives have given way to shorter, simpler forms because longer narratives are not applicable to the American scene. People no longer have the leisure to narrate them, and the original language used to tell the stories is no longer spoken. There also has been a shift from sacred to secular, from supernatural to realistic, and from communal to individualistic.[6]

Because the extended family no longer lives under one roof in America, traditional folktales, legends, and myths narrated after supper by peasant families in rural Poland have given way to memorates, or personal-experience narratives, related on special occasions such as holidays, birthdays, or weddings when people get together.[7] Storytelling also occurs in the workplace around the office water-cooler or during such repetitive group tasks as preparing a mass mailing; during leisure activities, for example among a group of mothers sewing costumes for a school's upcoming play; and in library or school programs featuring professional storytellers. But folk narratives in these settings are more likely to be occupational or regional than ethnic in nature. Thus the Polish-American family remains as the locus for ethnic folk narratives.

The transition from folktale to personal-experience narrative also has been noted in the storytelling traditions of contemporary Mexican-American, Italian-American, and Native American communities.[8] Frances

Malpezzi and William Clements argue that among Italian-American informants, traditional Old World narratives were too closely tied to a particular language to survive effectively in the New World. The formulaic nature of some stories (for example, the openings, closings, and magical spells recited by characters) did not translate nicely from the regional dialect into either English or the new pan-ethnic language, standard Italian. In addition, the New World offered competing forms of folk or mass entertainment, such as Italian-American puppet plays or mainstream American movies, radio, and television.[9]

The personal-experience narrative, then, has become an important narrative form in America's ethnic communities, a form that folklorists have often overlooked: "There are thousands of sagas created from life experiences that deserve, indeed cry for, recording. Here are precious oral narratives dealing with a series of great folk movements . . . and this migration should be described in terms of humanity as well as of mass statistics."[10]

These narratives, which Steven Zeitlin calls "family folklore," consist of "glorious moments carefully selected and elaborated through the years, tailored to the demands of the present."[11] Stories tend to emphasize eccentric relatives or sharp changes and upheavals in the family's history—the unusual rather than the predictable. In retelling and reshaping these incidents within the family circle, storytellers are making the unexpected or disastrous a part of the smooth, normal functioning of the family unit.[12] Like Old World legends, New World narratives are an important educational device; they teach the young about the ethnic community but within the context of the family rather than the larger society.

Memories of the Homeland

Stories about life in the old country and immigration to America were common among first- and second-generation Polish-Americans. One woman who had come to America at age thirteen in 1914, Kate Moch, recalled an unusual incident that happened to her family in Poland when she was a little girl:

> For Easter, we have, there was Polish style. We lived on a farm, and we walked to church like from here to Fredonia or more [about five miles]. And we live by the woods and we go to the river. We have, they call, not

river, but in Polish, *rzeka*. Sometimes the water was real deep. And we was going to church. See, Polish people take food to bless. They took eggs, bread, in the old country they have salt pork that they cook, sausage, and they make a cheese. And we take that to church and they bless.

And my stepmother, but do you know, it shows you how people was dumb in old country, to walk so far from here, carry a big basket I remember, a *big* heavy basket. She carry everything that far up there on her back!

SILVERMAN: Oh! On her back? All that way?

MOCH: Yeah. To carry that to church to bless. They couldn't take half of that— no, they carry *every*thing. Maybe about four or five dozen eggs, and the sausage, and the bread, and the horseradish, and everything carry to church.

And I was going with her, we were going through the river, and we didn't have no *bridge* there, we just have two boards like this, you know. [She indicates, with her hands, two narrow planks.] Two boards. And my younger sister fall in the water.

And we got her out of the water, and I have to go back home, I couldn't go because I have to take her home. I couldn't go to church with my mother, my stepmother.[13]

The story is embedded in a conversation about holiday foodways, a significant form of ethnic identity for Kate Moch. It is likely that she remembered the river incident because it occurred on one of the most important holiday weekends for Poles, Easter, and spoiled what would have been an exciting day for her.

A more recent immigrant, a thirty-two-year-old woman vividly recalled rural Polish funeral customs of the 1970s because one such funeral was for her boyfriend.

GABRIELLE MERTA: When there's an old person, we'd dress it in a *dark* [outfit], and we'd have a dark casket. If you have a young person, you dress it in *white*.

And in my case, my boyfriend got killed in Silesia when that accident happened. Fifty-three guys died underground in a coal mine. I was dressed as a bride, walking behind his casket with flowers.

So they do that for a young person because that person was not able to get married, so they have the bride walking. Then I had to throw the bouquet into the grave.

SILVERMAN: And if the person was much too young to have a boyfriend or girlfriend?

MERTA: They'd still do that. They'd have a little girl or a little boy walking behind the casket. And they have the casket being carried through the whole village to the church. And you have the band walking in front of it.

Then you have the boys carrying the cross, then you have the priest walking *right* in front of it. Then you have your casket, and the family walking behind it.[14]

Other accounts such as the following from Martha Steffan reveal the great lengths to which Poles in the old country would go to avoid domination by foreign oppressors.

With my father, you know, he was a ditch digger, and you were *never* supposed to look up when the big shots were going by.

Well, he heard them and he looked up, and a woman spit in his face and dragged him out of the ditch and had him horse-whipped.

A few months later, he was *drafted* and he wasn't going to fight for that *damned* country, so he *blinded* himself in one eye.

SILVERMAN: He *did?* He blinded himself in one eye?

STEFFAN: Yeah, so he wouldn't have to go [into the army]. But all his life, he had a fear of being deported.[15]

The Immigration Experience

Given the Polish peasants' dislike for their foreign rulers, many opted to make the arduous trip to America, a story frequently retold by their descendants. Martha Steffan recounted her mother's experience as a stowaway:

See, she got on this *boat,* she *had* no money, she *had* no food, she *had* no *change of clothes,* she lived *nine* days on milk from the *cows* that were on this boat. When they took the cows and everything off, there they found my mother in the corner.

SILVERMAN: After the cows were taken off?

STEFFAN: Yeah, and the guy says to her, "What's your *name?*"

"*Dunkirk.*"

"Where are you from?"

"*Dunkirk.*"

That's the only word [of English] she knew. So anyway, they took her off, fed her, and she ate so much, because she hadn't eaten in all those nine days.

So then they put her in a hotel, locked the door, and the next morning, they took her *out* and fed her breakfast. *Then* she had to take all that *shit* and stuff off the boat. I used to ask her, "How long did it take you?"

"I don't know. Four or five hours, half a day." She had to, uh, you know, take all that *manure* off and put it on the truck . . .

SILVERMAN: She had to clean it up?

STEFFAN: Yeah, that was her punishment. So then they *fed* her and they said to her, "Where do you want to go?"
"Dunkirk."
Naturally, that was the only word she used! [She laughs.][16]

Another elderly woman, herself an immigrant from Poland, felt the immigration experience was so important that she prepared cue cards in advance of my visit in order to jog her memory. The resulting account combines the repetition of key words, characteristic of oral narratives, with the cadences of a polished speech:

MARY MILLER: I came from the old country, that's from Poland, 1914. My mother and father, brother and *I* came. When we left Bremen, Germany, and came to Boston, Massachusetts, *not* Ellis Island. See, some of them came there, and then they came by train to Dunkirk.

SILVERMAN: Uh-huh.

MILLER: And the name of the *ship* that we came on was *Vaterland*. It was a German ship. V-A-T-R-L-A-N-D. Then of course, those people, when they first came, were very illiterate, as you know that. Some of them had never been to school, they didn't have schools.

Now, when we arrived in this country, when we came by train from Boston to Dunkirk, he [father] had a sister here, of course. Most of them had family here or something, somebody else that had preceded them here, you know? And then, they would write to them and tell them how great it was over here, and they were all poor, so that's the reason these people migrated here, was because of the work.

Well, the first thing they did was, my father worked in Radiator in Dunkirk, that was factory work, and the railroad. He done everything and anything that he could, you know, that paid money, any money, which was very little.

Rents were very cheap. In those days, they rented a house. [Speaking to herself as she consults her handwritten notes, "Let me see, what did I write here?"] Oh. When we got *here*, we encountered other people, different ethnics.[17]

The Tabakiery versus the Galiciuks

Because Poland was under foreign domination by three different rulers during the era of the great migration, immigrants initially retained their distinct regional identities when they arrived in the United States although they settled in contiguous neighborhoods. I collected more personal narratives about this factionalism than any other topic. In the

Polish communities of Dunkirk and Buffalo, New York, for example, immigrants from Prussian Poland clashed with the more recent arrivals from Russian and Austrian Poland. Prussian Poles, called "Tabakiery" because of their fondness for snuff, lived in a neighborhood apart from Austrian Poles, known as "Galiciuks" because they hailed from a region called Galicia. The result was the Hatfields versus the McCoys or sometimes Romeo and Juliet, as illustrated by the following poignant tale told by an elderly woman.

> I met such a *nice* guy, his name was Stanley Bobek, and every time he'd pick me up, by the time he got home he got beat up by Fourth Ward people, guys.
>
> So *then* I decided we'd meet under the *viaduct.* That was all right for a couple of weeks, but then they'd meet him on *top* of the viaduct and beat the hell out of him anyway.
>
> So I wrote him a letter, and I said, "It's no use." I liked that guy! And so, I wrote to him not to come any more. The last I heard, he was in Cleveland.[18]

Men as well as women related many stories about factionalism. One elderly man advised me that "Galaniery" was a slur on the Austrian Poles from Galicia, much the same as "Nigger" as applied to African Americans. Russian Poles were known variously as "Cossacks" or "Bolsheviki."[19] In her research in Boston's Polonia in the 1970s, ethnographer Ewa Morawska also collected accounts of intrafamily friction because of marriages between the offspring of Ruskie and Galicjany.[20] The factionalism continued even as Polish-Americans climbed from the working class into the middle class:

> ALOIS MAZUR: I remember when I was a young *judge,* at that time there were quite a few Polish-American judges. One of them was a fellow by the name of Judge *Zimmer,* Michael Zimmer. He came from the Erie, Pennsylvania, area—I'm sorry, from the mining towns of Pennsylvania. And then there was a Judge Kuczynski, who came from Black Rock [a section of Buffalo].
>
> And one time, Judge Zimmer got *very, very* angry and disturbed at something that Judge Kuczynski did, and he's relating the matter to me. I was a young judge of about thirty-three, thirty-four years of age.
>
> And he [Zimmer] says finally, almost in desperation, he says [adopts a gruff tone of voice], "Well, what do you *expect* from a Russian!"
>
> You know, he [Kuczynski] wasn't Russian, but he was from the Russian part [of Poland], you see?[21]

Poverty and Discrimination in Polonia

The new Polish-Americans were not contending only with intraethnic squabbles during the 1930s; they also had to cope with poverty. As Kate Moch, the mother of nine, recounted the following tale, her voice dropped significantly in volume when she spoke of her reluctant decision to make moonshine in order to make ends meet:

> But there was depression, there was *no* work. And there was—oh, that was hard. We lived on North Street. My Helen was born, then Eddie was born. And then when we moved back to Roberts Road, that big house across the street from the firehouse, on Brooks's. That big house, four-family house, we live there.
>
> And I was expecting my Jenny, and the landlady said to me, she says "Kate"—everybody was making moonshine—"Why don't you start making it?"
>
> And my God, I started making it, and the kids were small. I work like hell, because I think I was making it for about ten years, and we made a living. Otherwise the kids would probably starve.
>
> The kids were small, I didn't know how to talk English, either. But the fellows come in, and talk, and have a drink, and talk English, and I learned fast.[22]

Polish-Americans also learned about discrimination during the depression:

> ADRIANA ANDERS: I used to pay on our little loan book, my mother's, at the Loan. And one of the men, he was, I don't know what you call it, he was on the board there . . .
>
> SILVERMAN: Lake Shore Savings and Loan?
>
> ANDERS: But he also was a teller. He also was a teller at the bank. And he used to talk to me every time I'd come in. You know, we got friendly. He was an older man. We'd talk, and I once mentioned to him that my sister was graduating from Normal School. She was going to be a teacher.
>
> And he said, "You know, it's too bad her name is a Polish name, because she's going to have a hard time finding a job here in town. You know, if your name was changed"—or something like that.
>
> That's another thing I always felt bad about, because here we were, so proud of her. She was the first one in the family to graduate from college and everything, you know. [Speaking softly, "We were all so proud and everything."]
>
> And here, to get told that![23]

Despite discrimination and poverty, Polish-Americans were proud of their self-sufficiency and resilience, reflected both in stories about relatives and the informants themselves. They took pride in their ability to work long hours to further their business or educational plans in America. Wolf Tombak, owner of a bakery at Buffalo's Broadway Market, told the following story to a crowd at his stall as he demonstrated how to make an almond pastry ring:

> *Yummy, yummy!* The best baked goods money can buy. I'm an old-time baker, and I would leave the United States a million dollars, a billion! Best country in the whole *world!* [But there are] too many *lazy* people. When I start, I came to the United States, [I made] salad dressing and coleslaw at Main and Amherst Streets. Fifty cents an hour, eighteen hours a day, for ten years. And I worked for a living back when my twins were born. For ten years, seven days a week, I'm here. Nothing happened to me.
>
> People are lazy. They kick the bucket too early. Or they go in gin mills instead of going home to take care of the kids and the *wife.* Another shot and a beer, another shot and a beer.[24]

Tombak is seasoned by many years of experience with both the public and news media, who videotape him regularly, especially at Easter. His booming voice has the practiced, rhythmic quality of a storyteller at home with an audience.

Religious Legends

Polish-Americans' firm belief in the value of hard work went hand in hand with their faith in God. I collected nearly as many stories related to religious beliefs and practices as I did tales about factionalism. Many people recounted the Catholic Church's processions for various feast days in Polonia, but others focused on folk religious beliefs; a Polish girl was believed to have turned to stone, for example, after dancing with a holy picture.[25] Both in Poland and early Polonia, such pictures were believed to have special powers and for that reason there are legends about the pictures themselves, such as the famed portrait of Our Lady of Częstochowa in the monastery of Jasna Góra in Poland:

> The Polish, being a particularly religious and devout people, have as their patroness the Mother of Christ, Mary. They are especially devoted to her under the title of Our Lady of Częstochowa. Legend has it that this particular image of our Lady was uncovered hundreds of years ago by a young Pol-

ish orphan, who was subservient to a landlord in Russia. The lad returned the image to Poland, where it was enshrined in a locale called Częstochowa, from whence comes the title.

Some time later a Swedish invasion of Poland took place. To rouse the sentiments of the Poles, a number of Swedish soldiers removed the image from its shrine and attempted to carry it away. However, the horses were unable to pull the carriage upon which it was to be borne away. It was as if they were paralyzed. In anger, a Swedish officer drew his sword and slashed the image. The portrait actually bled. To this day all reproductions bear this scar.

Many miracles since then have been attributed to this Madonna.[26]

Some stories express strong belief in miraculous healings:

KATE MOCH: Well, I'll tell you a miracle now. I have a sister in the old country, younger than I am. A lot of people don't believe it [the miracle], but I do.

She couldn't see, she couldn't walk. And my stepmother told me that there was, on the *piscnize* there, a Święty Jan, St. John, statue. There was a St. John statue, and the water was dripping up there, like a little stream comes from the hill. And by that statue, my stepmother took my sister before sunrise up there. She wash her in that water, and she left a scarf there to wipe her. And my sister *walk,* and my sister could see, she got married, and everything.[27]

In addition to such accounts of cures involving a religious component, there were many recollections of illnesses and deaths in early Polonia, especially during the Great Flu Epidemic of 1918–19. Other accounts are of more recent origin, reflecting the belief that a loved one will make his or her presence known at the moment of death (chapter 5). One woman, Valerie Pawlak, recalled her mother-in-law's death:

It was a fall day, the leaves were beautiful, and I had sheets and pillowcases on the line. I looked out the window and there was no wind. There was this one pillowcase, a white one, that was without a clothespin, drooping.

I went outside and went down the steps to hang that pillowcase, and all of a sudden I hear, "Valerie! Valerie!"

And I went running, I went running down the sidewalk, because my father used to like to go to White Eagle Bakery, and he'd put rye bread in my mailbox and just toot [his car horn] or something or yell. So I figured maybe that was him.

I went down there, but there was nobody there, was nobody. So I went down there and said, "*That's* weird. There's no neighbors around—who's calling me?"

I come back up the steps. As I come up the steps, the telephone's ringing like crazy. I went to the telephone, and they said, "Ma got hit by a car, it doesn't look good." She did die afterward.[28]

Humorous Tales and Jokes

Although outsiders often associate Polish-Americans with "dumb Polack" jokes, Polish-Americans themselves tell them only in certain limited contexts such as joke-telling sessions among Polish-American men in taverns. Such jokes stereotype an ethnic group and perpetuate a negative image.[29] In the 1990s these slurs appeared on the bulletin boards of such computer services as Prodigy, prompting complaints from Polish-Americans and other ethnic groups concerned about similar jokes. Rather than the "Polack" jokes, Polish-Americans find humor in other narrative modes, such as the following tale recounted by Lucy Moch, whose parents frequently told it at home:

> There was a guy going to the market—this was in the old country. He was carrying a goose, and he was going to sell it.
> He met up with a friend, a neighbor. And this guy that carried the goose was deaf. He could talk, but he was hard of hearing, you know?
> So this guy says to him, "Jak się macie, Bartosiu?"
> See, this was short for Bartłomieju.
> He says in reply, "Mam gąsiora w koszu," meaning that he had a goose in the basket.
> Well, the friend knew he couldn't hear, so he says, "A jak się tam wasi moję?" meaning, "Well, how's your family?"
> And Bartłomieju says, "Talara mi dają," meaning, "They're giving me a dollar for her."
> And this goes on. The friend says, "A jak się tam wane dzieci moję?" You know, "How are your children?"
> And this guy don't hear him, and he says, "Łon zwiezany, łon nie słeci," meaning, "He's tied up, he won't fly."
> So that guy got disgusted with him, and he says, "Ah, Bartosiu, wyście bez rozumu," meaning, "Ah, you haven't got no brains!"
> And Bartosiu answers him by saying, "Jak go nie sprzedam, zaniosę go do domu" (If I won't sell him, I'll take him back home). [She laughs.][30]

In that tale, humor arises from misunderstandings caused by aural difficulties. Visual mistakes are at the heart of the following "drunken woman" tale related by the informant's son and his friends during parties in their Polish-American community:

KATE MOCH: One woman got drunk. She went out drinking, you know. She went, come home drunk. And she couldn't find the house. She went right to the stable where the *cows* was. And she lay down, fall asleep, by the cow. And in the morning, she opened the eye, like this [she squints]. She couldn't see nothing, only she see four tits was hanging. The cow, you know, in the morning, they got milk, they're heavy, you know. And she said [adopts a sweet, seductive tone of voice], "Hey, boys, one at a time!"[31]

Other Polish-American narratives resemble the "Pelt Kid" narratives of Native American tradition, "noodle tales" in which a person misconstrues information, resulting in comic effects.[32] In the following story, a sexually naive young man learns about the world:

> A farmer had a *son,* and they have a farm. He was a farmer. And the boy find a girl and decides to get married.
>
> And he says, the boy's sitting down, the father said to the boy, "You're getting married. You know, everything's—the woman is just like a *cow,* you take care of them when they have babies, like a mother and everything." And the boy said, "Well."
>
> So they move out on their own. And when he come back to the father once, the father asks, "How's the marriage?"
>
> So the boy says, "Well, father, everything was good, but I couldn't eat the afterborn [afterbirth]." [The storyteller laughs, explaining, "Cows eat the afterborn."] And the boy said he wouldn't eat that, he couldn't eat that.[33]

Unusual Personalities

Stories about unique family members in early Polonia are even more intriguing than stories about daily life. As Steven Zeitlin has observed, American families like to tell stories pinpointing personality traits, but these stories simultaneously stereotype personalities and reduce complex individuals to character types such as mischief-maker, hero, villain, or innocent.[34] Polish-American informants related a number of such "personality" stories, and in doing so they were indicating their own value systems, a worldview in which good, kind, decent, gentle people prevail. Kate Moch, for example, recalled how a mean uncle had tried to force her to marry a much older man:

> My uncle brought me [here]. See, I have two uncles in Washington, Pennsylvania. One was my godfather. And when I write to him, he brought me to this country, and he wants me to get married with a fellow he knew. He had a mustache, and he was twenty-nine years old and I was *sixteen.*

And the girls said to me, "Kate, are you gonna get married with that guy?" I said, *"What* guy?" They said, "The *organista,* he play in church." I said, "No, I don't wanna get married to *no*body. I'm too young to get married." And my uncle said, "Marry him. He's a good man, he's a good man." But I said to him, "This one, I show you that cousin of mine." See, that was his older *girl.* And I said to my uncle, "You want *him* in the family? You got older girl than I am, send her, get *her* and marry him. I don't want to marry an old man."

SILVERMAN: No. Thirteen years.

MOCH: Yeah, I was sixteen.

SILVERMAN: That would be thirteen years older than you.

MOCH: Yeah. I said, "No, I don't want to get married." So I told him. He gave up after that.

SILVERMAN: And so that didn't happen.

MOCH: That didn't happen, I didn't want him. Then I come to this city and I marry my *man,* he didn't have a damn thing.[35]

Other informants gave accounts of cheap cousins, granddaughters who are wonderful mothers, wealthy relatives, and saintly priests. And so the process of Polish-American storytelling continues, ever dynamic, ever in flux, creatively using bits and pieces of the past to construct narratives that are meaningful to a given family, within a certain culture, at a particular moment in time. Like the storytellers of old Poland, today's raconteurs are performers intent on orally transmitting information about their culture's values to the next generation.

8

"GUARDIAN ANGEL, STAY BY MY SIDE": FOLK RELIGION IN POLONIA

Anioł stróż, bądź przy mnie.

(Guardian angel, stay by my side.)
—Polish folk prayer

Catholic religious beliefs are inextricably woven into the Polish and Polish-American worldview (chapter 3). Many Polish-American oral narratives are of a sacred nature.[1] One of the most familiar Polish proverbs, for example, is "gość w dom, Bóg w dom" (a visitor in the home is God in the home), a saying that is often framed and either hung on the wall or placed in a windowsill of a home.[2] William Thomas and Florian Znaniecki have argued that the Catholic Church is "surrounded with a nimbus of holiness, an object of awe and love" for Poles because the most important events of individual, familial, and communal life occur there, as does instruction in the ethnic group's moral teachings.[3] These attitudes permeate daily life.

In the face of adversity, subjugation, and domination, religion historically provided an important source of cultural coherence and social unity for Poles; in America, the bonds fostered through religion compensated for their sense of isolation. Both in Poland and America, the Catholic Church featured a richly symbolic liturgical calendar:

Aside from more than a score of special seasonal observances . . . Mass was celebrated daily and church attendance was obligatory on Sundays. The faithful were also expected to confess their sins to the priest, perform Penance and receive Holy Communion at the very least once a year around Eastertime. All these devotional practices and many more observances connected with the Sacraments which marked rites of passage and the virtually innumerable feasts in honor of the Saints embedded the Polish immigrant in a collective spiritual life that celebrated community through common worship.[4]

Although a Polish-American's relationship with God is intense, it is also complex and mediated by priests, the Virgin Mary, and a host of saints who act as intercessors for the faithful. In Polonia's early years, there also were *wróz* or *wiedzący* (wise ones), holy men and women, who, although not witches, understood the natural order of things and worked within the Christian framework to give advice outside the realm of the priest.[5] Although by no means absolute, distinctions may be made between the Polish-American folk group's beliefs and the official Catholic religion. As Carla Bianco has noted with respect to Italian-Americans of peasant ancestry, "Folk prayers, the worship of objects and human vestiges, magic behavior patterns in pilgrimages and sanctuaries, miraculous letters and healings, the capture of witches on Christmas night are, at least potentially, mediators of Christian values. Though in a very narrow and elementary way, they are the only means of participating in the dominant and not otherwise understandable Catholic cult."[6] These religious beliefs of the folk group in the community rather than within the church are referred to by the Catholic Church as "paraliturgical customs."[7]

In the Polish-American folk community, faith is manifested through iconographic displays within the home as well as in yard and roadside shrines; beliefs in angelology and demonology, expressed respectively via beliefs in guardian angels and the evil eye; folk blessings for Christmas, Easter, weddings, and everyday use in the home; prayers to God, the Virgin Mary, and various saints for protection against illnesses and lightning; and miraculous cures, including the modern-day healing of a western New York state woman that the Vatican certified as a true miracle.[8]

Home, Roadside, and Yard Shrines

In Poland, peasants expressed reverence for God by way of numerous iconographic displays. Inside the home, there were small altars with a statue of the Virgin Mary or a saint as the focal point and surrounded by votive candles and flowers; outdoors, there were crosses or roadside shrines known as *kapliczki przy drozne* (chapels by the wayside). Ethnographer Sula Benet, who did fieldwork in Poland in the 1930s, noted that the shrines were common to all villages: "Each village has at least one, and sometimes more. The shrine is usually located at the very edge of the village, establishing a boundary line. A popular place is at the crossroads, because more people pass here and also because crossroads are believed to be a favourite haunt of evil spirits, who may be held in check by the beneficent influence of a sacred figure. The passer-by will stop to rest and pray at the shrine, and perhaps to leave an offering of flowers or green boughs."[9] Shrines also were constructed at the sites of suicides, murders, witch burnings, heavenly apparitions, springs believed to be miraculous, and the gravesites of those buried in forests or fields.[10] Such structures often were walled in on three sides, with a roof of shingles or wide planks topped by a small tower, glazed pottery ball, or iron cross. The most ancient shrines often contained a *Chrystus frasobliwy* (troubled Christ) figure, a carved statue of Jesus seated with his head resting in his hand.

Shrines at the village limits marked a parting of the ways; departing visitors would say good-bye to their hosts here, as would sons leaving home for military service. Most mourners accompanying a corpse on its journey to the cemetery also would bid farewell at the shrine. Occasionally, official village business might be conducted at the site or farmers might pray for rain there.[11]

Although the origin of these crosses and shrines is obscure, it has been hypothesized that they are a Christian sacralization of pagan rituals. This is suggested by the shrines' frequent placement near crossroads and borders, areas the pagan Slavs deemed unsafe.[12] Once Christianity was introduced to Poland, the Catholic Church attempted to make the sites sacred. During the Counterreformation of the seventeenth century, shrines in Poland became more numerous as a means for the Church to reinforce Catholicism. Their popularity continued during the following two centuries, not only as religious sites but also as family monuments.

Polish immigrants to America brought the tradition with them, especially in rural areas. In central Wisconsin, for example, farmers have constructed scores of shrines since 1857, when Poles first came to Wisconsin, at crossroads, roadsides, near churches, in cemeteries, and adjacent to homes. Builders of the earlier shrines and crosses were trying to re-create the monuments of their native villages in Poland, whereas more recent creations emanate from a desire to display beautiful religious statues no longer exhibited in contemporary American Catholic churches.

In western New York state, where an estimated 25 percent of all Catholics are of Polish descent, a number of Polish-American families have erected yard shrines highlighted by statues of the Virgin Mary, Jesus, or a saint.[13] One informant described her backyard shrine featuring the Sacred Heart of Jesus: "That's been here, I would say, my children bought me that for Mother's Day maybe about six years ago. The Sacred Heart is my favorite because of the burning heart with all His love, and I love people, and that heart shows."[14]

Indoor iconographic displays may juxtapose sacred and secular elements, a reflection of the homeowner's personal interests. In one home, for example, a display atop a television set featured a picture of Jesus and other religious artifacts, family photos, Buffalo Bills football memorabilia, and a cup decorated with the region's Concord grapes.

In addition to such displays, framed holy pictures of the Virgin Mary, Jesus, saints, or prayers often adorn the walls in homes of devout Polish-Americans. Such items are available through religious orders such as the Felician Sisters (Congregation of St. Felix of Cantalice), an order in the northeastern United States that originated in Poland, as well as stores specializing in religious items.

Demons and Angels: Evil Eye and Guardian Angel Beliefs

Early Polish-Americans, like their Italian Catholic counterparts and many other nationalities, shared in another universal folk belief, the evil eye.[15] Certain individuals, especially those marred by a scar or other physical deformity, were believed to be most capable of giving the evil eye to another person, although an ordinary person could unwittingly transmit it by a simple act of admiration.[16]

Although many superstitions from Poland dropped by the wayside in Polish-American communities, belief in the evil eye persisted for many years. "In Buffalo in 1910, many people still believed in the evil eye and in the possibility of casting a spell, even by a good person, unintentionally. Thus, one must not praise or admire a child or any growing thing too much or it might turn ugly or stop growing. If one could not restrain oneself, then one should preface or follow the words of admiration with the expression "na psa urok" (may the spell fall on a dog) or spit over one's shoulder."[17]

Too much praise also might mark a child or cause the child to meet a bad fate. To remove that possibility, one would transfer that ill-feeling to some other object by way of *uroki* (charms or spells).[18] As recently as the 1950s, red ribbons were worn by Polish-Americans anxious to ward off the evil eye.

> TOM GESTWICKI: I remember a lady living, when we lived on Gazelle Street, there was a lady living around the corner that *all* the neighborhood people thought she had an evil eye. And I guess, when I was much too little to remember, but my mother dressed me with, and put a little red ribbon if we ever had to go by the house, because that warded it off. Yeah, they were real firm believers in that, I just remember that lady.
>
> SILVERMAN: The evil eye . . .
>
> GESTWICKI: Yeah, that she could look at you and make you sick.
>
> SILVERMAN: Make you sick?
>
> GESTWICKI: Yup, um-hmm. Supposedly, the dog died after she cursed it or something.
>
> SILVERMAN: Your mother's dog? Or her dog?
>
> GESTWICKI: It would be my grandparents' dog. Yeah, they were real believers that that lady possessed some kind of evil.[19]

The evil eye also could be transmitted by jealous neighbors to farm animals, particularly cows who would then suffer from milk fever. To restore health to the animals, the entire family was supposed to participate in a search for the evil eye, believed to be one of the half-moon-shaped fungi that grow on trees: "To destroy the eye, cover yourself with a sheet and go at midnight to the tree and puncture the fungus with needles. Keep on doing this until the fungus falls to the ground. When this happens, the power of the 'evil eye' will be gone. But be careful not to touch the fungus, either now or for a certain length of time, else the cure will not work."[20]

In recent years, belief in the evil eye has virtually disappeared among Polish-Americans in the western New York communities that I surveyed; many informants dismissed it laughingly as a superstition of their immigrant ancestors. Yet belief in angelology remains strong, especially among parochial school students.

A study of children attending St. Stanislaus School in Buffalo in 1984 found that widespread belief in guardian angels operates at three levels of complexity as children grow older.[21] Among those up to age nine, guardian angels are imaginary figures introduced by parents, grandparents, or teachers as concrete beings with magical powers such as the ability to fly, shrink in size, see through walls, or become invisible. At about nine years of age, the child's conceptualization changes, and guardian angels become imaginary playmates and caretakers. But that, too, evolves as the child matures; by age eleven, the child refers to the guardian angel as "my good side," an indication that the values embodied by guardian angels have become internalized. The folklore associated with guardian angels helps transmit traditional values of the Polish-American culture, which emphasizes cooperation and refuses to equate the mere amassing of goods with goodness.[22] These values are in opposition to mainstream culture that champions individualism, competition, and materialism.

The Healing Power of God: Folk Blessings, Prayers, and Cures

Although guardian angels are associated primarily with children, Polish-Americans of all ages can invoke the aid of God against illness, imminent death, lightning, or other maladies through various blessings and prayers, either to God directly or through the intercession of the Virgin Mary, saints, or other figures.

Blessings are shared within the family circle at two important moments in the liturgical year: Christmas Eve and Easter morning (chapters 3 and 4). These blessings are led by the head of the family and feature the distribution of a ritual food: at Christmas, the opłatek, whose purpose is to bring about a spirit of forgiveness and unity, and on Easter Sunday, the hard-boiled egg blessed in church the previous day by the priest. Folk blessings also play a major role in rites of passage, such as the blessing for a happy, prosperous marriage given by the bride's parents to a young couple on their wedding day (chapter 6). Another folk blessing is given on a daily basis:

> AL MAZUR: I still do this. It's a cheerful thing. I come into the house, and I think it's one of the most beautiful customs. I'll say, "Niech będzie pochwalony Jezus Chrystus" (praised be to Jesus Christ). And the response is, "Na wieki wieków, amen" (forever and ever, amen).
>
> DOROTHY MAZUR: We always did that when we were young, every day.
>
> AL: But we sort of almost got to kid around about that. I'd come in and sing out, like I was a bishop [sings]: "Niech będzie pochwalony Jezus Chrystus!"
>
> DOROTHY: Our dogs would hide! When you leave the house . . .
>
> AL: When you leave the house, you would say—well, there's two responses

here. "Idź w Bogiem" (go with God), and the response would be "zostańcie z Bogiem" (remain with God).

DOROTHY: We'll still say that, if you walk in, like our children when they moved away and we walk into their homes, or even now, when they move from their apartment to a new home, we come in and say, "Niech będzie pochwalony Jezus Chrystus." When we bought our piece of property in the hills there, the cabin, and took your [Al's] mother up to see it, she walked in, she said that.[23]

The Mazurs also noted that both sets of parents used to have a holy water font at the door so that people entering the home could bless themselves, but they themselves no longer observe this practice.

Another informant whose family used the "niech będzie pochwalony Jezus Chrystus" greeting told me it was given because it was customary to do so. "They [people] had respect for the Lord. They were Christians, you know, and they'd come to your door, whether it was a man or a woman or what. Even if my father would go to the cupboard to get the whiskey out, and they'd have a shot, you know. But, when that man came to the door, 'Niech będzie pochwalony,' he'd always take his hat off."[24]

As might be expected when medical remedies were either unavailable or ineffective, blessings and prayers to cure illnesses have figured as prominently in the lives of Polish-Americans as they have in other folk communities. One folk cure involved the sign of the cross and the "Our Father" prayer.

KATE MOCH: My daughter lives on Roosevelt Avenue in Dunkirk. She had a boy, he was nine months old, and he was small. He was getting convulsions all the time. And he was just sitting. They had him to every hospital in Dunkirk and Children's Hospital in Buffalo and every place, and they thought he's gonna be, what do you call that?

SILVERMAN: Epileptic?

MOCH: Yes—no, uh, retarded. Well, I used to go to her, and he would sit on the couch, and he was shaking all the time, he'd get those convulsions. And oh, I'd hate to see, that baby was *so* sick!

My aunt used to live down here in Fourth Ward, and she was married to my father's brother. And I went to her and I talk to her, because she was from old country. And she said to me, "Kate, some day you take me there, and I'm gonna take the holy candle"—like they got in church, blessed candles . . .

SILVERMAN: Blessed candles?

MOCH: Yeah. Not the candle like this [points to small candle], they have regular *gromnicza,* they call it in Polish. And she took that candle to my daughter, and she melt the candle in a little pan, and she took holy water, and she make the cross like that [makes the sign of the cross] with a stick—broom.

SILVERMAN: With a broom?

MOCH: Yeah, make it . . .

SILVERMAN: Broom straws?

MOCH: Yeah, broom straw, make a cross. And she'd melt that, and put the water here in a little dish, and she'd take that candle and put it three times in front of him . . .

SILVERMAN: Over the little boy?

MOCH: Over the little boy. And she say a prayer, the "Our Father," and he *never* got sick after that! And he's twenty-six years old![25]

In some instances, the moon rather than a religious figure is invoked, suggestive of a pagan origin, as in the following prayer from Poland's Cieszyn region near Czechoslovakia and Silesia:

Witóm cie,
miesiónczku nowy,
od bolynio zymbów
e głowy.

(I greet you,
new moon,
from the pain of toothache
and headache.)[26]

A version of this prayer was recited by a Polish-American woman who told me that she learned it from her immigrant father; he prayed to the new moon so that he never would have a toothache and reportedly never did.[27] Another variant in Polonia eliminates all references to illness, thus transforming it into a simple greeting when one sees the moon: "Witam cię księżycu na wschodzie i na zachodzie" (I greet you, moon, in the East and in the West).[28]

More common than such prayers to the moon were those asking for the aid of the Blessed Virgin Mary, who occupied a place second only to that of her son Jesus in the Polish peasant's hierarchy: "The intensity of her worship is closely linked to the deep respect for human motherhood. Because of her tenderness, Mary is appealed to on behalf of the weak, the sick, the innocent, and those of high purpose, such as soldiers setting forth to battle."[29]

More church holidays honor Mary than any of the saints. May is Mary's special month, and Saturday her special day throughout the year; any tasks in which her help is sought should be done on Saturday. As elsewhere in the Catholic world, in Poland there are more churches named for the Virgin Mary than for any other heavenly figure. Miraculous pictures of her are venerated throughout the country, including the smoke-darkened Black Madonna of Częstochowa, the object of many pilgrimages and the subject of legends. The worship of Mary has continued in similar fashion in Polish-American communities.

Prayers to guardian angels and saints also are common in Polonia. One woman's father taught her a guardian angel prayer to be recited during bad weather:

> If it was a storm, lightning and thunder,
> Say this: "Anioł stróż, bądź przy mnie."
> That means, "Guardian angel, stay by my side."
> You'll never get struck by lightning.
> Even now, to this day, if there's a storm,
> I keep repeating that.[30]

"You Have a Saint": The Halasinski Story

Around the world, Catholics have prayed for centuries to saints and holy figures, asking for their intercession with God in difficult or seemingly hopeless causes. Such was the case in 1983 for Lillian Halasinski of Dunkirk, New York, who had an incurable illness and prayed for assistance to Mother Angela Truszkowska, a deceased Polish nun.[31] Her prayers were answered, and the Vatican certified the case as a true miracle, which led to the beatification of Mother Angela, the first step toward sainthood.

> LILLIAN HALASINSKI: It started in May. I was in the garden, and I fell right on a rosebush. My leg gave way. And so then I doctored it, and I went to a . . .[32]
>
> GERALDINE HALASINSKI [her daughter]: Chiropractor . . .
>
> LILLIAN: Chiropractor all summer . . .
>
> GERALDINE: She thought it was something from her spine.
>
> LILLIAN: Nobody seemed to help me. Then in the late fall I was in the hospital, dehydrated . . .

GERALDINE: In September and October, she lost sixty-five pounds in two months . . .

LILLIAN [speaking simultaneously]: That's one sign of diabetic neuropathy. You lose a lot of weight, and I lost sixty-five pounds. They kind of gave me up, that I won't make it. I kept on doctoring, and I landed in the hospital, and Sister Leocretia, a Felician sister, she came to visit me. She was giving communion to patients. And she told me to pray to Mother Angela. She gave me a prayer to Blessed Mary Angela. And I prayed from then . . .

GERALDINE: Two months . . .

LILLIAN: Yeah. Of course, I doctored, and the doctor finally gave up, and he says, "I can't do anything else for you."

I says, "Well, amputate my leg."

And he says, "Well, before I do, go first to the hospital."

GERALDINE: To see a surgeon.

LILLIAN: No, not . . .

GERALDINE: Oh, therapy, for therapy. He says there's one more thing he's going to try.

LILLIAN: And I went there, and my leg was in such terrible pain that they couldn't do anything. And that same night, at nine o'clock in the evening, I sat in the chair, my daughter was reading a book, and my husband didn't feel too good so he went to bed, and I could sense the presence of Mother Angela right in the doorway. It was so beautiful, the silence was beautiful, you can't describe it! You never want it to end. And suddenly, I had no pain, my leg was swollen in the first place, that was gone . . .

GERALDINE: She was scaly, peeling like a bad sunburn . . .

LILLIAN: And my leg was pink. And from that time on, I had no pain and it's twelve years now, January fourth.[33]

When Lillian Halasinski reported her miraculous healing to Sister Leocretia, she in turn told the Felicians, who asked the Vatican to investigate the matter. After waiting two years to ensure that she wasn't simply in remission from the illness, the Vatican began an inquiry:

LILLIAN: They sent a report to Rome, and there were five [Vatican] doctors, and they had to agree on all of that. They sent me all kinds of tests to go through. I had to go to Buffalo doctors . . .

GERALDINE: Neurologists, orthopedic specialists . . .

LILLIAN: And one doctor, what was his name?

GERALDINE: Phillips.

LILLIAN: Dr. Phillips. He said, "You have a saint." He says, "I have many patients with diabetic neuropathy. I don't know what to do with them. They're all in wheelchairs because that's not curable, that sickness."

In April 1993 the Halasinskis and a contingent of priests and Felician nuns from western New York state went to Rome for the beatification of Mother Angela, then to Kraków, Poland, to visit her burial site. Since then, the intense media coverage of Lillian Halasinski's cure has resulted in many requests to the Halasinskis and the Felician sisters for additional information about Mother Angela.

As of 1996, the Halasinskis themselves had distributed 1,775 prayers, 78 bone relics, 160 medals, 18 pins, 66 Mother Angela bulletins, 29 Catholic newspaper accounts, and 13 sets of photographs of themselves with Pope John Paul II. The relics taken from Mother Angela's bones are tiny chips, about the size of a pinhead, which are believed to have healing power: "They put it [the relic] on their pain, wherever they have the pain," Lillian Halasinski says. Each relic comes with an authentication statement from the postulator general in Rome.

Although many Polish-Americans employ such religious objects, folk prayers, blessings, and shrines in their daily worship, it should be noted that due to geographic mobility, an increasing number of them belong to parishes that are not ethnically Polish but rather multiethnic in character. One might assume, therefore, that the Polish religious traditions both in the church and home are dying away, but that is not the case. "They recall these customs and they want to maintain them because they're beautiful," Cornelian Dende says. "They recall going to church, for instance, on Holy Saturday with that little Easter basket with foods to be blessed. They were accompanied by their mothers. So now they'd like to find it in the church that they're frequenting. And so they approach the pastor. And if the pastor is a good pastor, if here's a need among the parishioners, he's going to try to satisfy it."[34] Within the Diocese of Buffalo, for example, the practice of the Holy Saturday święconka blessing has spread to non-Polish parishes in the English language, and so the process of adaptation continues. As they did in the Old World, Polish religious objects, folk prayers, and folk blessings coexist with the official Catholic faith and are modified to meet the contemporary needs of the New World faithful.

9

THE GARDEN OF HEALING:
POLISH-AMERICAN FOLK MEDICINE

Śmierć tego nie ubodzie u kogo szałwia w ogrodzie.

(Death will never sting him who has sage in the garden.)
—Knab, *Polish Customs*

Plants played an important role in the daily lives of Polish peasants.
Not only were they a source of food, but they also provided dyes for
clothing; inspiration for folk art decorative motifs; symbols of life, fertility, or other concepts for holiday and rite-of-passage celebrations; and
medicine.

Their use in celebrations, where they aided in the mental well-being
of participants by warding off evil, has been alluded to in chapters 3
through 6. For Corpus Christi Sunday, for example, wreaths as small as
the palm of a hand would be made of such herbs and flowers as *macierz-
anka* (thyme), hazelwort, stonecrop, *przywrotnik* (lady's mantle), sundew,
mint, *ruta* (rue), *stokroć margarytka* (daisy), and *barwinek* (periwinkle).
The wreaths were hung on the monstrance for the week following Corpus Christi and then taken home and hung on the wall above holy pictures or placed in the foundation of a new home to ward off evil spirits
and natural or manmade disasters.[1]

On St. John's Eve (June 23), which marks the summer solstice, *bylica*
(mugwort) played a key role. A garland of the herb tossed on a midsummer fire would render the thrower safe from all ill-fortune for the coming year. *Dziurawiec* (St. John's wort), *koszyczki Najświętszej Marii Panny*
(vervain), *łopian* (burdock), *leszczyna* (hazel), and *piołun* (wormwood)
were among the many herbs believed to have the power to protect homes
against witches and other evil forces, especially on this night. Herbs col-

lected before sunset on St. John's Eve were believed to have special potency in curing illnesses, which is why many children and elderly people searched for clover, *rumianek* (chamomile), and *podbiał pospolity* (coltsfoot) to ease rheumatism, arthritis, and lung problems.[2]

Plants also played prescribed roles in births, weddings, and deaths, having either symbolic or medicinal value. Rue represented maidenhood, grown by families with daughters of marriageable age. The night before her wedding, the prospective bride would cut down the rue, aided by her bridesmaids, and weave it into a wreath to wear to church the next day.[3]

Krawnik (yarrow) regulated menstruation, mugwort increased fertility, *boże drzewko* (southernwood) was believed to prevent miscarriages, and St. John's wort scared away evil spirits during childbirth. New mothers drank *melisa lekarska* (lemon balm) or chamomile tea, and infants slept with a sprig of *jemioła biała* (mistletoe) for pleasant dreams and wore shirts bearing southernwood and mugwort to prevent the evil eye. A death was announced to the community by means of a sprig of periwinkle and the name of the deceased person tossed on a doorstep, with the understanding that each household would then take the periwinkle and name to the next home until the periwinkle finally returned to the home of the deceased. Mugwort and wormwood were tucked around the body, which was incensed with juniper berries.[4] Polish mountaineers believed that *dziewanna* (mullein) was an aid to childbirth, and Polish-Americans in Milwaukee used it to cure farm animals of worms.[5] Still other Poles employed mullein to treat diarrhea, lung ailments, toothaches, warts, burns, and sore feet.[6]

Homemakers in Poland and in early Polish-American communities took various herbs and flowers gathered from field and forest to church to be blessed on August 15, the Feast of the Assumption of the Blessed Mother (Matka Boska Zielna, Our Lady of the Herbs). This blessing was a Slavic custom rather than part of the universal Catholic ritual.[7] It was believed that blessed herbs and flowers wished to be helpful to humanity, a belief reflected in a proverb, "Świeć i mnie! Co mogę to pomogę!" (Bless me also! I will help as much as I can!), supposedly whispered by plants as homemakers stood in front of them, deciding which to cut.[8]

The role of a Polish homemaker (*gospodyni*) was paramount in maintaining a peasant family's health. In Polish cities there were additional alternatives: physicians, barber/surgeons, city pharmacies or those of nearby monasteries, traveling salesmen, authors of books on herbal medicines, and even folk healers.[9] The education of early Polish physicians was, at best, inadequate, however. Medical education at schools in Kraków and Warsaw during the seventeenth and eighteenth centuries barely existed due to a lack of funding, resulting in a surplus of uneducated doctors who practiced medicine in the cities without proper diplomas.[10] In the country, where peasants were illiterate and far removed from any doctor's office, families relied on women's knowledge of teas, salves, and poultices to treat illnesses, information based on oral tradition. Rather than planting a formal herb garden, Polish women ranged through meadows, fields, and forests to supply their families' needs.

This tradition of self-healing persisted in Polonia throughout the early part of the twentieth century. Polish immigrants brought seeds or slips of plants with them to re-create the "outdoor apothecaries" of their homeland. One such garden in Connecticut featured mugwort, wormwood, southernwood, thyme, *żywokost* (comfrey), and iris roots, all transplants from the woman's home in the *górale* (highlands) of southern Poland.[11]

As late as 1925 in Buffalo and other Polish-American communities "wise" women and men set broken limbs and prescribed potions or ointments. In addition to such healers and self-doctoring, Polish-Americans urged their druggists rather than their doctors to prescribe remedies.[12] In Buffalo, for example, the Arko Herbs Company, a store that sold herbal remedies, existed for many years on Broadway on the city's Polish east side. Among the store's potions, shown to me in 1995 by a man whose late father had been a doctor, was a two-fluid-ounce bottle of thyme, a bitter-tasting liquid selling for 75 cents. The bottle's label advertised it as "a remedy for colic, cramps, diarrhea, dysentery, toothache and earache. Also for the relief of pain and gases in the stomach and bowels." Adults were advised to take one teaspoon diluted with water every hour or two until relieved; children's dosages were to be adjusted accordingly. The medicine was manufactured in Buffalo.[13] Polonians also occasionally turned to other ethnic groups for advice.

I tell you who had a lot of good medicines was the Indians. But I don't remember what they were. There were salves and all that from the Indians that they'd get in Irving. There was Indians, there used to be a railroad track, a streetcar track, that ran all the way through Dunkirk on the outskirts through Sheridan, all through Irving and all the way to Buffalo. And those Indians lived right along those tracks in shacks, 'cuz I can remember that. But they'd go to the woods, and they got all these—they didn't die of stuff. They had medicine of their own. Ginseng and whatever it was they called all those different leaves and teas.[14]

Early Polish-Americans made a thorough search for such medicines from all available sources because they had limited access to physicians but many illnesses. For that reason, prevention was primary:

> RITA DANNER: My grandmother was a very firm believer in nature. I guess all the old Polish people were and still are to today. She, instead of taking a vitamin or milk or anything else, she ate a clove of garlic every day of her life.
>
> SILVERMAN: Just raw?
>
> DANNER: Just a raw clove of garlic. I'll never forget that.
>
> SILVERMAN: Did she eat it at breakfast?
>
> DANNER: Any time. She'd just eat the clove of garlic.[15]

Despite such preventive measures, death was a frequent and untimely visitor to Polonia in the early twentieth century, particularly during the winter. "It was nothing to see a few children eight, nine, ten years old die," Mary Miller recalled. "And you had quarantines on the houses. And diseases were so widespread. There wasn't the medicine that you have today. I can remember one family, there was two girls, two sisters died—because the one girl got some kind of a sickness and she slept with the other girl, then the other girl died. In one week, two girls in that family."[16]

The worst time, recalled by a number of people, was the Great Flu Epidemic of 1918–19 that killed thousands, both in Europe and America. Given Polonia's lack of modern medical practices, the epidemic was especially deadly. According to Mary Miller, "Whole families would be dying, and they'd carry them out. Out back at St. Hyacinth's, there was a whole family that died. They kept taking them out of that house. You wouldn't even have a funeral because the priest didn't even want to go to the house for fear. That was how deadly it was. They took them out at night to the cemetery with the horse and wagon."

Folk remedies were tried with varying degrees of success, as indicated in a conversation between a native of Scranton, Pennsylvania, and his wife, born and raised in western New York.

> AL CLARK [to wife]: Do you remember when they had the first flu?
>
> ANN CLARK: Yeah.

AL: They had camphor, camphor bags. Did you have those?

ANN: No. Camphorated oil?

AL: No. *Camphor* in a little sack like, they used to wear around their neck. It was supposed to . . .

ANN: Oh, no, I didn't use that one.

SILVERMAN: And what was that one for?

AL: That was for the flu, to combat the flu. But they did have that.

ANN: They all *died*, though.[17]

A variant of the camphor bag did, however, prove successful for another woman. She bought small blocks of camphor for use both at home and work and placed some of them over the heat register in her bedroom and pinned others to her work clothing, a treatment she believed effective because she didn't catch the flu.[18] Other patients tried different remedies:

MARY MILLER: When you got that flu, you first started with a terrible headache and a congestion, and you just ached all over, and your mouth was all coated. And it was an awful sickness, true. My mother took whiskey, put honey in it, and pepper, and maybe bacon grease or something, because I know it was quite greasy. But she gave us whiskey.

SILVERMAN: To drink?

MILLER: Yes, children.

SILVERMAN: Like a cough medicine?

MILLER: Yeah.

SILVERMAN: I've heard that.

MILLER: Hey, we survived that. Nobody in our family died of the flu.

Whiskey combined with several other ingredients also was believed to help cure the common cold.

KATE MOCH: A lot of people, they make whiskey, honey, and butter. And warm up together, and that's supposed to be, a lot of people put onion in it, and it's supposed to be good for a cold, too.

SILVERMAN: Now is that something you drink, or . . . ?

MOCH: Drink, drink, drink.

SILVERMAN: And it's whiskey and honey and butter and . . .

MOCH: And onions fried. Onion, that's supposed to be good for colds, too. Honey is good for a lot of stuff.[19]

Rita Danner still drinks whiskey and honey with tea and lemon whenever she gets a cold, with excellent results: "You sweat a cold out. You drink that as hot as you can, and you get under the blankets, boy, and

I'll tell you, in a couple of hours you get up and you're wringing wet. You change clothes and do it right again. And it does work."[20] Other cold remedies included homemade chicken soup and a combination of lemon extract and candy:

ROSE LEHR: For a cold, my mother used to take licorice and that rock candy.

RITA DANNER [daughter]: Oh yeah, that's a good one.

SILVERMAN: What was that?

LEHR: And lemon.

DANNER: Licorice, black licorice, and rock candy—you've heard of rock candy?

SILVERMAN: Sure.

DANNER: And what? Licorice, rock candy, uh, what else did she put in there? Water and lemon extract. Pure lemon.

SILVERMAN: That worked?

LEHR: She boiled it for about twenty minutes . . .

DANNER: Boil it . . .

LEHR: And then put it in a bottle.

SILVERMAN: And that worked.

LEHR: In two or three days, the cold was gone.

A drink of whiskey, honey, and lemon also was used for coughs.[21] There were other cures as well, such as human urine, valuable because it is sterile.[22]

MARTHA STEFFAN: When all three of us kids were coughing, my mother called Doctor Sullivan, and he said, "Mary, I could give you some cough medicine, but I'll tell you something that will work better. Let your kid pee in a glass and drink that pee."

SILVERMAN: No kidding.

STEFFAN: In two days the cough was gone. The sore throat was gone. But how I used to *hate* to drink *that!*[23]

For the congestion of a chest cold, sometimes the patient would drink a teaspoon of turpentine.[24] More commonly, a poultice would be applied to the chest, such as goose grease, snake oil, or onions. "We used to take onions and fry them," Mary Miller said, "did you ever hear of that? With a flannel cloth and wrap that around you. That's another cure for a chest cold."[25] Still other Polish-Americans suggested camphorated oil or lard. "We used to have melted lard, and put it on a woolen cloth and lay it there [on the chest], and keep it on overnight, and that was supposed to really help."[26] Lard also was used for burns, but for cuts, rashes, and sores there were other home medicines.

KATE MOCH: You know what they grow outside, they call *babka?*

SILVERMAN: Uh-huh.

MOCH: You know its green leaves, plain green leaves, they're kind of heavy?

SILVERMAN: Yeah.

MOCH: Those are good to put on sores, too.

Known in America as the weed plantain, *babka lancetowata* has been used since ancient times by Polish women to treat skin disorders. Its fresh, crushed leaves were applied to cuts, burns, furuncles, and skin inflammations, which were then covered by a clean cloth. When its leaves were mixed with lard, salt, and soft bread, the mixture was used to cure boils and ulcers; the juice of the leaves was effective against fevers and bee stings; and the crushed leaves were applied with egg white to snake bites.[27] There was another treatment for cuts in addition to babka. Kate Moch recalled her days on a farm in Poland:

> You see this big cut? [Shows her hand.]
>
> SILVERMAN: In your hand?
>
> MOCH: Yeah. You know what I did? I was a healthy girl, I want to do everything. We have rye, we plant rye. We didn't have nothing, no machinery, no nothing, so we cut with a scythe, you know, that little one, that's what they call a scythe, and I cut myself on it. Big piece of [flesh], chunk of meat. And my father *see* it, and he run in the house, and he get the *bread.*
>
> SILVERMAN: Bread?
>
> MOCH: Bread, and wait, wait! He put the bread, I guess he went and *wet* it, *pee* on it, and he cut it out and it [the flesh] grew with no trouble.

Human urine continued to be used in this country not only for cuts but also for rashes such as roseola.

> I guess when my grandmother was younger, my mother was a young girl yet, they had a baby in the family that was born with roseola on its cheek. And how can I explain roseola? It's a very red, uh, crusty swelling rash on its cheek. I mean, it was as big as the baby's cheek. And it was very, very ugly. Well, Grandma said she had taken the baby's diaper with the urine after the child had urinated and taken that diaper with the urine and placed it on this baby's face constantly, and it cured it. It took the rash completely away without any scarring.[28]

The spice rack in a Polish-American home also provided cures, such as one for cold sores cited by Rita Danner: "I use this until today. I tell everybody about it. My grandmother would take cotton balls and soak them in vanilla. And it works. In a little plastic bag, you just fill it up with little balls of cotton and vanilla extract. Not imitation, it's got to be real vanilla, and dab, dab. Takes it right away. No scarring, no nothing." For boils, common food items such as cabbage were applied to the spot to draw out the pus.

> KATE MOCH: In old country, when I was small and my brother was small, we had boils, they call them carbuncles, and my brother have right here. [Points to her face.]
>
> SILVERMAN: On his face . . .
>
> MOCH: And I get right here. [Points to her arm.]
>
> SILVERMAN: And you got one on your arm.
>
> MOCH: Yeah, and you know what to put? They put cabbage leaves, warm. They *warm* the cabbage leaves, and they put the cabbage leaves, and they come to the boil, the big root [of the boil] after.
>
> SILVERMAN: And you could just . . .
>
> MOCH: Just pull out after, the root. But that *hurts!*

In a similar manner, bread was soaked in warm milk and then placed over a boil with a bandage to hold it in place until the mixture cooled, and it would "draw out the poison."[29]

Wormwood was used in both the Old and New World to cure stomachaches.

> SILVERMAN: It was a plant? Was it made into a tea?
>
> AL AND DOROTHY MAZUR: Yup.
>
> DOROTHY: The taverns here would have a bottle of whiskey with a part of that in there so when you came in . . .
>
> AL: Not whiskey, vodka.
>
> DOROTHY: Vodka?
>
> AL: Yeah.
>
> DOROTHY: Or whiskey. My mother said they had whiskey, too, and they used to have that soaking in there, and men with stomach problems would ask for that. That's what it is.
>
> AL: They used to harvest the thing and then put it up in the attic to dry.
>
> DOROTHY: I may have some, my mother's.
>
> AL: It is very bitter, terrible stuff. I suppose the way to cure a headache is to hit yourself over the head with a hammer, and that's the equivalent of it.

For infants who had stomachaches or couldn't sleep, Polish-American mothers believed that chamomile tea was effective; if babies had colic, a few drops of catnip and fennel were added to their water bottles. For children who had the mumps, pork fat was applied to the swollen area and a cloth tied over it for several days to reduce the swelling.[30]

Fresh garlic (*czosnek*) also was important in a home apothecary. It was hung over a door to drive away illnesses and evil spirits, a belief reflected in the proverb "ucieka jak czarownica od czosnku" (runs like a witch from garlic).[31] The garlic bulb was used to cure headaches; chopped and eaten either raw or cooked with food, garlic was also believed effective against high blood pressure or cholesterol.[32]

The liquor cabinet provided a potion to ensure healthy teeth.

MARTHA STEFFAN: My father had his own remedy for his teeth, his own toothpaste.

SILVERMAN: What was that?

STEFFAN: You won't believe it.

SILVERMAN: Try me, go ahead.

STEFFAN: A shot of whiskey in the morning. That's all it is.

SILVERMAN: So you gargle the whiskey...

STEFFAN: And then you swallow it. At night, the same thing. And I tell you, he had beautiful teeth and beautiful *gums*, hard. Because when he took that whiskey in his mouth, he'd make such awful faces, us kids used to laugh. In the morning, especially. At night we were sleeping. He'd repeat that twice a day. I tell you, he had beautiful gums, beautiful teeth when he died at age sixty-five.

By the time World War II began, more and more Polish-Americans were turning to doctors, prescriptions, and hospitals rather than their ancestors' herbal medicines, in part because the younger generation was better educated and more able to afford medical care. Many informants referred to folk remedies in the past tense, noting that they themselves had abandoned such treatments years earlier. Yet there is a revival of interest in medicinal herbs, both on an ethnic and regional basis, as evidenced by the proliferation of books, articles in popular magazines, and speakers available to address groups. Sophie Hodorowicz Knab, an immigrant, is a nursing instructor and also the author of numerous articles and books dealing with Polish herbs. Her mother practiced folk medicine at their home in western New York state:

SOPHIE KNAB: The first herb that I saw her using was the plantain for boils and hard-to-heal areas, and people have told me stories about how they used it to heal incisions. And my mother used nettle for treatment of arthritis. I remember her writing to Poland, asking for the nettle seeds to plant in her garden, and she had nettle growing in her yard for years and years.

SILVERMAN: That used to grow wild in the fields though, right?

KNAB: Right, yes. But here, she was having a hard time because nobody was selling the herbs, at least in Dunkirk they weren't.[33]

As an adult, Sophie Knab developed an interest in Polish folk medicines. Very little information was available in the English language, however, so she researched Polish texts and later began writing, lecturing, and planting a Polish herb garden in her backyard. Her presentations often include a display of herbs that many Americans of Polish descent would recognize, such as comfrey, plantain, and wormwood. "What the display does is," she says, "it simply reminds people of the herbs that their mothers, fathers used to grow in their gardens, and they'll recount stories for me about how their dad made a wormwood tea, you know. So people not only enjoy looking and reviewing these things for themselves, but some people want to buy some of the herbs from me, which I'm not selling because they are strictly for display."

Still others inquire about the herbs not because they recognize them but they remember stories about folk medicine and healing told by parents or grandparents. As Sophie Knab observes, "Frankly, a lot of fourth generation people are looking for alternative medicine other than the medicine we know, Western medicine. I think they are more willing to experiment and try different things." Even among Polish-Americans who prefer "Western" medicine, folklore plays a role in their medical treatment. Oral narratives about the advantages or disadvantages of various prescription drugs, surgical procedures, or doctors circulate widely within ethnic, occupational, and regional groups. Although many members of Polonia have exchanged the backyard apothecary for the hospital, folklore continues to contribute to their mental and physical health.

Sophie Hodorowicz Knab of Grand Island, N.Y., in her Polish herb garden next to *bylica* (mugwort), a tall, spiky plant, in 1995.

Celebrated under a tent outdoors, this 1991 polka mass was part of the Eden, N.Y., Polka Festival. The celebrant was the Rev. Mark Skura; music was performed by the City Side Band of Buffalo.

Denise Szatkowski of Alliance, Ohio (left) teaches polka dancing to her daughters Chris and Kayla at a 1995 polka festival in western New York state.

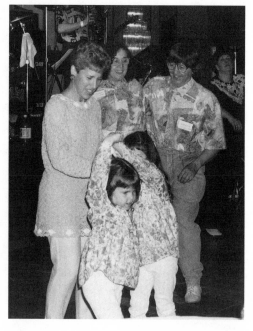

Like many other "commuter ethnics," Jane and Ed Bognaski of Syracuse, N.Y., drove 150 miles to suburban Buffalo to attend a 1993 Dyngus Day dance.

Buffalo's Merry Tatra Dancers, a Polish-American folk dance group, circa 1958. Leader Daniel Collins is at the far right. (Courtesy of Daniel Collins)

(Opposite) Więz Dance Ensemble member Andrea Makowski and a partner at a 1995 performance.

Wycinanki at a multiethnic folk arts festival in western New York state in 1979.

Pin-style pisanki made by inscribing wax designs on egg shells, then dipping the eggs in a dye made from onion skins, water, and vinegar. These pisanki were made by Henia Makowski for an Easter egg festival in Cheektowaga, N.Y., in 1992.

(Above) Pierogi at a Christmas
wigilia, 1994.

(Right) Joe Rozen boiling
pierogi.

Joe Rozen's daughter, Lori (right) and his sister, Jane Henderson, make the pierogi for the family wigilia in 1995.

At his family's Christmas wigilia in 1994, Jim Rozen helps himself to
kapusta (sauerkraut soup), watched by sisters Julie and Lori.

Monike Poslinski and Jeff Wini-
arski demonstrate how to make
chrusciki for shoppers at the
Broadway Market in Buffalo on
Palm Sunday 1993.

Ed Tarnowski cuts up hard-boiled eggs for Easter barszcz at his social club, the Kosciuszko Club of Dunkirk, N.Y., in 1993.

Daniel Kij, Lackawanna, N.Y., in 1997. He is among the many who use personal computers to discuss Polish-American customs via the Internet.

10

POLISH FOLK SONGS:
SEEDS OF A NEW MUSICAL STYLE

We are family,
Polka family,
We're the best of friends
Getting together now and then.
—"We Are Family," Polka Family Band

The concept of family always has been an integral part of Polish-American life, finding expression over and over again in the group's folk music and dancing. In the early days of Polonia, before the advent of "ethnic" recordings, immigrants shared a wealth of folk songs, many of which were Easter hymns or Christmas kolędy (chapters 3 and 4).[1] Beyond these, however, were songs of Polish nationalism, old country occupations such as farming, immigration, friendship and love, and rites of passage such as birthdays, weddings, and funerals.

These songs were performed primarily within the family, the Polish-American community. A glimpse into that era was offered by one remarkable folk musician, Albert (Al) Clark (né Wisniewski) of Dunkirk, New York. To avoid joining his father in the coal mines near Scranton, Pennsylvania, Clark left home at age sixteen to work first as a galley hand on ships plying the Great Lakes and then as a bugler in the U.S. Navy before moving with his wife, Ann, to Buffalo's Polish community and finally to Dunkirk, where he was employed as a machinist. At every stop he expanded his repertoire of folk tunes; he did not formally collect them, however, until he retired in his sixties, when he learned to play the clarinet.[2]

He recalled that Scranton's large Polonia enjoyed a lively musical tradition during the 1910s and 1920s. "When they had picnics or anything, we always had a three- or four-piece band, and they used to play these Polish numbers at these outdoor picnics. This was from the church socials, you know what I mean? The group would get together on a Saturday afternoon, and they'd have a little platform for dancing, and then they'd have this four-piece orchestra, drink beer, and have all these Polish dishes."[3]

Unlike today's amplified, brassy-sounding polka bands, the early "orchestra" of America's Polonias might have consisted of a concertina, violin, string bass, and clarinet, a combination referred to as the *wiejska* (old village) style of eastern Poland. This instrumentation derived from Polish villages, where one might find violins, cello, a small double-bass, drum, flute, and occasionally a dulcimer, accordion, or bagpipes performing for village festivities.[4] Such wiejska groups were common in western New York state's Polish-American communities in the early twentieth century.[5]

Merrymaking at a church social or picnic might include the performance of "W Poniedzałek Rano" (On a Monday morning), which in seven verses celebrates the ups and downs of a farmer's weekly life. The first verse follows:

W Poniedzałek rano!
Kosił ojciec siano,
Kosił ojciec, kosił ja,
Kosiliśmy obydwa,
Kosił ojciec, kosił ja,
Kosiliśmy obydwa.

(On a Monday morning!
My father and I seeded the hay,
Sowed the seed, father and I,
Sowed it when the sun was high,
Sowed the seed, father and I,
Sowed it when the sun was high.)[6]

The song, according to Clark, proceeded thus: "They seed the crop, they cultivate it, then on Wednesday, they harvest it, then on Thursday, they take the crop to market, Friday they sell it, on Saturday, they drink it [the profits] all up, then on Sunday, they go to church and *cry* about what they did."[7]

At Polish-American community events, another nostalgic look at the homeland came from the Polish national anthem, "Jeszcze Polska Nie Zgineła" (Poland shall never die). It celebrated the bravery of General Dąbrowski's legions marching from Italy to Poland in 1797, just after Poland's final partition by Prussia, Russia, and Austria. Composed by Józef Wybicki and Michał Ogiński, the anthem quickly passed into the folk musical repertoire of many immigrants who hoped Poland's regions would someday be reunited, a feat not accomplished until the end of World War I:

> Jeszcze Polska nie zginęła,
> Kiedy my żyjemy.
> Co nam obca przemoc wzięla,
> Szablą odbierzemy.

Chorus:

> Marsz, marsz, Dąbrowski,
> Z ziemi włoskiej do polski
> Za twoim przewodem
> Złaczym się z narodem.

> (Poland will not perish,
> While we live to love her;
> What the cruel foe has ravished,
> We'll regain through power.

Chorus:

> March, march, Dąbrowski,
> From Italia's fair lanes,
> Back to join the nation
> Back to Poland's broad plains.)[8]

As might be expected, songs about immigration were dear to the first- and second-generation Polonians, such as "Zrobił Góral Krzyż Na Czole" (The mountaineer made the sign of the cross on his brow).[9] The first and fourth verses are as follows:

> Zrobił góral krzyż na czole,
> Wyruszył do drogi
> Żegnal ojca, żegnal matkę
> I rodzinne progi
> Żegnal ojca, żegnal matkę
> I rodzinne progi.

I pojechał w świat daleki
Od Tater kochanych
Między ludzi mu nieznanych
W Stanach Zjednoczonych
Między ludzi mu nieznanych
W Stanach Zjednoczonych.

(The mountaineer made the sign of the cross on his brow,
Preparing for his journey
Bidding farewell to father and mother
And to his birthplace
Bidding farewell to father and mother
And to his birthplace.

And he left for the distant world
Far from his beloved Tatra
To live among strangers
In America
To live among strangers
In America.)

Another immigration song, "Jechal Jeden Polak" (A Pole was journeying), performed during the 1940s in Detroit for folklorist Harriet Pawlowska, speaks of a young man's desire to seek the "big, wide world." But like the singer in the previous song, he, too, strikes a poignant note of longing for his homeland as he concludes:

W Ameryce dobrze
Czy mały czy duży.
Piwka się napije,
Piwka się napije,
Cygara zakurzy.

W Ameryce dobrze
I śmiało i śmiało.
Ale w Ameryce,
Ale w Ameryce
Poczciwości mało.

(American life is fine
No matter who you are.
There's beer to soothe dry throats,

There's beer to soothe dry throats,
Cigars to puff with ease.

American life is fine
In freedom's atmosphere,
But here in America,
But here in America
Life can be most lonely.)[10]

Songs of Friendship and Love

But strangers became friends in the new American Polonia. Whether at home or on a picnic, they sang about their comrades with such songs as "Jak Się Macie, Przyjacielu?" (How are you, friend?), a tune about the vicissitudes of daily life:

Jak się macie przyjacielu,
Jak się macie wraz?
Jak się miewa wasza żonka,
Cały domek wasz?
Bartłomieja głowa boli,
Wszystko idzie wszpak,
Tak i Kuba nam powiada
Że i u was tak.

(How are you friend,
How are you all?
How is your wife,
And your little home?
Bartholomew has a headache,
Everything is going wrong,
Yes and Jacob says that
It's the same at his house.)[11]

Another lively folk melody sung at various gatherings had several sets of lyrics, but most commonly was sung as "Miała Baba Koguta" (The old woman who had a rooster).[12] It begins as follows:

Miała baba koguta,
Koguta, koguta,
Wsadziła go do buta,
Do buta, hej!

(Once there was a baba who,
Baba who, baba who,
Kept a rooster in her shoe,
In her shoe, hey!)[13]

Because Polonia's church socials provided an opportunity for young men and women to meet, love songs such as "Malarz Maluwiej" (The artist is painting) and "Maniu, ach Maniu" (Mary, oh Mary) were popular. "Malarz Maluwiej" praises the girl's beauty:

Malarz maluwiej
Wiedny i nocny,
Evey malowie
Dziewczynka ocziej,
Ooh-la, lah-lah-lah,
Ooh-la, lah-lah-lah,
Ooh-la, lah-lah-lah-lah.

(The artist is painting
Day and night,
And he painted
His girl's eyes.
Ooh-la, lah-lah-lah,
Ooh-la, lah-lah-lah,
Ooh-la, lah-lah-lah-lah.)[14]

In "Maniu, Ach Maniu," a young man begs a girl to love him:

Maniu, ach Maniu,
Ach dajże buzi raz.
Słodkie twe usta
Więc pozwol jeszcze raz,
Będziemy szczęśliwy
Ty będziesz kochać mnie.
Przekonaj się, ja kocham cię,
Więc całuj, prosze cię.

(Mary, oh Mary,
Oh give me a kiss once.
Sweet are your lips
So once more,
I will be fortunate

If you will only love me.
Believe me, I really love you,
Give me a kiss, please.)[15]

Informal music-making also took place in Polish-American homes. Al Clark's brother, an accomplished musician on the banjo, xylophone, and piano, often got together with two cousins to play "for their own amazement" rather than for church socials, christenings, and community dances. On these occasions or in taverns, drinking songs would be performed, such as "Od Jakuba":

Od Jakuba, do Jakuba
Wypieme wszyse finisz.
Od Jakuba, do Jakuba
Wypieme wszyse finisz.

Chorus:

A kto nie wypije!
Daj mu cztery kije.

Łupu cupu, łupu cupu
Niech po polsku żyje.
Łupu cupu, łupu cupu
Niech po polsku żyje.

(From Jacob, to Jacob
We'll all drink to the end.
From Jacob, to Jacob
We'll all drink to the end.

Chorus:

He that won't drink,
Give him four lashes.

Łupu cupu, łupu cupu
Let us live like Poles!
Łupu cupu, łupu cupu
Let us live like Poles!)[16]

The men also enjoyed what Al Clark termed "risqué songs," tunes with a double meaning such as "Wszytke Rybky" (All the fishes):

Spitała się pani
Młodego doctora

Ci liepi dac z rana
Ci liepie z wieczóra.
'Z wieczoze dobrze dac
Bi się lepiej spało,
A w rano proprawicz
Bi się pamiętała.'

Chorus:

Wszystke rybky
Spioł wie zozé,
Jumptary, jumptary a,
Moja stara
Spac nie moze
Jumptary, jumptary a.

(The young girl asked
The doctor
Whether to give it in the morning or at night.
"At night give it well
And you'll be able to sleep better,
And then in the morning you should give it as a reminder."

Chorus:

All the fishes
In the sea,
Jumptary, jumptary a
My old man [lady]
Can sleep no more
Jumptary, jumptary a.)[17]

Rites of Passage and Hymns

Of course, unlike Al Clark's relatives, there were many musicians who did perform in public, especially for weddings. As in the old country, these were occasions for great feasting and singing at home: "The guys with the accordion and the bull fiddle would be waiting at the—most of the receptions were at the homes. They didn't have them in a hall. It would be a big affair at home, where they picked up the rug and did the dancing in the parlor. You know, they cleared it out. This was the thing."[18]

Light-hearted tunes with a lively tempo such as "Gdzesz Był, Jasienku" (Where were you, Johnny?) set the stage for dancing at such events. The song, which teases a young man for staying out all night, begins as follows:

Gdzesz był, Jasienku?
Gdzesz był do rano?
U dziewczyni, u jedynie,
Sama niedawno.

(Where were you, Johnny?
Where were you 'til morning?
At my girlfriend's, my only girlfriend's,
Myself not long ago.)[19]

Even more traditional at Polish-American weddings was "Dwanaście Aniołow" (The twelve angels), sung during the oczepiny (chapter 6). Unlike many of the other folk songs included here, "Dwanaście Anio- łow" is again being performed today at a number of weddings because the czerpiny is regaining its popularity. I have collected several variants of the song, including the following sung by Paul Urbanik of Dunkirk:

Dwanaście aniołow, na roz kwitnej rozy
Dwanaście aniołow
Dwanaście aniołow
Pannie młodej służy.

Pierwszy anioł niesie lilije pachniącą
Pierwszy anioł niesie
Pierwszy anioł niesie
Drugi anioł niesie swiece goryjącą.

Trzeci anioł niesie mirtowy wianeczek
Czwarty anioł niesie
Czwarty anioł niesie
Słubny pieszcz oneczek.

Piąty anioł niesie, słubne posłuszeństwo
Szosty anioł niesie
Szosty anioł niesie
I błogosławienstwo.

A szesciu aniołow słoja nad jej głowa
Trzy mają wianeczek

Trzy mają wianeczek
Jak by na królowa.

Obejrzy się Marys, na wysoko wierzy
Dwanaście partloni
Dwanaście partloni
Twoj wianeczek z biergy.

(Twelve angels, on a blossoming rose
Twelve angels
Twelve angels
Serving a young maid.

The first angel carries scented lilies
The first angel carries
The first angel carries
The second angel carries a hot candle.

The third angel carries a myrtle wreath
The fourth angel carries
The fourth angel carries
A wedding ring.

The fifth angel carries a wedding vow of obedience
The sixth angel carries
The sixth angel carries
The blessing.

And six angels are looking out over her head
Three have the veil
Three have the veil
As though for a queen.

Look Mary, on the high heavens
Twelve ushers
Twelve ushers
Will take the bride's veil off.)[20]

The angel imagery in this wedding song reflects the central role of Catholicism in the lives of Polish-Americans. The Catholic Church, including both the Roman Catholic Church and a splinter group, the Polish National Church based in Scranton, also fostered a deep appreciation of Polish sacred music. This was especially true in the Polish

National Church, which celebrates masses in Polish rather than Latin. Immigrants who supported the church spoke Polish at home and wanted their parochial schools to educate youngsters in the Polish language and customs. These "Polish schools," generally open on Saturdays, taught young people how to read, write, and speak the Polish language.[21]

Parochial schools carried out this mission in cities that had large Polish populations until the 1970s, when dwindling enrollments and fewer priests and nuns forced a number of parochial institutions to close. Christmas kolędy and sacred songs in particular were taught to students until recent years. According to Robert Hora, "I remember always everything in church was Polish and English, and masses would be in Polish sometimes, and sometimes the homilies would be in Polish. The traditional hymns, the nostalgia, remembering when I was a little kid, certain Polish hymns—you know, 'Serdeczna Matka.' "[22]

A favorite hymn during mass especially at communion time, "Serdeczna Matka" (translated as "Soft-Hearted Mother" or "Beloved Mother") asks for aid from Mary, protectress of the Polish people. One rendering is as follows:

Serdeczna Matka,
Opiekunko ludzi,
Niech cię płacz, sierót
Do litości wzbudzi.
Wygnańcy Ewy,
Do ciebie wołamy,
"Zmiłuj się zmiłuj,"
Niech się nie tułamy.

(Soft-hearted mother,
Guardian of our country,
Don't cry, orphans
For mercy she inspires.
All the exiled children of Eve,
To heaven we cry,
"Have pity, have pity,"
We will not be homeless.)[23]

Mary also was invoked in a Polish funeral hymn that is still sung, "Witaj Królowa Nieba" (Queen of heaven):

ROBERT HORA: When I was little, I recall that they used to sing that hymn, and then they would turn the crank, and as they were singing the hymn, the body would gradually go to the grave, which was very emotional. As time went on, they stopped the lowering, but they continued to sing the hymn. The last time I remember that sung was at my mother's funeral, that was about twenty years ago, but they didn't lower the body into the grave, but they all gathered around. And the organist would accompany the priest to the cemetery.

SILVERMAN: And they would just sing it a cappella?

HORA: And they would sing it a cappella, right. So that was a traditional song that was sung to the Blessed Mother as a form of protecting the loved one, taking care of the loved one into the next world.[24]

A version of "Witaj Królowa Nieba" as performed in western New York state is as follows:

Witaj Królowo Nieba i Matko litości,
Witaj Nadziejo nasza w smutku i żałości.
K'Tobie wygnańcy Ewy wołamy synowie,
K'Tobie wzdychamy płacząc z padołu wieżniowie.
Orędowniczka nasza racz Swe litościwe
Oczy spuścić na nasze serce żałośliwe.
I owoc błogosławion żywota Twojego
Racz pokazać po zejściu z świata mizernego.
O łaskawa, pobożna, o święta Marya,
Niechaj będą zbawieni wszyscy grzeszni i ja.
O Jezu, niech po śmierci
Ciebie oglądamy,
O Maryo, uproś nam czego pożądamy.
Uproś nam żywot wieczny grzechów odpuszczenie,
A przy śmierci skon lekki i duszy zbawienie.

(Hail queen of heaven and mother of mercy,
Hail our hope in sadness and sorrow.
Toward you, we children of Eve call,
Crying in this valley of tears.
Our intercessor, lower your merciful eyes
On our saddened hearts.
And show us the blessed fruit of thy womb
After we leave this wretched world.
O gracious, pious, O holy Mary,
May all we sinners be saved including me.

O Jesus, may we see you after death,
O Mary, obtain what we desire.
Obtain for us eternal life and remission of sins,
A light death and salvation of our souls.)[25]

Births as well as deaths were noted in folk songs. In Polish-American communities, "Sto Lat" (One hundred years) was commonly sung for one's birthday, sometimes preceded by the mainstream American "Happy Birthday" song but on many other occasions on its own. Families often ask polka radio deejays and polka bands to play "Sto Lat," whose lyrics are:

Sto lat, sto lat,
Niechaj żyje, żyje nam,
Sto lat, sto lat,
Niechaj żyje, żyje nam,
Sto lat, sto lat,
Niechaj żyje, żyje nam,
Niechaj żyje nam!

(A hundred years, a hundred years,
Let him live, live let him,
A hundred years, a hundred years,
Let him live, live let him,
A hundred years, a hundred years,
Let him live, live let him,
Let him live!)[26]

The pairing of "Sto Lat" with "Happy Birthday" suggests the Americanizing influence that became manifest during the 1930s in Polonia's music. On the airwaves in Buffalo, for example, Polish musicians put their talents to work in an American genre: the radio commercial. One such radio jingle, although the creation of the mass media, passed back into the realm of folk music, orally transmitted for thirty or forty years and readily sung by several folklore interviewees. It is "Kolipinski's Theme Song," played for many years on a Saturday morning radio show to promote Kolipinski's furniture and appliance store.[27] The first two verses are as follows:

Verse 1:

Gdzie wesoło już od rana, na Broadwaju, na Broadwaju,

Kolipinski firma znana, na Broadwaju, wierzcie mi.
W sklepię ludzi jak w kosciele, pełno wrzawy ruchu wiele,
Każdy gość jest ucieszony, i sumięnnie obsłuzony.

Chorus 1:

Tra ra ra Kolipinski meble ma.
Tra ra ra i na spłaty chętnie da.
Tra ra ra więc nie czekaj pospiesz się.
Kolipinscy na Broadwaju oczekują cię.

Verse 2:

A wiec prosi piekne panie, Kolipinski, Kolipinski,
Wyrzucily reczne pranie, Kolipinski radzi wam.
Bo do prania sa maszyny, bez wusiłku odobriny.
Prać maszyną to wygoda, recznie prać to ráczek szkoda.

Chorus 2:

Tra ra ra, Kolipinski Maytag ma.
Tra ra ra, i warunki dobre da.
Tra ra ra, więc nie czekaj pospiesz się.
Kolipinscy na Broadwaju oczekują cie.

(Verse 1:

Every morning things are happy, here on Broadway, here on
    Broadway,
At the famous Kolipinski store on Broadway, take my word.
Like a church our store is crowded, so much life, so full of action,
Every client is contented and is served with satisfaction.

Chorus 1:

Furniture, Kolipinski has it all.
Tra ra ra and he'll make your payments small.
Tra ra ra, hurry down and don't delay.
Kolipinski they await you here on old Broadway.

Verse 2:

Dearest ladies, he will tell you, Kolipinski, Kolipinski,
Rid yourselves of those old washtubs, Kolipinski urges you.
Now machines can do your laundry, without effort all your laun-
    dry,
Washing by machine's a pleasure if your dainty hands you treasure.

Chorus 2:

Tra ra ra, and he has a Maytag too.
Tra ra ra, easy payments just for you.
Tra ra ra, hurry down and don't delay.
Kolipinski's, they await you here on old Broadway.) [28]

By this time, Polish immigrants and their children and grandchildren were enjoying a new Polish-American form of music whose origins were falsely attributed to Poland—the polka. [29]

11

AN AMERICAN ORIGINAL:
THE POLKA

Polka persists as a modern, urban couple dance because it embodies a style that is not too esoteric and can be understood by other urbanites as an identity marker.
—Charles Keil, Angeliki V. Keil, and Dick Blau, *Polka Happiness*

The polka occupies a central position in Polish-American culture; it is what Robert Plant Armstrong terms an "affecting presence" because it is accorded special treatment by the culture's participants.[1] Many fans approach the music with a frenzy akin to religious devotion, immersing themselves completely in "polka happiness" for days at dances, festivals, or even on polka cruises.[2]

Despite its strong affiliation with Polonia, the polka originated not in Poland but rather in Czechoslovakia during the nineteenth century. According to one account, in 1830 a Czech servant girl named Anna Chadimova, from the town of Kostelec on the Elbe River, invented the lively peasant dance in 2/4 time, naming it "polka" because it reminded her of the way a Polish woman, or *polka,* would dance, with a skip and a slide.[3] Other researchers discredit that as a myth, but they do stress that the polka's development coincided with the rise of European nationalism and the transformation of peasants into the working class as they left farms for the cities. The polka, then, is "people's music."[4]

From Czechoslovakia, dance teachers took the polka to Paris and London, where it became the rage as a "salon polka" in 1844.[5] Disseminated internationally from those cities, the polka quickly took root in the New World, becoming the national dance of Paraguay and developing into distinctive regional styles among Mexican-Americans, the

Papago and Pima of Arizona, German-Americans, Czech/Bohemian-Americans, Slovenian-Americans, and, of course, Polish-Americans.

It is important to note that the polka is both an ethnic and class identity marker and has a strong base in the working class. Several folklore interviewees have noted the disparity between "high C" and "low C" culture in Polonia. "High C" adherents are generally well-educated professionals who encourage the performance of Chopin's music rather than the polka music of blue-collar workers. In Binghamton, New York, for example, "The Poles are the *kulturists*. Their idea of Polish is the *krakowiak*, the Polish dances. We have some dance groups down there; they don't dance the polka, they dance the krakowiak."[6] The same holds true in Buffalo, but for many other Polish-Americans the polka is an important part of their ethnic heritage. As one promoter told me, "I played in my own band when I was a young kid, my two brothers and I. I think you'll find that in a lot of these polka bands, music was very important to the parents. Taking music lessons was just a part of life."[7]

From "Folk Music Soup" to Polka

How, exactly, did the "folk music soup" of Polish immigrants become the polka? Its genesis remains uncertain because much historical research needs to be completed. An example of such research has been provided by Mark Kohan, a musician and Polonia historian who offers an intriguing account of the transmission process by which the folk song "Małgorzatka" (Margaret) evolved into both a polka and an oczepiny song.[8] Kohan notes that the song has been traced to the sixteenth century and was originally sung by students at the Jagiellonian University in Krakow. Its lyrics focus on the age-old problem of dating, in this case for Poland's fighting elite, the Husars, and a young girl named Margaret:

Za górami, za lasami,
Tańcowała Małgorzatka z husarzami.
Tańcowała Małgorzatka z husarzami.

Przysedł ojciec, przyszła i mać,
"Chodź do domu Małgorzatko, chodź, już czas spać."
"Chodź do domu Małgorzatko, chodź, już czas spać."

"Niepódę ja, idźcie sami,
Niechaj ja se potańcuję z husarzami,
Niechaj ja se potańcuję z husarzami."

(Beyond high hills, beyond forest,
Danced our lovely Margareta with the Husars.
Danced our lovely Margareta with the Husars.

Came her father, came her mother,
"Come home Margareta," they implored her, "do not dance with them."
"Come home Margareta," they implored her, "do not dance with them."

"I will not come, father, mother,
I must dance this joyous evening with the Husars,
I must dance this joyous evening with the Husars.")[9]

According to Kohan, the original melody and lyrics as given have been recorded by Lenny Gomulka and the Chicago Push on Chicago Records, but during the 1950s another Chicago musician, Li'l Wally Jagiello, modified and "Americanized" the lyrics for the polka. Kohan believes that the earlier variation takes away some of Margaret's innocence: "In this version, which Li'l Wally more than likely knew as a poem, Margaret and her parents are now Polish-American, mixing the Polish and English language to create a humorous situation. It is highly unlikely, however, that Husars were found in Chicago in the 1950s." The Li'l Wally version is as follows:

Za górami, za lasami,
Tańcowała Małgorzatka z husarzami.
Za dwa dolary: Hej! Za two bucks!

Przyszedł ojciec, przysała matka,
"Chodź do domu, chodź do domu, Małgorzatka."
Za dwa dolary: Hej! Za two bucks!

"Ja nie pójde, idźcie sami,
Bo ja pije i tańcuje, z husarzami."
Za dwa dolary: Hej! Za two bucks!

(Beyond the hills, beyond the forest,
Danced lovely Margaret with the Husars.
For two dollars: Hey! For two bucks!

Came her father, came her mother,
"Come home, come home, Margaret."
For two dollars: Hey! For two bucks!

"I won't come home with you,
I'm staying here to dance and drink with the Husars."
For two dollars: Hey! For two bucks!)

The song still exists, with altered lyrics and played in a major key rather than the original minor key, as the unveiling ceremony song "Spadła Wiśni." The words, however, have been changed to tell the bride what to expect from marriage:

Spadła wiśni, widzieliśmy,
I podarła fartuszczek, szywaliśmy. (2x)

Jeden trzymał, drugi trzyma
A ten trzeci co doleci, porozrywał. (2x)

Czy ci rada, czy nie radać,
Musisz kochać i szanować, tego dziada. (2x)

(We all saw you fall out of the cherry tree,
Now you've torn your apron and we're sewing it together. [2x]

One is sewing, the other is folding it
And the third isn't helping by tearing it. [2x]

Will you be happy or not?
You'll have to love and honor that old man.) [2x]

The alteration of existing material—in this case, folk melodies and lyrics—for new purposes is a constant feature in the folklore transmission process. Polish immigrant musicians played a vital role in this effort, helping to forge a new, Polish-American ethnic identity in the early twentieth century.[10]

The Polka Goes on Record

Polish immigrants had opportunities to perform in bands for weddings, christenings, and other community activities; they also organized church choirs and singing societies, such as Chopin's Singing Society in Buffalo, before 1900. But there were other, newer performance opportunities in New York City and later Chicago. As both Charles Keil and Victor Greene have pointed out, the polka is, to a certain extent, the product of mass mediation.[11]

America's recording industry grew up alongside the polka, blues, jazz, and other musical styles. As early as 1900, major record companies such as Victor, Columbia, and Edison began catering to the demands of ethnic immigrants by recording music from "the homeland." In 1901, for example, Berliner, Columbia, and Edison issued catalogs containing a variety of music in the Polish, Irish, Italian, Hebrew, and Spanish languages. Significantly, class consciousness already played a role in the record companies' decision-making process. They used their best ethnic recording stars to cut folk songs aimed at poorer immigrants but recorded opera for those more wealthy.[12]

With the outbreak of World War I, record companies were forced to stop recording in Europe and looked to homegrown American ethnic talent instead. Columbia set up a studio in Chicago in 1915 and discovered Frantisek Przybylski and his Polish Village Orchestra, which recorded "Dziadunio," later known as "The Clarinet Polka." The Sajewski Music Store in Chicago played the role of matchmaker, finding local artists willing to record ethnic music for the major labels.[13]

Although it is true that the ethnic music was thus, in Marxist terms, "commodified," a product of capitalist recording companies eager for financial gain, the new record albums were a social and emotional boon for America's Polonias. The new music, as Victor Greene has observed, enabled Polish-Americans to deal creatively with the problems presented by immigration: adjustment to a new land, strangers, the English language, and pressure to assimilate.[14] This musical creativity on the early 78–rpm records was expressed as a composed and arranged band sound reflective of northern and western Poland; a more rural *gorale* string ensemble style emanating from the highlands of eastern and southern Poland; and experimental novelty and comedy acts, "accordion soloists, singers brought in from the street, vaudeville xylophone wizards, and virtually any specialty act with a Polish name on it that might sell more than a few hundred records."[15]

Among the Polish-American orchestras that recorded in the 1920s were Leon Witkowski's Orkiestra Witkowskiego, Franciszek Dukla, Ignacy Podgorski, and Ed Królikowski, known as the "Polish Paul Whiteman" because of his big-band sound. In both live performances and recordings there was a noticeable shift in instrumentation after 1915, with the sound of stringed instruments, especially violins, giving way to accordions and wind instruments.[16]

The end of the Roaring Twenties was a seminal period for the Polish-American polka, a time Charles Keil calls "a moment of ethnic truth" when Polonians had the opportunity to perform on radio and records as Polish-American musicians. Keil theorizes that they chose to meld Poland's folk melodies with dance forms already popular in America: the polka, oberek, and waltz.[17] Two key recordings of that period were the polka "Na Około Ciemny Las" (Around the dark forest) recorded for Victor Records by Franciszek Dukla on December 7, 1926, and the January 1927 recording of "Zaręczyny, Część 1" (The engagement, part 1) by Ukrainian fiddler Paweł Humeniak for Columbia.[18] In 1928 Ed Królikowski formed a polka band and began a radio broadcast the following year.

The Eastern- versus the Chicago-Style Polka

During the 1930s, business was booming for recordings in Polish; in 1931, for example, Victor released 176 records in its Polish series.[19] During that era, the first of two major Polish-American polka styles, the so-called eastern polka, emerged. Its performers were members of a folk community who had a wealth of musical material from which to choose: folk melodies from Poland; big band tunes, Dixieland, blues, and jazz, all part of the African-American heritage; mainstream white Anglo-Saxon-Protestant American popular songs; and material from Italian, German, Irish, and other earlier immigrant groups.

The resulting eastern-style polka, as performed by Walt Solek (the "Clown Prince of Polkas"), Ray Henry, Gene Wisniewski, Frank Wojnarowski, and Bernie Witkowski, reflects this musical mélange. With its emphasis on written arrangements and bright tempos as in the big bands, it attempted to appeal to the second generation of Polish-Americans, those familiar with Benny Goodman, Duke Ellington, and Count Basie. Yet it clearly bore the stamp of eastern Europe, with its Bohemian polka beat and folk melodies from Poland.[20] During the 1930s and 1940s this polka style prevailed, but by the early 1950s a new polka sound was emanating from Chicago: the so-called Chicago style. Credited to Li'l Wally Jagiello, it slowed musical tempos to the point that polka disc jockeys returned his records marked "Defective—Too Slow."

Li'l Wally maintains that the polka was never intended to be played so fast that people could not dance to it: "Eastern style may be musicians' music, but I don't play for musicians—I play for the public. The public wants to hear melody, lyrics."[21] The Chicago or "honky" style also emphasized the old village songs, the concertina, no written music, and freer musical phrasing, all a radical departure from the eastern style.

Within a decade, the Chicago style spread eastward to New York and Connecticut.[22]

Why this change in polka style in the 1950s? Charles Keil believes it represents working-class Americans' coming to terms with, and transcending, the "polak" stereotype. Keil also notes that a similar movement to a "dirtier" blues style was occurring simultaneously in African-American music.[23]

After World War II the heyday of big band music was over, although it continued to be popular for many years. During the 1950s young adults were attracted to the freer, less arranged style and new instrumentation, especially guitars and growling saxophones, offered by early rock-and-roll performers such as Chuck Berry and the western swing style of Bob Wills, which emphasized arrangements featuring horns, fiddles, and saxophones. A gutsier, from-the-heart, "honky" polka style was evolving at the same time and offered an ethnic alternative to young Polish-Americans.

Between the 1930s and 1970s, then, eastern and Chicago polkas were performed in a context that stressed the home and neighborhood. The following comments by Valerie Pawlak are typical of those of many ardent fans: "I was brought up with Polish music. My dad came from Poland when he was only a baby. But my dad played the accordion, and he'd fill in for bands. . . . My mom went to Buffalo to work, and she met my dad at a dance at Saints Peter and Paul. And my dad always told me he fell in love with her because she had a red and white polka dot dress on, which are the Polish colors. . . . We used to go to weddings or they'd hold Polish dances at Dom Polski, a dollar a dance."[24]

Community functions were influential for many future polka musicians and those who wrote about the polka. Steve Litwin, who writes a column on the music and plays the concertina, recalls, "When I was a kid, you always were taken to the weddings. I always spent most of my time sitting next to the stage watching the musicians, learning the music, trying to sing the songs. That's what I wanted to do."[25] Two musicians now in their forties remembered Buffalo's polka tavern scene in the 1960s as a source of inspiration:

> ED SKOCZYLAS: We used to go, when we were growing up, to Chopin's. We'd go there on a Wednesday night, Friday night, Saturday and Sunday. Four nights a week, and you couldn't walk in the place!
>
> TED SZYMANSKI: Big Steve played there on Wednesday nights when I was a kid, seventeen or eighteen. We used to get in there, pay 50 cents at the door, and you could hear rock-and-roll music in one part on Friday, or Polish

music in the back. And it was probably fifty-fifty. Then, the next day, Saturday, they'd just have the Polish music in the front, with the rock and roll
back there. Sunday would be the same thing. And for every day, they'd draw
pretty big crowds.

ED: It was packed. Then you'd go across the street to the Warsaw Inn. There
was another band playing there . . .

TED: On Friday and Saturday. If you didn't want to go there, you'd go down
to the Plewacki Post, and they'd have a band there.[26]

The Chicago polka scene was equally lively during the 1950s, according to the internationally renowned musician Eddie Blazonczyk, whose
parents owned the Mountaineers' Tavern: "We featured two- , three-
piece polka bands there. I grew up listening to this. And then later on
my mother purchased a place called the Pulaski Ballroom in Chicago.
And there we featured polka music five nights a week. And I listened
and grew up on such bands as Eddie Zima, Steve Adamczak, Li'l Wally,
Frank Yankovic, you know, all types of polka music. And I just fell in love
with polka music."[27] Polish was still the language of choice for Blazonczyk's parents, other Polish-American families, and many polka musicians at the time. He remembers being called "DP Edziu" in the third
grade because he spoke Polish at home.[28]

Polka Deejays as Cultural Gatekeepers

The Polish language also prevailed on America's polka music radio
programs, which began in the 1930s. Because the announcers generally solicit their own advertising, the programs transmit information about
Polish-American businesses as well as polka music: "It was in '30 or '31,
around there. The first polka program over the air and I was one of the
men that played on it," recalled Walter Kapinos. "It was live music, too.
Seven of us got in one little room. . . . The leader of the band, his name
was Benny Makuchowski. He ran the music but he also was soliciting
business. . . . If a fellow ran a grocery store, he [Makuchowski] would
say, 'Well, give me a couple dollars and I'll play it on the air for you. I'll
advertise your establishment.'"[29]

As with mainstream American radio in the 1930s, live bands on polka shows were soon replaced by recorded music. Yet the Polish language
remained a staple for many years, used not only to introduce songs but
also to dedicate them for birthdays, anniversaries, or other special family events.

Polka deejays have played a vital role in the transmission of Polish-American folk music. They serve as the gatekeepers of the culture in their communities, a fact well known by bands. "It [interest in polka music] depends on whether or not they have radio stations that play the music, whether that radio station plays stuff that's fifty years old, or stuff that's new," observed Hank Guzevich of the Polka Family Band.[30]

The Influence of Other Musical Styles on the Polka

Announcers and columnists have a bird's-eye view of a polka landscape, which is changing rapidly in response to the musical tastes of its audience, as it did in earlier years. Like Li'l Wally in the 1950s, a number of polka bands are now turning nostalgically back to their Polish ancestors for musical inspiration.[31] Eddie Blazonczyk, for example, composes songs based on the old gorale tunes that he heard during seven trips to Poland: "My roots and my feeling for my type of music comes from the *goralski* field, which is, like here in the United States, would be like bluegrass compared to country and western."[32]

Blazonczyk, the recipient of a 1998 National Heritage Fellowship and an award from the American Folklife Center for his recordings featuring Polish folk melodies, recalls "Mountaineers' Polka" (Goralska polka), the "Tu Lu Lu Oberek" (Tam pod krakowem), and "Grajcię Mi Skrzypeczki" (Violins play for me), all from the Zakopane or Kraków regions of Poland, as influencing his musical style.

The Polka Family Band also draws upon the gorale sound such as the "Gorali Polka" and folk songs such as "Zosia" and "On Monday Morning," but other musical forces also are at work:

> I listen to a lot of classical music like Brahms, Mozart, Beethoven—all of them. That's very influential because that's basically the structure and foundation of music in general. And the early polka music, I think, the early guys who played back in the 1940s and 1950s, they were structured more as *readers* and they came from a whole different school. So as they learned, they learned more from the standpoint of being technical. And so a lot of the early music *sounded* like classical music, even though it was polka music.[33]

Even more pervasive than classical music, however, is the interplay between the polka and country-western music. In Wisconsin, for example, country-western has had a profound effect on "Dutchman" German-Bohemian polka bands since the late 1920s.[34] Fans, columnists, and musicians themselves referred to this phenomenon many times during the course of my fieldwork. One fan told me that the polka is his favorite dance, followed closely by country and western music; another described his daughter's wedding as featuring two bands, one polka, the other country; and a country-western band in Buffalo found itself playing for the oczepiny ceremony at a Polish-American wedding in the 1980s, relying upon handwritten chords and phonetically spelled Polish words.[35]

On the national level, polka stars such as Eddie Blazonczyk and Jimmy Sturr acknowledge their musical debts to country music. Sturr, whose group was the first polka band to perform at the Grand Ole Opry in Nashville, called that concert "the most exciting thing I've done in years. Picture four thousand country fans. All of a sudden, this little old polka band comes out! We had a good time."[36] With Sturr's new emphasis on fiddles, he believes his musical style is akin to Cajun and Tex-Mex music.

The same cultural crossover is apparent with the fans who serve as dance teachers in their communities. Jean and Frank Osora of Middletown, Connecticut, teach both the polka and country-western line dancing at the local senior citizens' center: "We've got tapes from some of the polka bands, and we play them for our country lessons, because you can do line dancing with any kind of music. I do it with rock, with polkas, modern, whatever. And I tell them, you don't have to do it to one song, you can ad-lib and use what you have at home. But they also made polkas out of country music and other kinds of music. You can make a polka out of anything."[37]

Commuter Ethnics and Polka Hoppers: The Global Community

Musical versatility is becoming a hallmark of polka musicians, who creatively adapt the music of their ancestors to contemporary needs. Gone are many of the nightly, or even weekly, polka dances in many Polish-American neighborhood taverns, churches, and social clubs. One former polka musician who now heads a "commercial" band that plays a few polkas, some rock-and-roll numbers, and "a little bit of everything," attributes the decrease in performance opportunities to stiffer DWI laws that penalize drunken drivers, the high cost of hiring live bands as opposed to a disc jockey, and the changing musical tastes of the younger MTV crowd: "You've got younger kids in the Polish social clubs now, non-Polish members. So Saturday night comes along, and the old Polish regime comes out and sits in the corner. They don't drink much because they're getting older. The young kids are spending money like crazy. So the club is not stupid. It says, 'Let's try a rock-and-roll night.' It's a bread-and-butter thing for the clubs."[38]

The demographics of the remaining weekly dances have changed in a similar manner; the audience is composed largely of older adults. But the old sense of the okolica, the neighborhood "family," has been continued and geographically extended in a new performance context, the annual polka festival, which draws hundreds or even thousands of fans from the United States and Canada. I call these individuals "commuter ethnics" because they willingly hop in their cars to travel to a Polish-American event; the participants call themselves "polka roadies," "polka people," or "polka hoppers."[39]

Regardless of the term employed, polka hoppers make new friends and consider themselves part of an extended family. According to Steve Litwin, "We have friends in Minnesota, we see them once a year at Seven Springs in July. They've been to our house, we call them all the time, and we exchange Christmas gifts." Another polka hopper observes that the extended polka family is a harmonious grouping: "This is the only dancing we know of where you're going to find them as babies on up to eighty, ninety years old. And they all mix and get along good together. You'll never see a fight or an argument at a polka dance. And they'll hug you and kiss you, they're so glad to see you again. It's wonderful."[40]

What is perhaps even more unusual compared with other musical styles such as rock and roll or classical is the camaraderie between polka performer and fan. "No matter where you go, what dance or festival, when the band is done, you'll see them walking tables, talking to people," reports Steve Litwin. "They know their fans by their first names and last names. They know the cities they live in. I met Eddie Blazonczyk in the late 1960s, and the man never forgot my name. And all the bands are like that."[41] My observations at festivals confirm this. Polka musicians on break spend their time socializing with the audience rather than isolating themselves in a dressing room backstage.

The Intersection of Sacred and Secular: The Polka Mass

The sense of kinship among Polish-Americans has extended from the secular to the sacred sphere with the introduction of the polka mass at weekend festivals. An outgrowth of the Second Vatican Council's revisions in the 1960s that saw the development of folk masses, mariachi masses, rock masses, R&B masses, and jazz masses, polka masses originated in 1972, when Father George Balasko, himself a polka musician, first celebrated a polka mass in Lowellville, Ohio. The concept was popularized thereafter, both nationally and internationally, by Father Frank Perkovich in central and northern Minnesota. He celebrated a polka mass at the Vatican for Pope John Paul II in 1983, and since then the practice has spread throughout Polish-American communities.[42]

A live polka band provides the music for a mass. Usually, the band will distribute a printed program containing lyrics for the entrance, offertory, communion, thanksgiving, and recessional hymns. Responses may be sung or spoken for the various mass parts such as the gloria, gospel acclamation, offertory response, and great amen. Generally, musicians replace the lyrics of well-known polkas, waltzes, or other popular songs with an appropriate sacred text, although on occasion a new melody is composed for a specific set of sacred lyrics. The choice of music is generally left to the performers' discretion, although they may consult with the priest.

The resulting mass may have an eclectic combination of musical styles. For example, one polka mass by the Polka Family Band included "At This Sacrifice," a sacred version of the country hit "Blue Eyes Crying in the Rain"; "Serdeczna Matka"; and a Polish folk song, "Jak Szybko Mija-ja Chwile" (How quickly time flies), traditionally sung to herald the new year. It also featured a reflection of the Polka Family Band's interethnic, Polish-Mexican heritage, "Adios Reina Del Cielo" (Farewell queen of heaven), which, like its Polish counterpart "Serdeczna Matka" implores Mary for her blessings.

Another Polish-American polka band has pushed the boundaries of experimentation in the genre of religious music even further. The Dynatones' *Chapter VII* was a concept album that retold the life of Jesus. Although band member Larry Trojak considers it to be the group's best work, some polka show hosts shunned it: "One polka disc jockey won't play it. Maybe some people feel that religion doesn't mix with polkas. I know a lot of people who weren't crazy about the idea of a polka mass until they went to one. Perhaps people who don't like the idea see the polka as being limited to happy snappy music with lyrics about a guy in a bar getting shit-faced. A lot of it is this way, there's nothing really wrong with that aspect of it. But it can be about a lot of different sides of life."[43]

The Great Polka Debate: Polish or English?

Hymns for the Polka Family Band's polka mass were performed in Polish, English, and Spanish, a reflection of America's multicultural present that carries over to the performance of Polish-American polkas in the secular sphere as well. Because so few contemporary third- or fourth-generation Polish-Americans speak Polish, bands perform at least half of their material in the English language. Still, "Polish makes the polka." "Your hard-core polka fanatics, even if they're not Polish and they don't understand Polish, they will *not* want to listen to a band that plays all English," observes Hank Guzevich. "Because polka music just sounds—*Polish* music just sounds better in Polish."[44]

In composing polkas, Guzevich, who admits that even he is still studying the Polish language, will write one line in Polish followed by its English translation so a non-Polish-speaking audience can try to learn the Polish words. Another strategy is to select easier Polish words deliberately so fans can learn them phonetically, as so many musicians themselves now do.

The polka community, however, including musicians, boosters, and festival promoters, remains divided over whether the English language is preferable to Polish for polka lyrics. Those who support English view the polka as a pan-American musical style transcending all ethnic affiliations rather than a marker of Polish-American identity. The pan-American approach is taken by the president of a seven-hundred-member polka booster group. "The purpose of our club is to promote polka music. . . . We are *not* Polish. We are polkas, you know? Our whole interest is polkas. We do have people of different descents. We have German people, we have Italian people, we have Irish people, we have people of all descents in our United Polka League. We are not a Polish group, we are a polka group. This is our whole purpose."[45]

Promoters generally are in agreement. According to one from Phoenix, Arizona, "As much as I love the Polish and the music, I was thinking of starting a campaign to take the Polish out of polkas and just make it English because most of the younger kids and people don't understand what they're singing. I've got a lot of friends that I've brought, and they say, 'God, this [music] is unbelievable. Why do they have to sing in Polish?' It's part of our background and I love it, but I think if we're going to keep polka music alive, we should think about *not* having the Polish as predominant as it is."[46] A Syracuse promoter also believes that the English language is essential to the survival of polka music and that even more creative adaptation will be necessary, perhaps a fusion of polka and country music or performances pairing a polka band and a country-western group.[47]

Involving the Next Generation

If there is one point of universal agreement among polka fans, performers, and promoters, it is the necessity for including youngsters in the polka music scene. One young mother at a festival explained that she was teaching her daughters, ages four and seven, how to polka dance because she and her sister had learned and she wanted to carry on the family tradition.[48]

Promoters such as Stan Kozak and Tom Warzecha admit children under age seventeen free of charge to their festivals. This offers an important outlet for families to experience polkas together, because most weddings (formerly an opportunity for family polka dancing) are now for adults only. Musicians who tour nationally are keenly aware of the movement to encourage family unity.

> I see it more, like in Pulaski, Wisconsin. Those parents—they're farmers, you know, for the most part—and they're hard-working people. In the wintertime, where do they go? They can't go anywhere. So when the season for the festivals comes in, they bring their children. They do not leave their children at home.
>
> And I have asked them this, I have said, "Gee, you guys bring your whole families." And they said, "You know, this is one time when we get out of the house, where we're together as a family, and we still have our Polish heritage that carries on."
>
> And they want to give that to their children. And so they're starting them young, and who knows? Maybe in their teens, they may say, "No, I don't want to listen to this, I want to listen to something else." Because that has happened, I've seen it happen a lot. But they *still come back* to the polka.[49]

A twenty-five-year-old polka deejay has noted the same phenomenon among her radio audience. Many of her former high school classmates who once preferred rock and roll are now getting married, and they call her for advice about appropriate polkas to use for their weddings.[50]

These anecdotes suggest a life-cycle theory of folklore usage. Children are brought up in the folkways of a particular culture but rebel during their teens in an effort to establish an individual identity. Once that is accomplished, young adults have the opportunity to reflect on their identity within the group. Quite often, as suggested by the deejay, marriage will trigger such reflections, particularly if individuals marry outside the ethnic group.

Once their family is begun, new parents ponder their roles in the folk group and cautiously test the waters. If they are Polish-American, they may prepare the foods for the traditional Christmas Eve wigilia supper. Yet because of family responsibilities they may be unable to participate in other forms of folk expression, such as polka dancing or music (which would explain the decrease in attendance by adults in their twenties and thirties). Once their children are grown, parents can again participate in the life of the folk community until old age or illness curtail their activities. At this point, a new generation begins the cycle anew.

Outsiders as Polka People

Whether the life-cycle theory is actually occurring with respect to Polonia's polka community is open to debate. In the Buffalo area, observers generally agree on the graying of polka people, but there are striking exceptions: adult newcomers from other racial and ethnic backgrounds. One African-American man, a polka dancer since 1982, loves the events because of the polkas' "peppy music and lyrics," the card games and Chinese auctions associated with some gatherings, and the sense of community involvement through the parishes.[51] A thirty-four-year-old Irish-German-American from Buffalo, a confirmed rock-and-roller wearing a tie-dyed beret, corduroy jacket, and blue jeans, fell in love with polka music when his company sent him to a polka festival to handle the stage lighting:

> The name of the band escapes me, but they opened up with "Grand Illusion." And that's a Styx tune, an old rock-and-roll band, and I'm like, "Wow, this is incredible." I set up the light board almost in the kitchen, nowhere in sight of the stage. . . . Well, then, Gus [Guzevich] of the Polka Family Band comes up and says, "Can you move the light board?"
>
> I'm going, "Aw geez." I said, "I've got a hundred foot of cord, I can move it wherever you like." And he goes, "No, for tomorrow night at least, I'd like you out by the stage." So this escalated . . . to where I'm part of the polka celebration here. I was even requested to make up T-shirts for this show and sell hats here. It's turned into something where I just have a good time.[52]

To encourage prospective polka people to enjoy themselves, there are a number of local booster groups and fan clubs in Polish-American communities in addition to national organizations such as the International Polka Association, incorporated in 1968.[53] Some, such as the United Polka League of the Mohawk Valley, attract a crowd to events by offering free polka dance lessons culminating in a "graduation party" featuring pastries, cakes, nonalcoholic beverages, and polka recordings.

There also are regular meetings and polka dances, and if the organization is nonprofit, proceeds are donated to charities. "We try to promote at least one polka dance a month each year," says Edward Sabloski. "We bring in the best polka bands in the country. You name the band, and we have them. We have Grammy Award winner Eddie Blazonczyk coming in April 23. . . . We have brought bands in the past like Happy Louie, Marion Lush, the top bands."[54] Sabloski notes that innovation is encouraged on the polka dance floor, with rock and roll or figure dances such as the Chicken Dance, Silver Slipper, and Bumpsy Daisy as favorites with younger dancers. The newer steps are often learned at an out-of-town festival and then taken home, where the polka hopper informally instructs others.[55] Thus, folklore is transmitted anew.

Polkas Go Online

There is a new twist to the transmission process. Personal computers and the Internet have turned the information highway into a roadway for ethnic Americans eager to learn more about their heritage.

> We started a newsletter on the Internet. . . . we now have an alt.music.polkas newsgroup on the Internet, and there's also an accordion mailing list which has a lot of polka people on it. We're currently putting an E-mail list together of musicians, polka fans, and it's pretty much scattered from California to Florida, up into New England. A lot of older musicians we didn't even realize were on the Internet. And besides my column in the newspaper [the *Polish-American Journal*], I'm now doing an on-line column that I distribute by e-mail.[56]

With the entrance of polka roadies into the high-tech world of PCs and the involvement of younger adults at festivals in Ohio, Massachusetts, Pennsylvania, and southern Ontario, long-standing stereotypes about the audience for Polish-American polka music are being abandoned. No longer are its listeners exclusively older Polish-Americans who still live in Polonia. For the promoters of polkas, that represents both a fresh challenge and a new opportunity to reach a broader audience.

12

REINVENTING THE REEL:
POLISH FOLK DANCES IN POLONIA

Hej, Mazurze, bij nóżkami,
I daj ognia podkówkami!

(Hey, Mazurze, who's that prancing,
Put some spirit in your dancing!)
—"Hej, Mazurze," in *Treasured Polish Songs*

Like the Polish-American polka, the folk dances of Poland are being creatively adapted by today's Polish-American folk community
to serve new needs. The process of adaptation is not new, however. Because of its Central European location, Poland has been crisscrossed by
friend and foe alike over the centuries, ranging from warring Cossacks
and Teutonic knights, merchants in the amber trade, Italian artisans,
and French royalty.[1] The result is an intermingling of cultures, particularly in the area of dance.

For Polish peasants, the chief occasions for dancing were between
Christmas and Easter, when there was little farm work to be done; Carnival, the Thursday before Ash Wednesday; Easter Monday (Dyngus
Day); Whitsuntide, the day of the Green Feast when dancing took place
at homes decorated with green leaves; Corpus Christi, a day for religious processions and festivities; St. John's Eve; Midsummer's Eve,
when young people jumped over fires and danced around them and
garlands with lights were floated on streams and rivers; and the Harvest Home (Dożynki), a day of dancing to mark the harvest.[2] In addition, dances were commonplace at christenings and weddings:

If you have the good fortune to be invited to a wedding you will be sum-
moned the day before the ceremony by young men with gay ribbons in their

hats who, clicking their heels together at parting, say "Stand with God." To this you reply "God lead you." The house to which you go is made of wood ... the sound of music comes from the house and you find several fiddlers playing on two- or three-stringed fiddles and a double-bass not much larger than a cello. Probably the players are gypsies. . . . [The bride] is brilliantly dressed . . . dancing begins, the bridegroom inviting the women guests. The men stamp vigorously, the gay skirts swirl in dazzling patterns. The girls dance in high laced boots, their Sunday footwear, or everyday shoes made of one piece of leather with a thong to wind round the leg.[3]

Each region of Poland developed unique dances, some of which later became so widespread as to become national dances. Those considered national are the *polonez*, the *mazur, kujawiak, oberek,* and *krakowiak;* a widely known regional dance is the *taniec góralski* (mountaineers' dance).[4]

The polonez is a procession in 3/4 time used to open dances at aristocratic and court balls. According to legend, it first was used in 1573 by noblemen at the ascension of Henri III to the throne of Poland. It may have derived from an older folk dance of the peasants, the *polski*.[5] The polski, also a processional dance, features striding steps, with the accent falling on the first beat of the measure, embellished by bows, turns, bridges, and chains. It originated in Wielkopolska and was danced only by peasant men as a receiving line for ancient Polish tribes.

By the seventeenth century, the polski-cum-polonez became associated with the court, exemplifying the influence of a subordinate class (peasants) upon the dominant aristocracy (the szlachta), much like the later movement of the Polish-American polka from working class to middle class. Like the polka, the polonez also spread internationally and became known in Italy as the *polacca,* in Germany as the *polonäse,* and in its most familiar form, the French *polonaise*.[6]

The mazur or mazurka, originally a folk dance in 3/4 time from the Mazowsze region that like the polonez later became a ballroom dance of the szlachta, features a strong accent on the second beat and a number of distinctive dance patterns. Perhaps the best-known mazurka is the national anthem, "Poland Shall Never Die."

The kujawiak, a dance in 3/4 time of moderate tempo, is usually accented on the second and third beats at the end of a measure. It originated in the Kujawy region of western Poland.

The oberek, still danced by Polish-Americans, came from peasants in the Mazowsze region during the eighteenth century, becoming popular throughout Poland by the end of the 1800s. A dance in 3/8 time, its accent usually falls on the third beat. Its name, derived from *obracać się* (to turn), appropriately describes its whirling, fast nature.

The krakowiak originated in the city that was the home of Poland's kings for centuries, Kraków. Played in 2/4 time with a syncopated rhythm, the dance features exuberant slides, stamps, kicks, cries, and jumps punctuated by the sound of jangling metal coins on the men's leather belts.

Among the regional dances, the góralski of southern Poland's Tatra Mountain region is a colorful expression of local culture. Unlike other regions, the Tatra dances feature men and women performing separately, the men in the dominant role with spectacular leaps. Góralski used to be performed around a fire, the men facing inward and beating the ground with *toporki* (hatchets) used by mountain climbers. Accompanied by a song from onlookers, the dance features steps reminiscent of the Cossacks, waving of toporki, and jumps over the fire, which may have been part of an initiation ceremony into the region's robber bands.[7]

These national and regional dances are among those that survived the journey to America's Polonia. Although it is beyond the scope of this chapter to present a complete history of Polonia's folk-dance movement, it should be noted that these folk dances have been performed by relatively small numbers of Polish-Americans while the polka became the dominant dance of the community.

The Formation of Folk-Dance Groups in Polonia

Churches and Polish-American social organizations were at the nexus of Polonia's folk-dance movement in the 1930s and 1940s. One such dance group existed at Corpus Christi Church in Buffalo. Daniel Collins, the dance ensemble's leader, recalls, "They had a lady over there that tried to set up a group, my neighbor . . . she started teaching me some of the steps. She gave up, and so the group was on their own. And so we started. We kept it up a little bit. Then I heard about PNA [Polish National Alliance], and they had more regular rehearsals so I joined that. Then after a little while I started teaching, myself."[8]

The Corpus Christi group learned the krakowiak, oberek, and gorale, but Collins expanded the repertoire, adding the mazur, polonez, and a regional dance called the *komaka* later when he formed the Polish Folk Dancers sponsored by the Polish National Alliance. He taught five nights a week at various churches in Buffalo and its suburbs, emphasizing to young men that folk dancing, with its lifts and acrobatic moves, could be a masculine activity. The ensemble, like most current groups, danced to records or tapes rather than a live orchestra or band.

On most occasions the dance group performed free of charge for church and civic events, with as many as three performances per weekend, a reflection of public interest in ethnic folk dancing during the 1940s and 1950s. To maintain the attention of an American public of various ethnic backgrounds, Collins's dancers also performed tangos, calypsos, and Hawaiian numbers. His sources of choreographic inspiration also point to the influence of mass media: "At the time, I didn't really understand Polish, and I would go to the Rivoli on the East Side. They'd have Polish films, and I'd go and sit through a movie two or three times because of the dance sequences and get my ideas from that and from books."

After breaking away from the PNA because of its restrictions on the dance group, Collins formed the Merry Tatra Dancers, which performed in Detroit, Erie, and Rochester and at the 1964 World's Fair as well as in the Buffalo area. Once again, interethnic influences were apparent, not only in the performers' varied ethnic and religious backgrounds (Polish, Irish, German, Indian, Jewish) but also in the Tatra Dancers' interaction with a Macedonian dance group. "We were dancing together at some place," Collins remembers, "and I thought it was rather unusual, both groups clicked. Usually, you stuck to yourself, even if you changed in the same room. But with the Macedonians, we just clicked. I needed boys, so they joined my group, a few of them, and then I danced with their group."

The Polish and Macedonian dance groups were part of Buffalo's lively folk-dancing scene during the 1950s, which also included ensembles of Native American, Irish, Japanese, Mexican, Israeli, and Italian origin. In addition to live performances with these groups at such events as the International Institute's annual Folk Ball, the Tatra Dancers gained exposure on television. They were featured on three Buffalo television stations: WGR-TV's "Pic-a-Polka" program; WKBW-TV's "Time to Polka"; and, with the Chopin's Singing Society, in a series on WBEN-TV.

The Tatra Dancers disbanded during the 1960s after Collins had surgery that necessitated a change of career. Tastes in dance music also were changing. "It faded," he recalls. "People would care to see it, but the interest wasn't there with the young people. I mean, there was rock and roll, and they didn't want their ethnic background. They didn't want to seem to be a greenhorn. They wanted to be American, so they'd rather do rock and roll and jitterbugging than Polish folk dancing."

Contemporary Folk-Dance Ensembles

Still, Polish-American folk-dance ensembles have continued. Janet Stanek, the thirty-four-year-old leader of Buffalo's largest current Polish-American folk-dance ensemble, Więz, was only five when she first danced in a local Polish-American folk-dance group. The ensembles included the PNA's Garland Dancers, Gniezno, Cieszyn, the PCC (Polish Community Center) Dancers, and Biały Orzeł. All eventually folded because of "quibbling, low membership, or what have you."[9]

Like Collins, Janet Stanek stresses that organizational sponsorship of a dance troupe can have a stifling effect. "What happens is these organizations become like moms and dads to you, and they don't give you a whole lot of money but they give you a whole lot of rules." Such a problem spurred Stanek to quit the Solidarity Dance Ensemble, which she had founded twelve years earlier, to establish a new dance group with two other dance instructors in 1994:

> We didn't have a sponsor, and we searched for a sponsor. We put a couple of prospectuses out to get a sponsor, but no one wanted to sponsor us. So we decided, okay, we'll do it anyway. And we literally started it with my Discover charge card. And now we have people asking if they can be our sponsor, and we turn them down because we have learned that *not* having a sponsoring organization has made us so much more fun. . . . We are able to do what we want to do, to do performances, pick our dances, our choreography, membership drives, when we want to.

The ensemble, appropriately named "Więz" (a bond or kinship), depends both upon joint decisions by the three leaders and active participation by parents and grandparents, who are called upon to help sew costumes and arrange publicity in order to reduce expenses. Costumes, which can cost $200 apiece, have been donated by some organizations; others are purchased from stores or handmade. Parents are asked to provide white shirts or blouses in addition to a $7.50 monthly fee for each dancer.

The fifty members of Więz are in three groups ranging in age from four to their late thirties. Nearly half of the children's group (ages four through eight) and the youth group (ages nine through fourteen) are boys. There also is an adult group for those fourteen and over. The ensemble's repertoire includes national dances (the mazur, polonez, krakowiak, and kujawiak), as well as such regional dances as the *trojak*, a "trademark" because no other local dance group performs it, and two regional mountaineer dances, the góralski and the *zywiec*. A recent innovation is a choreographed version of the Polish-American polka, a well-received addition in response to the local community's interest in that dance.

The improvisational, creative adaptation of existing material is evidenced by Stanek's choreographic process. "If I have the music in my head and I'm driving in my car," she says, "sometimes I will choreograph the dance while I'm driving somewhere. The question is, 'Do I remember it in class'? Sometimes, more often than not, I'll choreograph on the spot, because I've been doing it for so many years that I can. I know the music and I know the steps and I know the level of the dancers that I'm dealing with." Another important source of inspiration comes from regular visits to a guest choreographer in Erie, Pennsylvania, Stanek's former dance instructor from the Polish National Alliance's dance instruction course at Alliance College: "He gives us a little bit of a different twist, which helps me liven up all the other dances as well."

The twelve boys and girls in the children's group start with easier dances, but to prevent boredom from setting in they are introduced to more difficult dances such as the krakowiak. "When they finally graduate to the next group, they know the stance, they know the position, they know the steps, they have rhythm already," says Stanek. The youth group's twenty-four members can handle difficult dances, although there is a challenge to make dances appealing to both sexes. "Boys don't want the romantic dances, they don't want the *slow* dances. They want to show off on stage. . . . The mountaineer dance is by far the boys' favorite because they use these axes that are stage props, but they get to do all kinds of stuff with them, and it pulls in the biggest audience response. It always is our show-closer for that group, big-time."

Dances selected for a particular program depend upon which Więz group is performing and the program's expected length. If the adult group is involved, the stately polonez, which opened many parties and balls of Europe, will begin the program. If all three age groups perform, the younger ones dance early in the program "before they get antsy."

Moxie and Creative Adaptation: Ingredients for Success

The Więz Dance Ensemble was named "Citizen of the Year in Culture" in 1995 by the local *Am-Pol Eagle* newspaper and has performed for many colleges, community festivals, and Polish-American organizations, including a special performance when Lech Wałęsa visited Buffalo in 1994. Stanek's account of that performance reveals both the necessity of "creative adaptation" and the moxie that a folk-dance ensemble must have in order to thrive:

> He came to town in October, we begged and pleaded to be able to perform. We were told, "No way, Secret Service won't allow it." We finally were allowed to come in costume and participate in the banquet as far as seating all the guests, and the next day to go to church and form a processional in costume. . . . But when we were in church, I said, "You know, I've got to give it one more shot."
>
> We were told to wait and see. We sent somebody to go get the music, and they said, "Okay, dancers in the back of the hall. You've got two minutes to get on, get off, get out."
>
> We had to practice. . . . Literally, we practiced in a stairwell. . . . We did it once through, came back out, and the intro was perfect. Apparently, we fit very well into what they needed as well, because they said in the intro that the president of Poland was asking, "Where are your young people?" And the answer is, "Here they are."
>
> So as much as we begged to get the show, it did Buffalo a good service too, because it showed the president that young people are involved in the Polish community here.[10]

Performances such as these give the young dancers poise and self-confidence, which is especially critical for boys, who Stanek says are more self-conscious about dancing in public than girls. "I walked into the boys' dressing room afterward—my son is in the group, so I'm allowed there— and I heard, 'Ah, they just loved us! They just ate us alive! Yeah, we were *great!*' And you laugh to yourself, but this is fantastic for a nine-year-old boy to think that about dancing on stage."

The performances also are a cultural identity marker for Polish-Americans to the world at large. Stanek doubts that there will ever again be "lots" of Polish folk-dance groups—"You'll see little groups here, like from Polish Saturday School, but they're seasonal and they don't go out and perform"—but she sees performance opportunities at ethnic festivals and in other cities such as Philadelphia and Chicago. Stanek predicts that within a few years her group will be known nationally.

Polish immigrants' folk songs and dances have undergone a dramatic transformation during the twentieth century, moving from the small-scale setting of the private home and okolica into a larger sphere, that of the mass media and public festivals. Polish-American musical and dance traditions are competing with rock music and other mainstream American musical styles for the attention of young people who are the potential future musicians, promoters, and fans. If these musical forms are to survive, performers and promoters must continue to develop strategies for reaching this audience.

13
GAMES PEOPLE PLAY:
FOLK ARTS, CRAFTS, AND RECREATION

Mój ty miły bednareczku, pobij i dzieżeczkę,
A ja zato ci wyszyję bielusią chusteczkę.

(O my darling little cooper, please repair my butter churn,
And for you I will embroider snow white kerchiefs in return.)
—"Mój Ty Miły Bednareczku," in *Treasured Polish Folk Rhymes,
Songs, and Games*

As the epigraph indicates, folk arts and crafts were an integral part of Polish peasant life. Not only did they provide such essentials as homes, furniture, cooking utensils, and clothing, but they also allowed for the expression of creativity and ethnic identity. That identity was both regional and class-based in nature. For many years there was a dichotomy between the folk art of Poland's working class and the professional culture of the wealthier because feudalism prevailed for so long, isolating rural peasants from the civilization of the cities and preserving their folk art.[1]

Regionalism was evident in the various styles used in embroidery, woodworking, pottery, textiles, and *wycinanki*, the paper cut-outs glued to the walls of peasants' cottages.[2] Decorative wooden vessels, for example, were hallmarks of Podhale, Kurpie, and the mountainous portion of Silesia, all known for fine wood carving. In the Kurpie region, wycinanki were made as single open-work cutouts, while in the Łowicz region, a layered look was favored. Among folk costumes, several well-known regional costumes, each with distinctive fabrics, colors, and stripes or other geometric patterns, include those of the Cracovians (often referred to as the Polish national costume), Sącz, Mazovia, and the Podhale mountaineer.[3]

Quite often, folk artisans put their skills to work for utilitarian purposes. Examples included pottery, metalwork buckles, and carved chests, tables, stools, and benches, many of them also decorated with painted floral or geometric motifs. On other occasions, the Catholic faith inspired artistic creativity, such as religious sculptures, Kraków's Christmas *szopkas* (nativity scenes), and the carved wooden *kaplicas* (wayside shrines) that dotted the Polish countryside.

Seasonal and rite-of-passage celebrations also called for specially created objects of ritual significance. For her wedding, a girl would receive the married woman's embroidered cap, or czepek, usually made by her godmother and later reserved for special occasions such as church services, folk festivals, and, finally, her burial.[4] Village women also gathered the day before the ceremony to bake a ritual wedding bread known as *korowaj* or *kołacz:* "Some breads took a round form, some were flat and each was decorated with various bread dough symbols. Tiny bread dough doves, rosettes, crosses, swirls and plaits, these are the basic elements of Polish bread ornamentations."[5] It was considered necessary for every wedding guest to receive a piece of the korowaj as a sign of goodwill toward the newlyweds, much the same as the wedding cake in America today. The proverb "bez kołaczy nie wesele" (without a kołacz, there is no wedding) was widely believed.[6]

During the long winter months when outdoor work was suspended, Polish peasant families prepared for their two major holidays, Christmas and Easter, by making special decorations. In the nineteenth century, when whitewashed walls became common in peasant cottages, young girls made wycinanki before Christmas, a custom that continued into the twentieth century as recorded by Sula Benet: "Paper cutouts are prepared, to be used as a frieze on the walls or as a border around the table-cloth."[7] The paper was first folded and then cut, originally with sheep shears, into freehand mazes of stylized, intricate designs featuring geometric designs, trees, flowers, roosters, hens, rabbits, stars, and human figures. Among the most elaborate were the wycinanki of the Łowicz area west of Warsaw, which had symmetrical layers of papercuts of various colors glued to form roosters, peacocks, or flowers.[8]

Another characteristic wall decoration at Christmas was the *pajak* (spider): "Chandelier-like ornaments are fashioned of coloured paper and straw, to be hung from the ceiling. These are known as *pajaki*, spiders, because some of them have the spreading effect of a spiderweb. . . . The spiders are among the most characteristic decorations of the Polish peasant's home."[9]

The best-known of the pajaki is the *dziad* (old man or grandfather). Fashioned from a bunch of wheat tied at one end and opened, umbrella style, to allow the grain to form a lacy border, the dziad was hung over the Christmas Eve wigilia table. On New Year's Day, the dziad was carried during greetings to friends and neighbors; it was beaten with a stick while the verse "na szczęście, na zdrowie" (for your good luck, for your good health) was repeated. It later was strewn in the fields where cabbage would grow in the spring, with the hope that the cabbage heads would be as large as the dziad, or placed under a cow in the stable to ensure the abundant delivery of calves. More recently, the New Year's greeting has been chanted, and mixed nuts have replaced the wheat of the dziad as a symbol of hope for a bountiful harvest in the year to come.[10]

The Christmas tree, called the *podłaznik* or *sad,* was introduced to Poland in the 1700s. The top part of a fir would be cut and hung upside down from the ceilings of Polish homes; decorations included apples and nuts wrapped in gold or silver foil, gingerbread figures, ribbons, paper flowers, and ornaments of paper or beads.[11] The tree also featured *swiaty,* "worlds" or "spheres" made of colored Christmas wafers, believed to represent Jesus and redemption.[12]

Better known to the world outside Poland are the decorated Easter eggs (*pisanki*), traditionally made by girls and young married women during festive evening gatherings in the weeks preceding Easter.[13] The earliest Polish pisanki, discovered near Opole in Ostróżka, date from the tenth century.[14] Numerous magic properties have been attributed to eggs the world over; they are regarded as a protective charm against illness, death, or the evil eye.[15] As a symbol of life and the rebirth of spring after winter, eggs figure in fertility cults in many countries from Christmas until the summer solstice. From the tenth to the twelfth century in Poland, pagans placed eggs on the tombs of departed ancestors, a custom known as *rejkawska.*[16] Until World War II, Polish young women presented decorated eggs to their favorite suitors.[17]

Each region of Poland developed its own techniques for decorating eggs.[18] They include pisanki (from *pisać,* "to write"), raw eggs ornamented with various designs.[19] In addition there are *kraszanki* (from *krasc,* "beauty"), hard-boiled eggs dyed a single color, blessed by the priest and then eaten on Easter Sunday; *wyklejanki* (from *klej,* "to glue on"), hollow eggs to which bullrush pith and colored yarn are glued; *nalepianki* (from *nalepiać,* "to stick on"), hollow eggs to which colored paper, straw, or fabric are glued; and *malowanki* (from *malować,* "to paint"), hollow eggs painted with a multicolored pattern.

Traditionally, eggs are colored in dyes prepared from plant materials such as onion skins, used throughout Poland, which gives them a yellow, orange, or brown color, depending on the type of onions used. Other plant materials differ from region to region, according to local plant life. Straw and saffron give a yellow color; crocus petals, orange; red beets or plums, the red color symbolic of Jesus' blood and a favorite color for dyed eggs; grass, moss, and spinach, green; logwood or sunflower seeds, blue; blackberries, purple; alder cones or coffee, brown; and alder bark or walnut shells, black.

The decorated hard-boiled eggs were not only objets d'art but also the focus of games in the village square, fields, or cemeteries. In one egg-rolling game for two couples, four participants were seated on the ground in a square. Each couple rolled their egg back and forth diagonally across the square, attempting to break their opponents' egg. When this occurred, a new couple with a new egg replaced them, and the contest continued until only one couple remained.

Skill in egg-tossing was measured in a second egg game for older youths. Hard-boiled eggs were tossed into the air until only one uncracked egg was left. Still another game involved cracking hard-boiled eggs. Each player hit his or her egg against the shell of an opponent's egg until one egg cracked, thus eliminating that player. A new player entered the game, and the competition proceeded until only one uncracked egg remained.[20] As a culture where manufactured toys and games were not readily available or affordable, Polish peasant society prized such games stressing inventiveness, many of them reflective of the rural, agricultural nature of the community.[21]

Games popular among Polish children throughout the year included "Wilk i Gęsi" (the Wolf and Geese). One child would play Mother Goose, surrounded by her clinging "goslings"; opposite Mother Goose was the wolf, who dug a hollow. He would engage in the following conversation, starting with Mother Goose:

Na co ten dołeczek?
Na ogienieczek.
Naco ogienieczek?

Na wody grzanie.
A naco woda?
Na talerzyków umywanie.
A naco talerzyki?
Na gąsek krajanie.
A gdzie masz
gąski?
U ciebie za
pasem!

(Why this little hollow?
To make the embers glow.
Why the little fire?
Hot water I require.
Why make the water steam?
To wash the dishes clean.
Why the dishes, please?
For carving up the geese.
And just where are the geese?
Back of you, those little geese!)

Upon concluding the rhyme, the wolf would lunge forward to try to capture the goslings, taking the captives to his den. The game would continue until all were captured.[22]

In another chasing game involving "frogs" and "storks," two children playing storks had to chase the frogs on one leg in an attempt to capture them. If successful, the captured frogs were brought back to the stork's nest. If the stork ventured into frogs' safe zone, however, the stork was captured. The game ended when either all of the frogs or all of the storks are captured.[23]

Circle games also provided much entertainment. One, much like the American "Simon Says," featured a child dressed as "Father Virgilius" in a high paper hat, shawl, and glasses, who taught the other children how to dance, jump, sneeze, wipe their noses, and other motions, all the while singing the song "Ojciec Wirgilius" (Father Virgilius). Children would line up in a row, twigs in hand, for another game featuring the folk song "W Poniedziałek Rano" (On a Monday morning [ch. 10]). As they sang about making hay, they went through the motions of mowing, raking, drying, pitching, stacking, and hauling hay, finally "resting" in a circle when they reached the last verse.[24]

Folk Arts, Crafts, and Games in Polonia

Given the rural, agricultural nature of many folk arts, crafts, and games, it might be expected that many did not survive the transatlantic crossing intact. Indeed, many times during my fieldwork among Polish-Americans I felt as though I were engaging in what Bruce Jackson has called "salvage folklore," material that "is always collected in radically different contexts than the ones in which it was formerly learned and performed. The stories remembered now are not necessarily representative of the stories told then."[25] This was especially true of the games and arts and crafts lore, as illustrated by the following conversation with Kate Moch:

> Did you ever make those feather ticks, the pierszyny?
> MOCH: Yeah.
> SILVERMAN: How do you make those?
> MOCH: Well, I tell you, I had one [one] time. I didn't like it, because I couldn't fix the bed nice. So I make the quilt, and after that we didn't want it. I like blankets.

At that point, realizing that I seemed disappointed, she continued with a description of pierszyny: "Those, you fill it up with feathers, you buy a lot of good feathers, they send me from Poland, uh, thirteen pounds of feathers. I make *five* big feather tick pillows. But I don't like feathers, I sleep on different kind of pillow."[26]

In a similar vein, Martha Steffan recalled the Easter egg-rolling game taught to her by her immigrant father:

> My father had his traditions like święconka, you probably have that, and rolling of the eggs. We couldn't wait til Easter Saturday, because he'd make a thing like that [with her hands, indicates a small slide], put it up against a chair or a box or something. Then we'd roll the eggs down, and my father would go like this [lightly taps an imaginary egg], and he'd know which egg was hollow and which one isn't. And if you *busted* the shell, that egg was yours. *Eggs* were something to *have* in them days! Today they don't care about eggs.[27]

Although egg-rolling games and the making of pierszyny provide examples of salvage folklore, other Polish arts and crafts continue to be practiced in Polish-American homes, particularly the making of pisanki colored with brown onion skins.

GABRIELLE MERTA: I take the onion peels, and I stick them in the water, and I stick my eggs in there. Then I bring it to a boil, boil for five minutes, and then just turn it off and leave it sitting there for fifteen minutes. They're nice and brown, and then you can take the little scraper—even a crochet hook—and scrape any design you want on it.

SILVERMAN: And that's how you put names . . . ?

MERTA: You put your names on, flowers, little birds, little moons, whatever you want to put on.

SILVERMAN: Are there any specific ones that you use on yours?

MERTA: Oh, I do everything on my eggs! I do usually the designs that we used to do in Poland, the little line across that goes, and then you put two lines across, around the egg, and then you put your little flowers inside and you connect the flowers with—you do, like, stencil work on them.[28]

For other Polish-Americans, the Catholic faith continues to inspire artistic creativity, as it did in the Old World. For example, one middle-aged woman, an amateur artist whose work is displayed in her home, has made ceramic sculptures of Jesus, sketches and paintings of religious figures, and even Christmas ornaments depicting a Felician nun believed to be responsible for a miraculous cure of the artist's mother.[29]

The secular world is also an inspiration. One man interested in woodcarving created gilded carved flowers, which he affixed to his garage door; a music stand; a clock; and a weathervane as well as a bathroom ceramic tile mural featuring a seascape, a reflection of his lifelong love for Lake Erie.[30] In modern Poland, although folk artists are not completely abandoning the forms of ancient sacred and ritual art, they are also concentrating on secular objects of interest to contemporary life.[31]

Although these examples were done by homeowners in their private residences, Polish-American folk artists also operate in the public sphere and create murals for churches, taverns, and other people's homes. Studies done by folklorists Kate Koperski and Mia Boynton in Buffalo's Polonia offer insights into the process of creation.[32] The wall-painting tradition by working-class artists began in Polish-American churches during the 1920s and lasted through the mid-1940s, later spreading to taverns and eventually, in the 1950s and early 1960s, to private homes. Church murals were supervised by professionally trained Polish-American artists such as Joseph Mazur of Buffalo, but those in homes and taverns often were done by church crewmen who worked under the supervision of the professionals. The murals represented a tradition that crossed the boundaries between sacred and secular themes and formal and folk styles.

There were important stylistic differences, of course, between sacred and secular murals. Those in churches often were created for parish anniversaries, and professional artists were in charge, relegating their less-trained crews to minor details. Home or tavern murals, painted by both the professionals and their subordinates, were more likely to be inspired by the memories of both homeowner and painter or by the postcards, magazines, and calendar art of popular culture. Nonetheless, in both the church and home murals there resided a common core of meaning for Polish-Americans based on a shared legacy of internalized experiences, values, and beliefs.[33] That sense of shared meaning, or community, was especially comforting to the generation of immigrants; the murals were aids to adaptation in the New World and offered them assistance in defining their identity.[34]

As Polish-Americans have begun to interact with other ethnic groups on a regular basis through intermarriage, shared occupations, and neighborhoods, the murals have reflected those historical changes. One completed in 1985 at a Buffalo soup kitchen, for example, depicts blacks and whites, men under thirty, and many children, a cross-section of the soup kitchen's clientele on Buffalo's East Side, now occupied by both African- and Polish-Americans. Here, community is a concept that transcends nationality and ethnicity.[35]

Polish-American Folk Arts Educators

The ethnic folk arts movement in the United States is receiving a boost from arts educators who present demonstrations to schools, libraries, and other groups and have displays at ethnic group festivals and multiethnic folk arts exhibits. Among the Polish-American exhibits, I have seen Christmas decorations, wycinanki, flax spinning, ritual bread dough making, and miniature wayside shrines of wood. The folk artist created the wayside shrines with a young man from Poland who came to America to visit his grandfather. For the artist, the miniature shrines encapsulate his family history.

CHESTER TYBOROWSKI: My mother would always say, she lived in the country [in Poland], she would say they'd stop along the roadside in the country and say a prayer. And I couldn't get it through my head, kaplica, what the hell's a kaplica? So I went over to Poland, I took my daughter and my wife, and I'd tell them about the . . .

SHARON TYBOROWSKI [daughter]: Kaplicas. So they're sort of like our signature pieces, wayside shrines, like our own family history.[36]

The backgrounds of the folk artists vary greatly. One older woman, a Polish immigrant, learned how to decorate eggs at home: "In Poland, in everyone's house around Easter, every house does this. Everybody, children, adults, they create eggs, and we decorate a lot, many, many of them to Easter baskets. Also in Poland, at Easter, godparents give baskets to godchildren. You usually give about six eggs to each godchild. Then we have to have many of them."[37]

A Polish-American man who was interested in making pisanki took another route. "I learned at a weekend of Polish culture at the Orchard Lake Seminary in St. Mary's College. The club I belonged to, the Polish-American Solidarity Club, we decided to reward some of our young dancers, and we took them on a trip, and some of us went along as chaperones. And I went as a chaperone, but primarily I went to learn how to do the Easter eggs. So I continue demonstrating them at our affairs."[38]

One younger Polish-American woman learned about egg decorating through two means. As a child, she learned from her mother and grandmother, who presented her with a miniature Easter basket filled not with candy but with a loaf of bread, a small coffee cake, decorated eggs, and other traditional Easter items. Later, she attended several thirty-day summer ethnographic and folk arts workshops in Poland, events also cited by two other Polish-American arts educators.[39]

As with the folk dance instructors described in chapter 12, contemporary folk artists do not rely exclusively on oral tradition for advice on creating designs. Generally well educated, they occasionally turn to other sources. "If I don't know how to make something or there's not even anyone to teach me how to make them, I'll go and I'll find books, pictures, patterns, and I'll try to read what I can about it and then reconstruct whatever it was that they did," explains one woman.[40]

What they share in common is exposure to the folklore at an early age, as Sharon Tyborowski describes: "I've always had an interest in art and folk arts, but a lot of it was just learning an appreciation of my customs and things from home. . . . I grew up in the time of the dumb Polack jokes, so when I was very young, sometimes I would let people make me feel bad about what my heritage was. After I visited Poland and really found out what the people were like and what the country was like, I decided that was never going to happen again."[41]

The future of folk arts education in Polonia, as in contemporary Poland, is dependent upon government support. The U.S. federal government has considered cutbacks in funding for the National Endowment for the Arts and other agencies that support folk arts programs, and Poland's government since the fall of communism has wrestled with similar budgetary concerns. The folk arts programs and regional museums supported by the communists cannot be as sure of financial aid now. One Polish-American artist who visited Poland in the early 1990s commented, "Those regional museums are closing. Some of those collections will be lost. It's a very sad thing, because you don't know what's happening. Some of the things, like the wayside shrines, are being stolen because of their value. It's a very unfortunate time."[42]

Despite the uncertainties of folk arts education in the public realm, in the private sphere of Polish-American home and community it is likely to endure because of a philosophy expressed by one folk artist: "What I demonstrate here, that's the old-fashioned way, so you can do it with very low cost or nothing, no pollution, no chemicals, just onion peels. And tools, you can make your own."[43] That simple formula for creativity has both the ingenuity of the Yankee and the thrift of the Polish peasant, the essence of the Polish-American artistic experience.

14

PIEROGI, KIELBASA, AND OTHER
SYMBOLS OF ETHNICITY:
POLISH-AMERICAN FOODWAYS

Lepiej wydać na piekarza, niż na aptekarza.

(Better to spend on the baker than on the druggist.)
—Zand, *Polish Proverbs*

In the Polish worldview, good and abundant food was believed to be essential for good health. Foodways also were, and continue to be, an important symbol of ethnic identity, a phenomenon noted by scholars of various ethnic groups.[1] In fact, foodways are among the most durable of all categories of ethnic folklore, persisting long after narratives and other genres have disappeared.[2]

Why do foodways demonstrate such durability? They are rooted in the family, the origin of an individual's earliest emotional memories of group membership.[3] As pointed out in previous chapters, Polish peasant culture privileged the family over the individual, which partially explains why the food preferences of the family and the larger Polish community would be maintained over many generations.

But foodways are not simply tenacious; they are socially mediated not only by the ethnic group but also by other factors, including regional groups, age, occupation, and one's stage in the life-cycle.[4] Among my Polish-American interviewees, for example, are a number of women who no longer make kielbasa at home because of the infirmities brought on by old age. They either rely on grown children who continue to prepare it or purchase their sausage at ethnic food markets.

As symbols of ethnicity, such foods are manipulated selectively to make statements about ethnic identity.[5] One Italian-American woman, for example, chose a traditional Italian menu, served in an informal buffet style, for her eldest daughter's wedding to a non-Italian to express disapproval for the match. The mother served an elaborate mainstream American formal dinner for the next daughter's wedding to an Italian-American as a way of demonstrating financial independence as a newly divorced woman.[6] Among the Cajuns of southern Louisiana, the crawfish is the emblem of both regional and ethnic identity.[7] Likewise, outsiders identify Polish-Americans, and they identify themselves, with particular foods such as kielbasa and pierogi.

It is important to distinguish between ethnic foods intended for consumption within the group and those prepared for the public. Richard Dorson classifies such folk behavior according to a four-tiered scheme: the presentational mode, the ethnic group's "public face" to outsiders; the historical mode, the group's actions in the civic setting to protect cultural identity; the communal mode, the group's "social face" in interactions with one another; and the esoteric mode, the "private face" of the ethnic individual.[8]

A slightly different typology is offered by Sabina Magliocco in a discussion of Italian-American foods. She differentiates among "esoteric foods" eaten by group members only; "display foods" such as spaghetti, identified by outsiders as typically "Italian"; "rechristened foods," mainstream American foods and beverages such as soda pop, which are given Italian-sounding names; and "pseudofoods" such as the large, round, wooden "cheeses" substituted for the real item in food-rolling games at Italian-American festivals.[9]

Borrowing from both Dorson and Magliocco, this chapter will use the term *esoteric* to describe food eaten by Polish-Americans within the ethnic group, both in the family and communal settings. Their presentation of "display foods" in public festivals intended both for ethnic group members and outsiders will be examined in chapter 15.

"The Best Cooks Were the Peasants": Foodways in the Old World

Because Poland was an agricultural country for many years, its population lived off the land but not always well. A customary peasant diet of the early twentieth century was described as "meagre, monotonous, high in starch and low in protein content."[10] Regionalism was as evident in Polish foodways as it was in folk dance, crafts, costumes, and celebrations; what was served depended upon what was available.[11] Like their counterparts in Italy and Germany, Poland's peasants ate little meat or poultry most of the year because those food items were scarce, reserved for weddings or major holidays such as Christmas, Easter, and the harvest festival.[12] According to one immigrant, "They usually had a cow and raised a pig or two, but the meat—I can't ever remember them eating any beef. They always sold their beef. Eating that was very seldom, until we came to this country."[13] Another immigrant recalled eating meat only two or three times in her thirteen years in Poland.[14] When a cow or pig was butchered, very little meat was wasted; even scraps became kielbasa, *kiszka* (ground pork steak with *kasza*, buckwheat groats), or *panas* (head-cheese). On those rare occasions, the Polish farmer also took care to send gifts of meat to the proper recipients according to established tradition.[15] If ducks or chickens were killed, the family might prepare czarnina (chapter 3) or *kurzy rosół* (chicken soup) from chicken parts.

Vegetables (*jarzyny*) rather than meats (*mięsa*) were daily staples in the Polish peasant diet. Potatoes, beans, beets, cabbage, tomatoes, cucumbers (fresh and pickled), and carrots were all eaten as seasonally available to the point of monotony. Kate Moch recalled with disgust that she had eaten mashed carrots for breakfast every morning in Poland. Another common dish served both for breakfast and supper was potatoes and homemade sauerkraut: "In old country, we make the barrel, because we have beams to the ceiling. We make this big barrel of sauerkraut. They bring the cabbage from outside, and they don't thrown the green leaves away. They *wash* the green leaves, and they have barrels, big barrels like they show on television here to take a swim.[16] They put the heads of cabbage in, way up to the ceiling, and they eat it three times a day."[17]

Cabbage, beets, and other vegetables were the featured ingredients in a variety of soups such as beet soup, cabbage soup, or *grochówka* (pea soup). Rice and kasza also were important dietary components; sometimes the kasza would be cooked and made into a filling for pierogi. Kasza also was served as a thick porridge cooked in either milk or water, with or without dried fruit; alternatively, it was highly seasoned and contained bits of meat, mushrooms, or gravy.[18] *Kluski* (noodles) and dumplings made of flour also were popular side dishes.

Mushrooms were an important food in Poland. Many varieties, such as *borowiki, maślaki, bedłki, pieczarki, trufle, smardze,* and *rydze,* grew abundantly in the wild and were picked for use either fresh or dried as a side dish, in soups, or with vegetables or rice.[19] One immigrant, an expert on mushrooms who has written for Polish-American newspapers and prepared exhibits for festivals, estimates that four thousand varieties have now been identified in Poland, including eighty listed as endangered species. In a rhapsodic tone of voice, she explained how her interest had developed during her childhood in Poland:

> I was a small child, I was going with my mom to the forest. And she always whispered in the forest, she never spoke loudly. So I asked her why she was whispering and she says, "Because we could wake up those midgets." Those little brownies? So see how small I was, with Mom, when I went to forest to pick up for the first time my mushrooms.
>
> It's a lovely moment to be in the forest early in the morning. It's so quiet, so peaceful, so beautiful. When you go to the forest before sunrise, you can just welcome the birth of the day, the sun rising, the shade, and the sunbeams and everything that you can see. It just grows in your heart and in front of your eyes. You just sit in the beauty of the day.[20]

Often, such mushroom-picking expeditions might begin as early as 4 o'clock on Sunday morning; by 7 A.M. the pickers would return home, just in time to go to mass.[21]

Although not generally a source of meat, the family cow provided milk on a regular basis, which also was made into butter or various cheeses such as *szarźjaski*. "It was made by curdled sour milk placed in a mesh bag and tied so it would drip," Mary Miller explained. "They'd tie it up so it would drip, you know, so it would just all dry. And when it was dry, they pressed it down, bag and all, usually because they didn't have weights of any kind. They had stones. They'd get big slab stones and press it down, so that it was a cheese that you could cut later."[22]

Butter and animal fats such as salt pork were indispensable to Polish cooking because of the flavor they provided, according to one Polish-American man whose father was a butcher:

> I think a lot of the cooking that came about, the foods, are reminiscent of the soul food here in that the best cooks were the peasants, and they learned how to cook with minimal things, the less expensive things. But the less expensive things usually were the tastiest, because it was the fat rendering, and the breads, and the vegetables. The wealthier people had the better cuts, but they were less flavorful. And so if you were a wealthy person, you would have hired a peasant to cook for you, because the peasants were better cooks.[23]

As Mary Douglas has observed, a complex series of associations governs a meal and puts its frame on a gathering.[24] For Poles as for other European peasants, meals were invested with an almost sacramental significance; eating was an intimate affair, and food could not be wasted.[25] The sacral character of food was especially apparent at the Christmas wigilia, which began with the sharing of the blessed opłatek, and the Easter morning swięconka, with its entire menu blessed by the priest. Because this food was believed to have great magical potency, waste or irreverent treatment of it was proscribed: "Bones from the meats are thrown into the well to keep worms from breeding in the water; crumbs from the table are carefully gathered and thrown into the garden; egg-shells are hung on fruit trees to improve the crop."[26] Similarly, crumbs from the Christmas wigilia table were saved to be sown in the garden in the spring.

Such festive yet solemn meals in an ethnic community require adherence to established rules and taboos regarding the colors of foods, number of different foods served, and specific food combinations. Japanese-Americans, for example, avoid serving four foods at a meal, except at a funeral, because of that number's association with death; foods should be presented in uneven numbers, with three, five, and seven especially favored.[27] Likewise, according to Polish tradition, the wigilia should feature an odd number of dishes, generally five, seven, or nine, to allow for the possibility of increase. The menu also should include representative foods from all of a farmer's produce sources because such representation would ensure the perpetuation of the food supply.[28]

The holiest of all foods was bread, the staple in the Polish diet and the secular counterpart to the body of Jesus.[29] An indication of bread's importance to Polish peasants is the number of taboos associated with its preparation. For example, a family's bread trough should not be lent to others because "bread is afraid of the outsider's household."[30] Darker, heavier breads were consumed as everyday fare. *Piękna pszenna mąka* (beautiful wheat flour), however, was reserved for holiday baking of *chleb* (bread) and *placki* (coffee cakes) such as the babka of Easter and the *strucla z makiem* (poppyseed coffee cake) of Christmas. There also was korowaj (chapters 6 and 13). Among eastern and southern Europeans, bread and salt commonly were presented to a couple entering a new home; more specifically, among Russians and Poles they were presented to newlyweds to symbolize prosperity and welcome.[31] Even on ordinary days, Polish cooks saved bread crumbs for binding, thickening, lining baking pans, and garnishing dishes.[32]

Changes in Polonia: Acculturation and Hybridization

Traditionally, foodways were the province of Polish homemakers and handed down orally for many generations. Once the immigrants crossed the Atlantic, however, their tastes in food and their methods of preparation began to change. For some, the old foodways served as a buffer to culture shock, a reassuring reminder of the Old World; others, however, changed their food habits as a way of easing the adjustment to life in the new country.[33] Those who retained the old recipes often improved them in the United States, where better ingredients were available.[34]

The importance of ethnic grocery stores, meat markets, and backyard gardens to immigrants cannot be underestimated. These sources provide ingredients not readily available otherwise. Immigrants also believed that garden vegetables were of higher quality than those from supermarkets and carried symbolic value, fulfilling the immigrants' dream of owning land.[35]

Polish-Americans have shopped for many years at large ethnic markets such as the Broadway Market in Buffalo, a facility on the city's East Side featuring meat and poultry vendors, grocers, bakers, and a restaurant. Until the 1970s, smaller towns relied on mom-and-pop stores to supply the needs of ethnic clienteles. "There used to be a lot of corner stores in Dunkirk, an awful lot," Joe Rozen recalls, "and they all seemed to have what their local clientele wanted. I know we could get the *śledzie* [herring] right at Tuczynski's Market, which was two houses away, or Chester Sobkowski used to have them, we could get them there. Same with the farmer's cheese that they made the pierogi out of. They always carried that."[36]

Shoppers who desired to buy a freshly killed chicken or duck could choose their poultry live at a meat market and then wait there until the butcher handed over the finished product in a neatly wrapped white-paper package. "When we were kids, we'd walk by Curley's Meat Market for shopping downtown," says Rozen. "My mother always got chickens there and had them delivered every Friday. And when we went in there and saw ducks, our eyes lit up. I said, 'Mom, get a duck, get a duck, make czarnina.' And so she did it quite often."[37]

Because supermarkets have replaced most small grocery and meat stores, many Polish-Americans have become "commuter ethnics" to satisfy their desire for ethnic food. They travel by car an hour or more to an ethnic food market in a large city, such as the Broadway Market, or to a restaurant that serves Polish foods.[38]

Traditional Polish cuisine is prepared less frequently now in Polonia than in the early years, a phenomenon also noted in other ethnic American groups.[39] That is because mainstream American foods or ethnic take-out foods are easier to prepare. Too, more women, generally the primary cooks in their families, work outside their homes. As a result, more Polish-American men are in the kitchen.[40] One man in his mid-thirties learned how to make stuffed cabbage rolls (gołąbki) and Polish-style barbecued hamburgers from his mother, recipes he prepares for his Irish-American wife and their children and at several Polish-American clubs.[41] Other Polish-American men gave me their favorite recipes for Polish foods, many of them soups or main courses that they themselves prepare. Still others find themselves at the stove because of tradition. One Polish-American social club that was once exclusively male has, for many years, featured Christmas and Easter meals cooked by the men for club members of both sexes.

Richard Raspa has noted that although ethnic foods in America are not cooked as often for economic or nutritional reasons as they once were in the Old World, they continue to serve celebrative ends. He describes the exotic food choices of Italian-Americans in Mormon Utah as "nostalgic enactment of identity."[42]

Although such revivalism may be partially accurate with respect to some Polish-Americans yearning to create a past that was never theirs, it is not the complete story. A number of foods cooked by peasant Polish immigrants have always been popular in Polonia, including gołąbki, kiszka, and kielbasa, whose preparation is a participatory event for the entire family.

> We used to stuff the sausage for our mother when we were kids. She'd cut up all the meat and season it and get the casing. Of course, we all wanted to help, so we'd all get the pair of scissors out, and you feed the casing through there and fold it back and hold it with your left hand, your right hand. You're putting in one piece of meat at a time, then squeeze it down until you had it full, then tie it up. That was a heavenly smell. She'd hang it across a broom handle to drain overnight in the kitchen and season it a little more that way.[43]

Another man noted the importance of proper seasoning and fat in the sausage: "If you have Polish sausage without any seasoning, you might as well throw it away. It's dry. You've got to have fat in it, too, to give it flavor."[44]

A popular condiment for Polish sausage is horseradish, especially if made at home or by a Polish food supplier. On a Palm Sunday at the Broadway Market, Wanda Skup demonstrated how to make horseradish by feeding the horseradish root into a machine.

> It's an old-fashioned grater, just electric. And the root looks like this, white, and we mix it with vinegar over here, and I put it in a jar.
>
> ED SILVERMAN: That's all there is to it?
>
> WANDA SKUP: First, they come in very dirty, and we have to wash them and clean it, see, like this. Then we grate it. That's the worst job. And most of what we have here today, we have the horseradish with no salt, no sugar, because lots of people can't eat sugar or salt, so that's why a lot of people like this horseradish.[45]

In addition to kielbasa and horseradish, another marker of Polish-American identity to outsiders is pierogi, perhaps because of their commercial availability both fresh and frozen. Many families prefer to make pierogi together at home in large quantities, especially for Christmas:

> PAULINE NEWMAN [daughter]: We just kept making them. Jane [Pauline's sister] makes the dough, and Kristan [Jane's daughter] was rolling it out, I was filling it, Mom puts it in the water and waits for them to cook up and then . . .
>
> JOE ROZEN [son]: We all come and eat them.
>
> PAULINE: The best part is the ones that break, because we love to eat them . . .
>
> STEPHANIE ROZEN: First I cook cabbage, today I fry the cabbage. And then I got the cheese mix, with the ricotta cheese. And then we got the potatoes and mixed a little with the cheese. So those two [her daughters] came over and make the pierogi. [She laughs.]
>
> SILVERMAN: How long does it take you to make all those?
>
> PAULINE: We had a big crew yesterday, so it only took us, what, about three-and-a-half to four hours.[46]

Pierogi fillings include sauerkraut, cabbage, cheese and potatoes, mushrooms, meat, apples, prunes, or blueberries. At a family gathering such as the one described, it is common to make upward of four hundred pierogi in one afternoon.

In addition to these public markers of ethnic identity, Polish-Americans also prepare esoteric foods intended primarily for consumption within a family or larger ethnic group rather than by outsiders. Chief among these are two soups, czarnina and Easter barszcz (a misnomer because it does not, as its name implies, contain beets).[47] A man preparing Easter barszcz for the święconka meal at the Kosciuszko Club in Dunkirk, New York, described its preparation.

> SILVERMAN: You start out with sausage water, right?
>
> ED TARNOWSKI: We put the eggs and sausage in there, you got a ham bone in there, and I use heavy cream . . .
>
> SILVERMAN: How much heavy cream do you put in there?
>
> TARNOWSKI: Oh, I've got a quart in there. Then I put horseradish in there, horseradish root.
>
> SILVERMAN: Horseradish root's in there. Okay.
>
> TARNOWSKI: Then I got a little butter in there. Then I put a little flour and water in there, to make it heavy.
>
> SILVERMAN: Do you measure this out or do you just figure it out because you know, it's all in your head?
>
> TARNOWSKI[laughs]: All in the head.[48]

The preparation of czarnina, described by one man as "chocolate soup" because of its color, begins with the cooking of a duck.[49] Then the duck's blood and vinegar are added, followed by flour to thicken the mixture. The soup is cooked until the duck is tender. Near the end of the cooking time, prunes or raisins may be added; sugar also is optional. Czarnina is often served with kluski.[50]

Kluski are another esoteric food item associated with family in the minds of many Polish-Americans. One woman who still makes kluski for her husband and children recalled her grandmother's method:

> RITA DANNER: When I was a child, we had a great big wooden table, and as long as I can remember, I always ate homemade noodles, kluski. And my grandmother would make the dough so that it would be like a cover for the table, like a tablecloth. That's how big it was.
>
> SILVERMAN: She covered the whole table?
>
> DANNER: The entire table, that it would lay two foot over each side, that's how much dough she would make for noodles. I'll never forget that.[51]

To prepare the dough, another woman explained that she uses six eggs beaten with a half cup of water and a teaspoon of salt, then enough flour "until it becomes real doughy, kind of hard." After that she kneads the dough for ten or fifteen minutes and then divides it into two balls, rolls each one thin, and cuts the dough into strips that are then boiled in salted water.[52]

Sweet doughs are turned into coffee cakes such as babka, a favorite at Easter, the poppyseed coffee cake made at Christmas, or *chrusciki,* strips of dough made from eggs, flour, and sour cream and shaped like bowties and deep-fried. Electric mixers and other machinery are among the modern methods of food preparation, as evidenced by a baker's chrusciki demonstration at the Broadway Market: "We put the dough through a machine, a thinnish layer. After we make that, we cut it into small squares with a pizza cutter, put little holes in the middle, and then we trim it like a bowtie. Then we fry them. We put them in peanut oil or vegetable oil, whichever is good, until it comes out crispy, like little bubbles on it. Then when it's done, that's what it looks like. We put a little powdered sugar on it, and that's all there is to it."[53]

Pasta-making machines or specially designed machines for chrusciki or pierogi are increasingly being used in place of the time-consuming, laborious methods that involve beating or pressing dough by hand. This is especially true in communal settings such as social clubs or small Polish-American commercial enterprises that are starting to wholesale their ethnic foods to supermarket chains.[54]

Other changes in Polish-American foodways are concessions to inter-ethnic marriages that result in increasingly busy families. One man, describing his family's wigilia as somewhat "hybridized," told me about a delicious vegetable casserole that has become a mainstay at the gathering and is brought by an Italian-American daughter-in-law.[55] In another family, a Polish-American woman is proud of the fact that her Irish-German-American daughter-in-law makes pierogi and keeps up other Polish traditions, even though she herself now buys pierogi.[56] The reverse also is true: Polish-American women who marry outside the group may adopt their husbands' foodways, as was the case for one woman who now serves a Swedish Christmas Eve supper including roast pork, boiled potatoes, and rice pudding (chapter 1).[57]

Alterations also have occurred with respect to the location of special meals, which have become virtually movable feasts in some instances. One German-American woman married to a Polish-American makes a trip to the Broadway Market each spring in order to buy a duck and duck's blood, which they then take to Florida for an Easter visit with the woman's sister and her Polish-American husband: "We have a Polish crumb coffee cake there and of course the hard-boiled eggs. And in the frying pan she has, she puts a hard-boiled egg, some ham, and Polish sausage and just lets it all get warmed through. . . . It's hard for them to get the things [there] that she would use for a Polish breakfast."[58] Another family continues to celebrate Easter at the mother's house, but the grown children and grandchildren eat in shifts because the house is too small to seat everyone comfortably at one sitting.[59]

Given the fact that today's Polish-Americans, unlike their ancestors in peasant Poland, are highly literate, it is no surprise that recipes frequently are written down. Many Polish cookbooks are available in the English language, and cooking demonstrations are an integral part of ethnic festivals. Still, during my fieldwork I observed several cooks working from a listing of ingredients scribbled on a scrap of paper, sometimes without the exact measurements given. The assumption was that the cook knew the proper oven temperature, cooking time, and amount of each ingredient. Alternatively, other informants store their recipes on home computers or have acquired them via a Polish hobby group on on-line networks such as America Online, Prodigy, or CompuServe.[60]

Although these second-, third-, fourth-, and fifth-generation Polish-Americans may no longer speak the Polish language, they retain the food vocabulary in the mother tongue, a phenomenon also reported among Japanese-Americans.[61] The Polish-Americans whom I studied still use "pierogi," "czarnina," "kiszka," "kielbasa," "kluski," and "gołąbki." That suggests that traditional foodways in both familial and communal contexts continue to bear meaning for many, although they may experience difficulty in explaining the significance of various foods used in holiday celebrations. Having heard that each Easter food carries a particular meaning, I asked a group at one Easter gathering about the meaning associated with the butter lamb, sausage, eggs, horseradish, and other items contained in the święconka basket taken to church. After considering the question for several minutes, they finally told me that they were not certain, but because their parents and grandparents had served the same foods, doing likewise was a tradition with them, too. Other folklorists may prefer a tidier explanation, but theirs was sufficient for me. I could readily observe that, as Robert Plant Armstrong would say, they accorded those objects special treatment within their folk community.[62] The foodways were so important, in fact, that a local Catholic priest was invited to bless the food before it was served.

Polish-Americans also stress the importance of transmitting their values about family and community, as expressed through foodways, to the next generation. Women who belong to Polish-American church groups, for example, often make pierogi and other foods to sell at parish functions. In addition to benefiting the church, the women are making a statement about their ethnic identity.[63] That also holds true at the familial level. Although foodways in the New World have evolved as the result of interethnic marriages and new food processing methods and ingredients, they remain a vital part of the Polish heritage.

15

ANCHORS AND PASSPORTS TO POLISHNESS:
PUBLIC FOLKLORE IN POLONIA

If we forget our Polish heritage,
we become nothing but ships in the
wind without anchors.
—Bishop Paul Rhode, 1934

Since 1978 residents of the large Polish-American community in
Cheektowaga, New York, have organized an annual festival promoting their heritage. Each August the event draws upward of twenty thousand visitors from Pennsylvania, Ohio, Massachusetts, and elsewhere in New York state for a weekend featuring an outdoor polka mass, polka dancing, performances by local Polish folk dance troupes, demonstrations by folk crafts exhibitors, and Polish food sold by commercial vendors.

The idea for the festival germinated after then–New York Governor Hugh Carey visited Cheektowaga to dedicate the town's new outdoor amphitheater. He suggested that because the community had a large Polish-American population a festival might succeed. Local organizers responded by enlisting financial support from banks, supermarkets, and smaller businesses that advertise in the festival program in addition to grants from the New York State Council on the Arts and the National Endowment for the Arts. Planning begins a year in advance so popular, nationally known entertainers can be booked for the festival, which costs approximately $25,000 to present.[1]

Farther downstate, Orange County's Polish-Americans hold their Onion Harvest Festival every five years on a weekend in August. The event, which originated in 1939, pays homage to the Old World tradition of dożynki, marking the climax of the county's onion harvest.[2] Held in farm country near the communities of Florida and Pine Island, New York, the Onion Harvest Festival is one of the largest exhibitions of Polish folklore on the eastern seaboard, drawing thirty thousand people. Professionally trained folk dance choreographers school three hundred local adults and children, many not of Polish descent, to dance in five different groups divided according to age. In addition, there is a choral ensemble composed of volunteers, a procession featuring the Onion Harvest Festival queen, a polka mass, and polka music by regional and nationally known bands.

Polish-American communities also host other events during the spring and summer travel seasons that are equally public in scale, designed to attract both local residents and tourists. Buffalo's Dyngus Day celebrations on Easter Monday bring in busloads of travelers from throughout the northeastern United States. They generally begin the day at Chopin's Singing Society, originator of the city's Dyngus Day parties, before moving on to other venues. To feed the large crowds, cooks at Chopin's prepare 1,200 pounds of sausage, color sixty dozen hard-boiled eggs, and ready five buckets of noodles for a casserole dish, among other items.[3]

Polka festivals from St. Patrick's Day through Labor Day weekend unite thousands of music lovers. Major festivals are held in Pulaski, Wisconsin; Seven Springs, Pennsylvania; New London, Connecticut; Ocean City, Maryland; and Chicago.[4] In smaller towns such as Dunkirk, New York, Polish-American social clubs like the Kosciuszko Club present weekend street dances that often coincide with a celebration by the larger community, such as the city's Fourth of July weekend festival.

Social organizations also present special events to generate interest in Polish heritage. In western Massachusetts, for example, the Society for the Preservation of Polish Culture offers free special programs and a coffee hour for the public. In western New York state, the Dom Polski Club in Dunkirk hosts a Polish night in October around Pulaski Day, an event featuring Polish food and polka music.[5]

What all these events have in common is a desire to present some aspect of Polish-American culture to both ethnic group members and outsiders. Polka music, a parade, or traditional arts and crafts may attract some.[6] Others may wish to share their traditions with friends outside the ethnic group. One Polish-American attorney, for example, brought a Jewish-American friend to Buffalo's Dyngus Day celebration the week after he had attended the friend's seder.[7] He believes the key to transmitting one's ethnic heritage is to engage participants in an activity. "When I went to the seder," he reports, "they had a custom where they hid the matzoh, and the kids would look for it. That kept the kids involved. And they had little kid songs. That's what they do here, too. I think the blessing of the basket is a lot of fun because you color the eggs and then you take it to be blessed. It's something the kids latch onto."

Other people are seeking to identify emotionally with a certain group when they attend an ethnic festival. As Sophie Knab remarked, "I think people want to feel special or different in some ways. And these are the things that anchor them here. You know, people will say, 'Well, we don't have any Christmas celebrations' or 'We don't have any Easter celebrations.' And they want to."[8] Polish-American festivals also afford an increasingly rare opportunity to speak in Polish with crafts exhibitors or musical groups (or to hear Polish being spoken), although most presentations are in English.

A sense of bonding with the ethnic group can occur simply through economic transactions, according to folk crafts exhibitor Lawrence Kozlowski: "Because it [the craft item] says it's from Poland, they have to buy that and that becomes their passport to Polishness. That's one thing I've noticed, not only here at the Cheektowaga festival but in Pittsburgh, in Philadelphia, at different festivals. There's the folklore and the ethnography and it has different meanings for different people."[9] He challenges the notion put forth by some scholars that current interest in the Polish-American heritage is a revival that began during the 1970s: "I think it's more of what we once did in the privacy of our homes, we're doing out for everyone to see now."[10] I, too, believe that one reason for the transition from private to public sphere concerns the availability of government money for ethnic programs.

Culture: Genuine or Spurious?

Since the 1970s, government funding of ethnic studies and folk arts programs has provided an opportunity for the public presentation of Polish-American culture. But such funding also has fueled a heated debate among both folklorists and folk community members over the issue of authenticity. Whose definition of "tradition" is presented, that of the folklorist or that of the community, and is the folk community united in its opinion of what constitutes "tradition"?[11]

Shalom Staub has argued that "authenticity" is not a word used self-referentially within a folk group.[12] I have found, however, that Polish-American festival organizers are keenly aware of the importance of authenticity. "We have worked very closely with Kate Koperski from Niagara University," one told me, "and then, of course, we have Sophie Knab, Judy Krauza, these are past committee members. Initially, we had several people from Polish organizations in the area. . . . And then, of course, if we work with Kate Koperski regarding the New York State and NEA grants, their background and their experience dictates authenticity. They *know* which of the craftsmen we should be getting, which ones will be funded and which ones will not."[13]

A similar concern about authenticity was voiced by Onion Harvest Festival organizers, who hired two graduates of Poland's only training institution for folk dance choreographers as the 1995 festival's artistic director and dance instructor. The artistic director, Stanisław Kmieć, was described by a festival organizer as a "purist" who observes traditions at home and has studied Polish culture extensively.[14]

Folklorists and anthropologists have vigorously debated the merits of authenticity for many years. In 1924 Edward Sapir described "genuine culture" as "the characteristic mold of a national civilization. . . . harmonious, balanced, self-satisfactory."[15] Twenty-six years later, Richard Dorson introduced the concept of "fakelore" to distinguish the Paul Bunyan legends and similar pseudo-literary forms from folklore, which was then in its infancy as an academic discipline in the United States.[16] More recently, in revisiting Sapir's conceptions of "genuine" versus "spurious" culture after their own fieldwork in Hawaii and Quebec, Richard Handler and Jocelyn Linnekin concluded that tradition, at any given moment, is not a core of inherited culture, its "commonsense meaning," but rather a process, a symbolic construction.[17]

Ethnic Americans are actively engaged in this process, what scholars term "impression management," selecting signals to create an ethnic identity.[18] Elderly East European Jewish immigrants have deftly improvised rituals blending Old and New World elements to create a meaningful lifestyle in their senior citizens' center in Venice, California. At a Latino festival in Washington, D.C., Latino groups target their food *kioskos* to three levels of social interaction: tourist exhibits catering to non-ethnics, street vendors selling traditional foods to Latinos, and family centers of food distribution uniting kin. To promote their community's Swedish heritage and develop tourism, during the 1960s Swedish-Americans in Lindsborg, Kansas, created a St. Lucia Festival featuring the self-conscious maintenance of traditions, revivals of ancestral customs from Sweden, and the creation of quasi-folk observances.[19]

These events are in what Richard Dorson termed the "public-presentational mode," establishing a favorable image confirming popular stereotypes. As one Polish-American newspaper editor put it, "The leaders of Polonia are trying to represent a set of positive values."[20] These decisions are carefully, consciously, and deliberately made, no surprise given the negative stereotyping of Polish-Americans due to the plethora of "dumb Polack" jokes. Suggesting that such jokes have created an inferiority complex among Polish-Americans, historian John Bukowczyk cites anti-Polish gags, routines, and skits by Rowan and Martin, Frank Sinatra, Phyllis Diller, Morey Amsterdam, Dean Martin, Joan Rivers, Johnny Carson, Steve Allen, Don Rickles, and Carol Burnett, as well as television shows such as "Laverne and Shirley" and "All in the Family" as portraying stereotyped Polish characters.[21] As many Polish-Americans have risen into the ranks of professionals and community leaders, they have desired to build a more positive self-image by drawing selectively from tradition, in some cases bypassing their peasant ancestors' humble customs—the source, in distorted form, of the anti-Polish stereotypes—in favor of "Polish high culture."[22]

An example from my fieldwork bears out Bukowczyk's theory. In Buffalo, many prominent Polish-Americans are members of Chopin's Singing Society, a cultural organization dedicated to promoting Polish heritage through concerts and special events. The society was the originator of local Dyngus Day party on Easter Monday. Festivities start on cue as soon as television cameras and photographers are ready. The well-rehearsed Chopin's choir, dressed in bright red blazers, one of the Polish national colors, begins a medley of American and traditional Polish songs, some in the English language, others in Polish. The brief concert is often televised live by at least one station. It is followed by short speeches from leading politicians and the blessing of Easter food by a young, articulate Polish-American priest fluent in both Polish and English.

The choir's polished performance each Dyngus Day is just one of many the group makes locally, nationally, and internationally. Since the 1970s it has staged reenactments of the dożynki, the St. John's Eve celebration, and wedding and holiday customs in public settings and on television; its members are skilled in dealing with the news media.

Yet the Chopin's Singing Society's vision of Polonia is not shared by all Polish-Americans. There is a split between proponents of "high C" and "low C" culture. According to a Buffalo Common Council member of Polish descent, "You will find ethnic music [the polka] created in an art form that might be looked down upon by certain people that like high C culture: Chopin music, Adam Mickiewicz lectures. You know where you find good low C culture? Polka music. But some consider it low-class, blue-collar. Those people have aristocratic pretensions although most of them are sons or daughters of peasants."[23]

Informants who described Polonia's low C culture admitted that it has an archaic quality stemming from the regional dialects and folklore of peasant Polish immigrants of a century ago. One Polish-American judge commented, "One day I was speaking with a visitor from Poland, and he said to me, 'You know, your Polish is very good, but you talk as if you came, like the people from World War I spoke.'"[24] Similarly, a Polish-American folk crafts educator discovered while on a trip to Poland that relatives there were shocked when she asked for pierogi: "They said, 'Why on earth would you want to have that kind of food?' What we didn't pick up on is that when our parents or grandparents came over here [to the United States], they made that kind of food because they had very limited incomes and that's what they could stretch to feed a family on. But that was really like the poor people's foods, certainly not delicacies by anybody's standards."[25] For these reasons, recent Polish immigrants who have studied about Chopin, Mickiewicz, and other leading figures in the "national" culture of Poland have little interest in affiliating with established Polish-American communities based on the peasant culture.[26]

Other ethnic American groups are coping with similar internal struggles in trying to shape an identity. Among Cajuns in southern Louisiana, for example, there is a sharp split along class lines between wealthier, more formally educated "genteel Acadians" who advocate speaking standard French to promote ethnic identity and "proud coonasses" who often speak a Louisiana French dialect or no French at all and emphasize the rowdier side of Cajun life: heavy drinking and eating, gambling, cockfighting, and barroom brawls.[27]

In Hawaii, the competing definitions of "Hawaiian tradition" range from an eclectic version presented by Hawaiian nationalists to that of the small, rural Hawaiian community of the "pure" Hawaiian, comparable to the archetypal Polish peasant. The latter variant, however, is not typical of the experience of most Hawaiians today. Many have intermarried, do not speak the Hawaiian language, and live in cities rather than rural areas. Both versions of ethnic identity converge and influence each other.[28] The same process is occurring in America's Polish communities, where lectures about Chopin's music coexist with polka nights. It is too soon to predict whether Polonia's high C and low C variants will remain distinct entities or merge into a new, "middle C" culture.

The Reinvention of Ethnicity by Individuals

Such cross-fertilization is likely to continue among ethnic Americans of the third and fourth generations as they construct new ethnic identities built upon the traditions of their immigrant ancestors. Although occupational, regional, religious, and many other identities are available to every individual, ethnic identity is rooted in a common language, food, music, and other tangible markers and has a special emotional appeal. In an era when families are increasingly splintered due to geographic mobility, an ethnic group is an alternative source of affective ties.[29]

An ethnic identity evolves as part of a dynamic, creative process, "something reinvented and reinterpreted in each generation by each individual."[30] Folklore interviewees described their sense of ethnicity in various ways; only one, a Polish immigrant, called herself Polish.[31] Some said they were Polish-American, others claimed to be Americans of Polish descent. This dual allegiance was explained as follows: "I would be very proud to say I'm Polish-American, sure. American-Polish, whatever. But I would have to favor America also because in 1944 I went to the service, and I was in the service for a couple of years, so I served my duty and that was it."[32] One Polish-American maintains that his immigrant ancestors welcomed, and even expected, their descendants to make such a transition, adding, "I'm not terribly into holding onto traditions that have no personal meaning. If it's something we did at home, because we want to do it, I have nothing against that."[33]

Ethnicity, then, is derived from the meaning it has for individuals within the context of the family and ethnic group as expressed through folklore. In both public and private settings, today's Polish-Americans are searching for an ethnic identity in ever-greater numbers. Echoing the sentiments of a number of interviewees, the pastor of Buffalo's leading Polish-American Catholic parish explained: "What I see today is a younger, more enthusiastic generation intent on preserving customs and in some cases the language. There's an interest in genealogy today and a movement for a one-world concept, but not in the sense of everybody giving up what they had. There's an adverse reaction to the concept of the melting pot."[34]

That is not to suggest that most Polish-Americans are transmitting their folklore to the next generation. The future of their heritage depends largely on individuals whom Wsevolod Isajiw calls "ethnic rediscoverers," people socialized into the general society's culture who have developed a symbolic relation to the culture of their ancestors.[35] Their brothers or sisters may not take any interest in the subject, but they themselves may have visited Poland, studied Polish-American cooking, crafts, or music, or taken courses in the history of Polonia and eastern Europe. One such "rediscoverer" feels that ethnicity effectively combats alienation and loneliness and provides a sense of history: "Most people don't know where their grandparents came from. They never traced their family roots. And so they're brought up in a void, a vacuum."[36] For the interviewees, having a Polish-American ethnic identity, shaped by folklore adapted to the needs of each generation, fills that void.

What Does It Mean to Be a Polish-American?

In the years following World War II, many changes occurred in Polish-American communities, both geographical and class-based in nature. As John Bukowczyk has noted, many Polish-Americans left working-class inner cities for middle-class suburbs and the industrial Northeast for California; in turn, Hispanic- and African-Americans moved into Polonia's old urban neighborhoods.[37] During the 1990s, when I was conducting fieldwork in Buffalo and its suburbs, I observed this phenomenon on the city's East Side, the home of Polish-American churches, social clubs, businesses, and the Broadway Market for many years. With the shift of the Polish-American population to the suburbs, East Side churches are being closed because of declining membership, social clubs and businesses are relocating to nearby suburbs that they deem to be safer, and the Broadway Market is reconsidering its marketing plans in light of the community's increasing population of African-Americans.

In addition to these changes, I found that fewer postwar Polish-Americans are learning the Polish language and more are marrying outside the ethnic group, two factors that would argue against the transmission of the folklore to the next generation. Yet the folklore continues to be transmitted; in fact, I discovered non-Polish-American spouses who are enthusiastic proponents of traditional culture in several families. What is the impact of intermarriage upon ethnic folklore usage? More research is needed.

The effect of the mass media upon traditional folk cultures also requires further investigation. Bukowczyk argues that the advent of television in the 1950s "supplanted local, regional, class, or ethnic customs, traditions, and folkways with a national culture for the first time in American history."[38] Although it is true that many Polish-Americans were following "The Adventures of Ozzie and Harriet" with great interest, I do not believe that television supplanted regional, class, or ethnic folkways with a national culture. Regional, class, and ethnic customs coexisted with the new national culture, a trend that still continues. Nor did television give America its first national culture. That distinction belongs to radio, which began to provide nationwide news and entertainment programming during the 1920s.

Although both radio and television promoted the development of a national culture, they also offered air time to ethnic groups for the development of special programming, which, contrary to Bukowczyk's theory, exposed both group members and outsiders to the ethnic group's culture. Polish-American radio programs were on the air by the 1930s and featured polka music (chapter 11); similarly, by the 1950s, local television stations were beginning to broadcast ethnic music programs. Radio and television stations still broadcast programming for ethnic audiences. Do these programs promote additional interest in ethnic folklore among group members and outsiders? Again, the question invites further research.

Mass-media programs, the popularity of home computers and the Internet for special-interest "Polish culture" newsgroups, and the increasing performance of folklore in public arenas such as Dyngus Day parties, polka weekends, and ethnic festivals all suggest that the Polish-American community is actively redefining its public image, selectively drawing upon the folklore of both rural peasant ancestors and the Polish-American working class to overcome negative stereotypes of the "dumb Polack."

But what does it mean to be Polish-American, especially because so many people have traded life in the okolica for mainstream American suburbia? The question is difficult to answer because Polonia includes not only the descendants of the peasants but also two groups of more recent arrivals: "displaced Poles" who came after World War II and "Solidarity refugees" who emigrated during the 1980s. These groups have felt little affinity with the established Polonia, preferring the "national" culture of contemporary Poland.[39]

Despite this cultural fragmentation, my folklore fieldwork offers some preliminary answers. Easter and Christmas celebrations, accompanied by traditional foodways and music, remain important among the majority of interviewees. Many also observe Polish wedding customs, enjoy Polish-American polka music, or relate personal narratives of an ethnic nature; smaller numbers participate in Polish folk dancing, folk arts and crafts, and folk religion and medicine. To be considered Polish-American, I believe that an individual must participate in at least some of these folk-lore genres, but as Helena Znaniecka Lopata has asked, How ethnic does a Polish-American have to be in order to be called an "ethnic"?[40] Is it enough to speak a few words in Polish, attend a Christmas Eve wigilia, and dance the polka every weekend? Scholars need to give additional thought to this issue. Assuming that a person considers himself or her-self Polish-American and takes part in the folk community's life to some extent, why does it matter? I believe that for the individual, the folk group represents a second, extended family, an additional source of emotional ties; like genealogy, a group's folklore offers a sense of connection to one's past, as many people told me.

All Americans can claim kinship with one, or perhaps several, ethnic groups. My research among Polish-Americans suggests that although ethnic Americans may no longer live in the geographically isolated neighborhoods of their immigrant ancestors, an ethnic identity, devel-oped anew by each generation through folklore usage, remains an im-portant component of life.

APPENDIX:
THE INTERVIEWS

Anders, Adriana. Personal interview, 17 July 1991.

Asztemborski, Bob. Personal interview, 12 April 1993.

Blazonczyk, Eddie. Personal interview, 17 March 1995.

Bognaski, Ed. Personal interview, 12 April 1993.

Boruszewski, Emily. Personal interview, 1 March 1993.

Brogcinski, Jean and Robert. Personal interview, 20 Aug. 1995.

Budniewski, Ray. Personal interviews, 6 Feb. and 10 April 1993; telephone interview, 7 April 1996.

Ciesielski, Robert. Personal interview, 12 April 1993.

Clark, Al. Personal interviews, 10 June and 7 Nov. 1978, 6 Nov. and 23 Nov. 1979.

Clark, Ann. Personal interview, 10 June 1978.

Collins, Daniel. Personal interview, 17 March 1995.

Danner, Rita, and Rose Lehr. Personal interview, 20 Aug. 1995.

Dende, Cornelian. Personal interview, 26 Jan. 1996.

Dzięgielewska, Jadwiga. Personal interview, 19 Aug. 1995.

Franczyk, David. Personal interview, 12 April 1993.

Gabalski, John. Personal interview, 19 Dec. 1992.

Gawlak, Chris. Personal interview, 12 April 1993.

Gestwicki, Tom. Personal interview, 1 June 1991.

Gibson, Rose. Personal interview, 15 Jan. 1979.

Gordon, Fred. Personal interview, 12 April 1993.

Gorski, Dennis. Personal interview, 12 April 1993.

Graminski, Belle. Personal interview, 7 July 1991.

Griffin, James. Personal interview, 12 April 1993.

Grupa, Frank, and Ray Budniewski and Ed Tarnowski, personal interview, 10 April 1993.

Guzevich, Gus, and Hank and Nellie Guzevich. Personal interview, 19 March 1995.

Halasinski, Lillian, and Geraldine Halasinski. Personal interview, 12 Jan. 1996.

Hodorowicz, Józefa Zalewska. Telephone interview, 19 Jan. 1996.

Hora, Robert. Personal interview, 17 June 1991.

Jacobs, Delphine, and Felix Jacobs. Personal interview, 30 Jan. 1979.

Jeronczyk, Ed. Personal interview, 19 Aug. 1995.

Kij, Daniel. Personal interviews, 29 May 1995 and 26 Jan. 1996.

King, Bob. Personal interview, 19 March 1995.

Knab, Sophie Hodorowicz. Personal interview, 19 Aug. 1995.

Kohan, Mark. Personal interviews, 19 Dec. and 29 Dec. 1992; telephone interview, 20 Nov. 1995.

Kozak, Stan. Personal interview, 19 March 1995.

Kozlowski, Chet. Personal interview, 7 July 1991.

Kozlowski, Lawrence. Personal interview, 19 Aug. 1995.

Krauza, Judith. Personal interview, 29 March 1992.

Kupiec, Gertrude. Personal interview, 28 Oct. 1978.

Lemieux, Linda. Telephone interview, 21 Aug. 1995.

Litwin, Steve. Personal interview, 19 March 1995; telephone interviews, 30 Jan. 1993 and 16 March 1996.

Makowski, Henia. Personal interview, 29 March 1992.

Makowski, Dick. Personal interview, 29 March 1992.

Matthews, Michelle. Personal interview, 19 March 1995.

Mazur, Alois, and Dorothy Mazur. Personal interview, 14 Sept. 1991.

Merta, Gabrielle. Personal interview, 20 July 1991.

Miehl, Ted. Personal interview, 1 June 1991.

Mikoll, Ann. Personal interview, 13 July 1992.

Miller, Mary. Personal interview, 19 Aug. 1991.

Moch, Kate. Personal interview, 19 Feb. 1979.

Moch, Lucy. Personal interview, 24 Jan. 1979.

Nowak, Alton. Personal interview, 14 Dec. 1978.

Nowak, Thela. Personal interview, 14 Dec. 1978.

Osora, Jean. Personal interview, 19 March 1995.

Panowicz, John. Personal interview, 29 March 1992.

Pawlak, Valerie. Personal interview, 13 July 1991.

Pencek, Jack. Personal interview, 25 Aug. 1991.

Polak, Ron. Personal interviews, 21 July 1991 and 12 April 1993.

Poslinski, Monike. Personal interview, 4 April 1993.

Purol, Celia. Personal interview, 13 Feb. 1979.

Rozen, Joe. Personal interviews, 20 July 1991 and 24 Dec. 1994.

Rozen, Stephanie. Personal interview, 24 Dec. 1994.

Ruszaj, Florence. Personal interview, 21 July 1991.

Sabloski, Edward. Personal interview, 12 April 1993.

Saccone, Betty. Personal interview, 12 April 1993.

Sawka, Helen. Personal interview, 12 April 1993.

Sekula, Lucy, and Monica Sekula. Personal interview, 17 Jan. 1979.

Skup, Wanda. Personal interview, 4 April 1993.

Silverman, Edward. Personal interviews, 23 April and 20 Nov. 1995.

Snyder, Christine Kupiec. Personal interview, 10 July 1991.

Stanek, Janet. Telephone interview, 22 March 1995.

Steffan, Martha. Personal interview, 17 Aug. 1991.

Szatkowski, Denise. Personal interview, 19 March 1995.

Szymanski, Ted, and Ed Skoczylas. Personal interview, 21 July 1991.

Tarnowski, Chet. Personal interviews, 20 April and 22 Dec. 1992, 17 April 1995.

Tarnowski, Ed. Personal interview, 10 April 1993.

Tofil, Peter. Personal interview, 21 Feb. 1995.

Tombak, Wolf. Personal interview, 4 April 1993.

Tyborowski, Chester, and Sharon Tyborowski. Personal interview, 19 Aug. 1995.

Urbanik, Paul. Personal interview, 6 Feb. 1979.

Urbanik, Sophie. Personal interview, 8 June 1991.

Uszacki, Helen. Personal interview, 16 April 1995.

Warzecha, Tom. Personal interview, 12 April 1993; telephone interview, 25 April 1993.

Waszczuk, Lynda. Personal interview, 12 April 1993.

Wisniewski, Willy. Personal interview, 12 April 1993.

Wojcik, Patricia. Telephone interview, 21 Aug. 1995.

Zachary, Mary. Personal interview, 7 July 1991.

Ziegler, Gerry. Personal interview, 10 April 1993.

Ziosk, Dianne. Personal interview, 12 April 1993.

NOTES

Introduction

1. Lopata, *Polish Americans*, 1.

2. See, for example, Dundes, *Folklore Matters*, 35; Flores, "The *Corrido*," 166–82; and Oring, "Ethnic Groups and Ethnic Folklore," 23–44.

3. For historical overviews of American Polonia, see Kruszka, *History;* Bukowczyk, *And My Children Did Not Know Me;* Pula, *Polish Americans;* Greene, *For God and Country;* and Wytrwal, *America's Polish Heritage.* For accounts of the Polish immigrants' early years in Chicago and Buffalo, respectively, see Pacyga, *Polish Immigrants and Industrial Chicago;* and Falkowski, "Accommodation and Conflict."

4. For sociological overviews of American Polonia at two different periods in its history, see Thomas and Znaniecki, *The Polish Peasant in Europe and America;* and Lopata, *Polish Americans.* For sociological studies of Buffalo's Polonia, see two works by Niles Carpenter and Daniel Katz that deal with the community's post–World War I years: "The Cultural Adjustment of the Polish Group in the City of Buffalo" and "A Study of Acculturation." A more recent study of Buffalo's community is that of Eugene Obidinski, "Ethnic to Status Group." Sociological studies of the Polonia in Boston, Los Angeles, and Detroit, respectively, include: Morawska, *The Maintenance of Ethnicity;* Sandberg, *Ethnic Identity and Assimilation;* and Wrobel, *Our Way.*

5. Two book-length studies of folklore in rural Poland, both in the English language, deserve mention. They are Sula Benet's *Song, Dance, and Customs of Peasant Poland* (1951), an account of her fieldwork in Poland during the 1930s;

and Sophie Hodorowicz Knab, *Polish Customs, Traditions, and Folklore,* which is based on her library research (but no fieldwork) about customs in various regions of Poland in the early nineteenth century.

6. See the following articles by Zand: "Polish American Childways," "Polish American Folkways: Cures, Burials, Superstitions," "Polish-American Weddings and Christenings," "Polish Family Folkways in the United States," "Polish Folkways in the United States," and the booklet *Polish Proverbs.* These essays are collected in Obidinski and Zand, *Polish Folkways in America.*

7. See Pawlowska, *Merrily We Sing,* a good collection of songs from Polish immigrants in Detroit around 1940 but lacking context; Keil, Keil, and Blau, *Polka Happiness;* Davis, "Utica's Polka Music Tradition"; Kleeman, "Origins and Stylistic Development of Polish-American Polka Music"; Leary and March, "Dutchman Bands," in *Creative Ethnicity,* ed. Stern and Cicala, 21–43; Savaglio, "Big-Band, Slovenian-American, Rock, and Country Music"; and Walser, "The Polka Mass." The Polish immigrants' folk songs are contained in *Songs of Migration and Immigration,* ed. Spottswood.

8. Ainsworth, "Polish-American Church Legends"; Ainsworth, *Polish-American Folktales;* Clements, *The Types of the Polack Joke;* Barrick, "Racial Riddles and the Polack Joke"; Leary, ed., *Midwestern Folk Humor;* Fish, "Is the Pope Polish?"

9. Goldstein and Green, "Pierogi- and Babka-Making at St. Mary's"; Davis, "Old-Fashioned Polish Weddings"; Kolinski, "Shrines and Crosses in Rural Central Wisconsin"; Koperski, "Children's Guardian Angel Beliefs"; Boynton, "Community Murals and Religious Paintings," in *Folklife Annual 90,* ed. Hardin, 30–41; Koperski, "Building Community," in *Folklife Annual 90,* ed. Hardin, 42–57.

10. Coleman, "Introduction."

11. For an anthology of essays in ethnic American folklore, see Stern and Cicala, eds., *Creative Ethnicity.*

12. Etzioni, "The Ghetto," 258.

13. Ibid.

14. Lopata, *Polish Americans,* 179.

15. Ibid., 5.

Chapter 1: Life in the Old Country and the Mass Migration to America

1. Kruszka, a Polish immigrant and Catholic priest who played a leading role in the early religious life of Polish-American communities, first published his monumental history of the Poles in America, *Historya Polska w Ameryce* (Polish history in America), in serialized form in several Polish-language newspapers in the United States between 1901 and 1904. It was revised for publication as thirteen volumes published between 1905 and 1908; the quotation cited as an epigraph appears in the English-language translation. *History,* part 1, ed. Pula, 20.

2. The following account is based upon that of Kobielski, *Millenium*, 25.

3. The concept of "double faith" is discussed in Gimbutas, "Slavic Religion," 354.

4. Szczepanski thus divides Poland's history into four periods in *Polish Society*, 6–13.

5. The liberum veto was removed by the Constitution of May 3, 1791, but it was too late to stop the advances of land-hungry Russia, Prussia, and Austria, which already had claimed portions of Poland as their own.

6. This tripartite classification is taken from Barnett, *Poland*, 361–66.

7. The word *Pole* (field) itself reflects a concern with agriculture.

8. These statistics are contained in Wandycz, *Lands of Partitioned Poland*, 6.

9. Barnett, *Poland*, 13.

10. A detailed description of the homes is provided in Fox, *Poles in America*, 48.

11. Benet, *Song*, 20.

12. Greene, *For God and Country*, 16.

13. Benet, *Song*, 21. In *For God and Country*, Victor Greene also stresses the father's role as temporary manager: "The soil was ancestral land, not private property, and the father's task was to assure that the land would sustain the family members" (17).

14. Benet, *Song*, 21–22.

15. Lopata, *Polish Americans*, 3.

16. Malpezzi and Clements, *Italian-American Folklore*, 29. See Malpezzi and Clements, 29, and Bianco, *The Two Rosetos*, xiv, for discussions of this village spirit (*campanilismo*), which was pervasive among immigrants from Italy. Only after they arrived in America did they begin to develop a sense of national rather than regional identity; thus, many referred to themselves as being Sicilian or Neapolitan rather than Italian.

17. Wytrwal, *America's Polish Heritage*, 151.

18. For discussions of the influence of agriculture and the Catholic faith upon Polish culture, see Jędrzejewicz, "Polish Peasant Rituals and Seasonal Customs," 1–24; Benet, *Song*, 25; and Greene, *For God and Country*, 15.

19. These figures are given in Wandycz, *Lands of Partitioned Poland*, 11.

20. For a comprehensive description of Polish messianism, see Bukowczyk, *And My Children Did Not Know Me*, 5.

21. For details on "organic labor," see Barnett, *Poland*, 17.

22. Helena Znaniecki Lopata distinguishes between the folk culture of the peasants and the national culture espoused by the patriots, and later most Poles, after industrialization in Poland following World War I. In this study, I will focus primarily on the folk culture brought to America by the peasants, although a number of interviewees were conversant with the national culture. For additional information on folk and national cultures, see Lopata, *Polish Americans*, 6.

23. This poem is contained in Kruszka, *History*, 25.

24. Kuniczak, *My Name Is Million*, 2–5.

25. Kruszka, *History*, 26.

26. Kuniczak, *My Name Is Million*, 44.

27. See Wytrwal, *America's Polish Heritage*, 53, for a discussion of the contributions of these earlier Polish immigrants. Polish-American historian Miecislaus Haiman divided Polish immigration to America into three periods: colonial (1608–1776), political (1776–1865), and economic (1865–present). See Haiman, *Polish Past in America*, 1. His scheme, as reprinted in Zand, "Polish Folkways in the United States," 65, is used here with two modifications. First, 1870 (the end of the Franco-Prussian War) rather than 1865 is used as a cutoff date. Second, the economic immigration is further subdivided, following Lopata's scheme (*Polish Americans* 9, 43), to reflect the period of mass migration from 1880 to the 1920s, followed by the "displaced persons" who came after World War II and then the latest wave of "new Poles" since 1965, many of them political refugees from the Solidarity movement or *wakacjusze* ("vacationers"), temporary visitors earning money through illegal jobs for a better life back home. A total of 1,587,412 Poles emigrated to the United States between 1948 and 1990 (ibid., 43), but many of these, because of class and educational differences, prefer to live outside Polonia.

28. Fox, *Poles in America*, 59.

29. See Bukowczyk, *And My Children Did Not Know Me*, 7, for a discussion of this transformation in agriculture.

30. Wandycz, *Lands of Partitioned Poland*, 276.

31. Ibid., 195.

32. Bukowczyk, *And My Children Did Not Know Me*, 10.

33. Wandycz, *Lands of Partitioned Poland*, 276.

34. Further information about these settlements can be found in Kruszka, *History*, 33, and Wytrwal, *America's Polish Heritage*, 62. Also see Wytrwal, *America's Polish Heritage*, 65, for a discussion of the role of Polish immigrants in the American Civil War.

35. The function of "bowing letters" is explained in Thomas and Znaniecki, *The Polish Peasant in Europe and America*, 303–4.

36. This formulaic opening and response also were used to greet visitors to Polish-American homes for many years, according to folklore interviewees in Buffalo. The authors of these bowing letters were thus, in effect, attempting to replicate face-to-face communication.

37. Thomas and Znaniecki, *Polish Peasant in Europe and America*, 312.

38. In many other cases the immigrants themselves scraped together enough money for the journey. Poland's most impoverished peasants, of course, never could afford to emigrate.

39. Thomas and Znaniecki, *Polish Peasant in Europe and America*, 719.

40. Wytrwal, *America's Polish Heritage*, 111.

41. See, for example, Kruszka, *History*, 40; Lopata, *Polish Americans*, 36; Wytrwal, *America's Polish Heritage*, 101; and Pula, *Polish Americans*, 19.

42. Bukowczyk (*And My Children Did Not Know Me*, x) places the figure at 2.5 million, whereas Wytrwal (*America's Polish Heritage*, 79) offers a total of three million. Wandycz (*Lands of Partitioned Poland*, 276) estimates that 3.6 million Poles came from Prussia, Russia, and Galicia during the period. The figures given are from Greene, *For God and Country*, 45; see also Lopata, *Polish Americans*, 53.

Chapter 2: "The Old Neighborhood Isn't the Same Any More"

1. Zand, "Polish Folkways in the United States," 68.

2. Ibid., 69.

3. Bukowczyk, *And My Children Did Not Know Me*, 40.

4. For a discussion of these voluntary associations, see Bukowczyk, *And My Children Did Not Know Me*, 38–39.

5. Wytrwal, *America's Polish Heritage*, 157.

6. Taped interview with Alton Nowak, Dunkirk, N.Y., 14 Dec. 1978.

7. Greene, *For God and Country*, 31.

8. Taped interview with Mary Miller, Cassadaga, N.Y., 19 Aug. 1991. Mary Miller came to America with her parents and brother from Austrian Poland; both parents were fluent in German as well as Polish.

9. Wytrwal, *America's Polish Heritage*, 85–86.

10. For further information on the occupational history of the Polish immigrants, consult Wytrwal, *America's Polish Heritage*, 87; Fox, *Poles in America*, 69; or Zand, "Polish Family Folkways in the United States," 79. According to Zand, boardinghouses were stigmatized socially. To live in a boardinghouse was considered an undesirable way of life among poorer immigrants because "so many evils flowed out of it—quarrels between husband and wife, infidelity, desertions, neglect and bad example to children" (79). Widows and deserted wives who ran boardinghouses were especially ostracized. The institution ended during World War I, when the number of immigrants from Poland dropped dramatically.

11. Abrahams, "The Language of Festivals," 162–63.

12. Taped interview with Peter Tofil, Dunkirk, N.Y., 21 Feb. 1995.

13. Ibid.

14. For an extended discussion of the PNA nationalist/PRCU religionist split, see Greene, *For God and Country*, 67–170. Greene contends that this intra-group religious conflict was primarily responsible for the development of ethnic awareness among Polish-Americans. A shorter treatment also is given in Wytrwal, *America's Polish Heritage*, 181–84.

15. Greene, *For God and Country*, 11.

16. Bukowczyk, *And My Children Did Not Know Me*, 45–46.

17. Taped interview with Al Clark, Dunkirk, N.Y., 7 Nov. 1978, a former Scranton resident and Polish National Catholic who converted to Roman Catholicism.

18. Bukowczyk, *And My Children Did Not Know Me*, 70.

19. Carpenter and Katz, "A Study of Acculturization," 130.

20. Bukowczyk, *And My Children Did Not Know Me*, 71.

21. Zand, "Polish Folkways in the United States," 70–71.

22. Interview with Al Clark, 7 Nov. 1978.

23. Bukowczyk, *And My Children Did Not Know Me*, 73.

24. Kruszka, *History*, 314. In *The Joys of Yiddish* (xx), Leo Rosten notes that the Yiddish press also sought to make life in the bewildering New World easier by creating a dialect: "And so proud new patriots swiftly enlarged their vocabularies with such useful, everyday words as *vindaw* (window), *stritt cah* (street car), *sobvay* (subway), *tex* (tax), and *sax* (sex)."

25. As Kruszka argued (*History*, 317), "A living, natural, real language, which is spoken every day, needs this change. . . . In order to live, [it] must seek nourishment from the environment in which it lives, must constantly take in and absorb new elements, and eject and expel the old, worn out and used ones." This can be compared to the work of Stephen Stern and John Allan Cicala, *Creative Ethnicity: Symbols and Strategies of Contemporary Ethnic Life*, an argument for ethnicity as a dynamic, evolving force in American life; Michael M. J. Fischer, who also describes ethnicity as dynamic and reinterpreted by each generation ("Ethnicity," 195); and Anya Peterson Royce, who discusses the development of symbols by an ethnic group as either a blending of old and new elements or completely new symbols (*Ethnic Identity*, 150).

26. Klinkenborg, *The Last Fine Time*, 22.

27. See, for example, Royce, *Ethnic Identity*, 210; Stern and Cicala, eds., *Creative Ethnicity*, xiv; and Isajiw, "Definitions of Ethnicity," 121.

28. Taped interview with Lawrence Kozlowski, forty-two, Pittsburgh, at the Cheektowaga, N.Y., Polish-American Festival, 19 Aug. 1995. Kozlowski, the author of several Polish folk arts books in the English language, is a craftsperson who exhibits work at regional festivals and has studied traditional folk arts in Poland.

29. See Bukowczyk, *And My Children Did Not Know Me*, 118, and Lopata, *Polish Americans*, xviii, for further discussions of the "ethnic revival" in Polonia.

30. Gordon, *Assimilation in American Life*, 160.

31. Keil, "Class and Ethnicity in Polish-America," 37.

32. Bukowczyk, *And My Children Did Not Know Me*, 74; Lopata, *Polish Americans*, xix. Lopata contends that many scholars view Polonia with bias because they do not see evidence of a national culture, only the folk culture.

33. Bell, "Ethnicity and Social Change," 169.

34. Royce, *Ethnic Identity*, 232; Fischer, "Ethnicity," 195–96.

35. Lopata (*Polish Americans*, 153) notes that in 1900, 100 percent of Amer-

ica's Poles married other Poles. By 1940 that figure had dropped to just over 50 percent, and those Poles who married outside the group chose either Irish or Italian mates.

36. Taped interview with Jean Brogcinski, Hamburg, N.Y., at the Cheektowaga, N.Y., Polish-American Festival, 20 Aug. 1995.

37. Taped interview with Jack Pencek, Dunkirk, N.Y., at the St. Hyacinth's Church Festival, 25 Aug. 1991.

Chapter 3: Polish-American Easter Celebrations

1. Abrahams, "The Language of Festivals," 167.

2. Hobsbawm, "Introduction," in *Invention of Tradition,* ed. Hobsbawm and Ranger, 1.

3. Taped interview with the Rev. Robert Hora, parochial vicar, at St. Elizabeth Ann Seton Roman Catholic Church, Dunkirk, N.Y., 17 June 1991. Hora grew up in the Polish-American community of Cheektowaga, a suburb of Buffalo.

4. Benet, *Song,* 53; Knab, *Polish Customs,* 82.

5. Knab, *Polish Customs,* 84.

6. Interview with Robert Hora.

7. Taped interview with Tom Gestwicki, Dunkirk, N.Y., 1 June 1991.

8. These explanations for the ritual significance of the foods are given in "The Meaning of a Blessed Basket" and in "A Polish Easter Basket," a pamphlet distributed at "A Celebration of the Easter Egg in Eastern European Tradition," Cheektowaga, N.Y., 29 March 1992. The event's coordinators were Kate Koperski and Judith Krauza.

9. In the two Polish Catholic parishes of Syracuse, some of the blessed food is eaten on Holy Saturday afternoon. Taped interview with Helen Sawka, Depew, N.Y., at a Dyngus Day party, 12 April 1993. Another woman, a Polish immigrant, told me that parishioners at her former church in Poland used to leave all the blessed food except the bread and baked lamb in church to be distributed to the poor. Taped interview with Gabrielle Merta, Derby, N.Y., 20 July 1991. Gabrielle Merta grew up in a large family in Zywice, a town in southern Poland, and was baptized by Pope John Paul II when he served as archbishop of Kraków.

10. Benet, *Song,* 60; Jędrzejewicz, "Polish Peasant Rituals," 9.

11. Interview with Robert Hora.

12. Interview with Gabrielle Merta.

13. These hymns were found in two collections from the northeastern United States: *An Album of Polish Easter Hymns,* and Pieśni Wielkanocne: *Easter Hymns* (a hymnal).

14. I interviewed a number of adults who ate two or even three święconka meals on Easter Sunday. The first would be at their own homes, followed later

in the day by visits to their parents and/or spouse's parents. "We don't hear anybody complain, because it's good food," said Joe Rozen (taped interview, Dunkirk, N.Y., 20 July 1991).

15. This prayer was given by Helen Uszacki at the Easter Sunday święconka held at the home of her son and daughter-in-law, Alex and Jackleen Uszacki, Dunkirk, N.Y., 16 April 1995. Helen Uszacki provided the translation.

16. Taped interview with Kate Moch, Dunkirk, N.Y., 19 Feb. 1979.

17. Newall, "Easter Eggs," 12–13.

18. Ibid., 14.

19. Ibid., 26.

20. *The Kosciuszko Foundation Dictionary*, 101.

21. The definition of Dyngus as "switch" was provided by Chet Tarnowski, taped interview, Dunkirk, N.Y., 20 April 1992; and as "reed used in whipping" by Ann Mikoll, taped interview, Depew, N.Y., 13 July 1992.

22. Taped interview with Ed Bognaski at the Knights of St. John's Club Dyngus Day party, Cheektowaga, N.Y., 12 April 1993. Also see Benet, *Song*, 56–60, and Knab, *Polish Customs*, 106–13.

23. Pirkova-Jakobson, "Harvest Festivals," 275; Jędrzejewicz, "Polish Peasant Rituals," 16.

24. For a description of Lupercalia, see *Holidays and Anniversaries of the World*, ed. Urdang and Donohue, 68, and Schilling, "Lupercalia," 53.

25. Lukács, "Easter Whipping," 116.

26. Knab, *Polish Customs*, 110.

27. Pirkova-Jakobson, "Harvest Festivals," 275.

28. Taped interview with Chet Tarnowski, Dunkirk, N.Y., 22 Dec. 1992.

29. Interview with Ann Mikoll.

30. Benet, *Song*, 58.

31. Brooks, "The Bear in Slavic and Polish Mythology and Folklore," 108–9.

32. Lukács, "Easter Whipping," 117. In some regions of Poland, the splashing still occurs but not whipping, which takes place on Palm Sunday. Interview with Gabrielle Merta.

33. Taped interview with Lynda Waszczuk, twenty-eight, and Dianne Ziosk, thirty-six, of Oshawa, Ontario, at the Knights of St. John's Club Dyngus Day party, Cheektowaga, N.Y., 12 April 1993. They reported that they and their friends splash one another on Dyngus Day morning, as do many Poles and some Polish-Americans in Detroit. However, the custom died out during the 1960s in Buffalo and Syracuse, New York, and in Erie, Pennsylvania.

34. Dorson, "The State of Folkloristics," 89–92.

35. Interview with Chet Tarnowski, 20 April 1992.

36. Hobsbawm, *Invention of Tradition*, 6.

37. Taped interview with Bob Asztemborski at the Polish Falcons Club Dyngus Day party, Depew, N.Y., 12 April 1993.

38. Taped interview with Fred Gordon at the Chopin's Singing Society Dyngus Day party, Buffalo, N.Y., 12 April 1993.

39. Cadaval, "Making a Place Home," 215.

40. Speeches by then Erie County executive Dennis Gorski and then-Buffalo mayor James Griffin at the Chopin's Singing Society Dyngus Day party, Buffalo, N.Y., 12 April 1993. Both stressed the need to instill in youngsters a love of their ancestors' heritages via such occasions as Dyngus Day. Buffalo mayor Anthony Masiello, an Italian-American, appeared at the 1994 Chopin's party, but in 1995, when the society moved to the suburb of Cheektowaga, the mayor was replaced by Dennis Gabryszak, the town supervisor. The county executive continues to make an appearance at the new location.

41. Taped interview with retired Buffalo city court judge Alois Mazur, Buffalo, N.Y., 14 Sept. 1991.

42. Keil, Keil, and Blau, *Polka Happiness*, 19. Information about the polka as a Polish-American, rather than Polish, dance was provided by two interviewees: taped telephone interview with Steve Litwin, Binghamton, N.Y. (formerly of the Buffalo suburb of North Tonawanda), 30 Jan. 1993; and interview with Gabrielle Merta.

43. Taped interview with Tom Warzecha at the Rescue Fire Hall Dyngus Day party, Cheektowaga, N.Y., 12 April 1993. Warzecha was the promoter of the Syracuse Dyngus Day weekend first held in 1993. The success of the initial event, which drew more than 650, encouraged Warzecha to continue it annually.

44. Taped interview with Edward Sabloski, president of the United Polka League of the Mohawk Valley, at the Knights of St. John's Club Dyngus Day party, Cheektowaga, N.Y., 12 April 1993.

45. Taped interview with polka musician Chris Gawlak at the Polish Falcons Club Dyngus Day party, Depew, N.Y., 12 April 1993.

46. Interview with Chris Gawlak; taped interview with polka band leader Ted Szymanski at the Eden, N.Y., Polka Festival, 21 July 1991.

47. See Kalčik, "Ethnic Foodways in America," 38.

48. Taped interview with Ron Polak, leader of the Polka Pals booster group, at the Eden, N.Y., Polka Festival, 21 July 1991.

49. Taped interview with Mark Kohan, thirty-two, leader of the Steel City Brass and editor of the *Polish-American Journal*, Buffalo, N.Y., 29 Dec. 1992.

50. The Syracuse event, held on the weekend after Dyngus Day so as not to conflict with Buffalo's parties, features polka and country-western bands, T-shirts, buttons, flowers and pussywillows for sale, and folk dance ensembles, according to Tom Warzecha (taped telephone interview 25 April 1993). See also Curran, "Buffalo Has Dyngus Day Spirit," B-2.

51. Tom Bauerle, "Breakfast with Bauerle" talk show, WGR–AM Radio, Buffalo, N.Y., 12 April 1993. During the one-hour call-in program, most listeners

chose Chopin's as their favorite Dyngus Day party. Curran, "It's Tough to Pick Favorite Spot," B-2.

52. Taped interview with Ron Polak at the Knights of St. John's Club Dyngus Day party, Cheektowaga, N.Y., 12 April 1993.

53. Items from the menu at the Kosciuszko Club święconka, Dunkirk, N.Y., 10 April 1993. A club director, Ray Budniewski, noted that for the święconka and other special club functions men rather than women traditionally do the cooking, apparently a reflection of the club's original male membership.

54. Taped interview with Geraldine Ziegler, vice president of the Kosciuszko Club, Dunkirk, N.Y., at the club's annual Holy Saturday święconka, 10 April 1993.

55. Myerhoff, *Number Our Days*, 10.

Chapter 4: The Christmas Cycle and Minor Holidays

1. Taped interview with Dorothy and Alois Mazur, Buffalo, N.Y., 14 Sept. 1991.

2. Interview with Robert Hora.

3. Benet, *Song*, 99; Jędrzejewicz, "Polish Peasant Rituals," 5.

4. Taped interview with Emily Boruszewski, Buffalo, N.Y., 1 March 1993; also see Benet, *Song*, 98–99.

5. Unconsecrated bread wafers like those used in communion, the opłatki may be a modification of an earlier ritual bread known as *podpłomyk*, a thin, flat bread given to neighbors as a goodwill gesture. Knab, *Polish Customs*, 36–37.

6. Interview with Gabrielle Merta.

7. Taped interview with Stephanie Rozen, Dunkirk, N.Y., at her family's wigilia in her home, 24 Dec. 1994. A widow, Stephanie Rozen invites all four of her children and their spouses as well as her grandchildren and great-grandchildren to the celebration.

8. Interview with Stephanie Rozen.

9. Jędrzejewicz, "Polish Peasant Rituals," 4–5.

10. Benet, *Song*, 97.

11. Interview with Robert Hora; Rozen family wigilia, Dunkirk, N.Y., 24 Dec. 1994; Contoski, ed., *Treasured Polish Christmas Customs and Traditions*, 45–46.

12. Benet, *Song*, 104; Jędrzejewicz, "Polish Peasant Rituals and Seasonal Customs," 6.

13. Interview with Stephanie Rozen.

14. Benet, *Song*, 94.

15. Interview with Stephanie Rozen.

16. Interview with Kate Moch; also see Benet, *Song*, 101–4, for a description of these customs.

17. Interview with Gabrielle Merta.

18. Interview with Emily Boruszewski.

19. Interview with Robert Hora.

20. Interviews with Alois Mazur and Joe Rozen. Some families also place a piece of opłatek at a place set for a deceased relative (interview with Emily Boruszewski).

21. Interview with Dorothy Mazur.

22. Telephone conversation with Ray Budniewski, 7 April 1996.

23. For further information about this Polish caroling tradition, see Bazielichówna and Deptuszewski, "Guisers of Koniaków," 497; Bazielichówna, "Further Notes on the Polish Guisers," 254–61; and Bartminski, "Polish Christmas Carols," 88.

24. Interview with Steve Litwin, 30 Jan. 1993.

25. Bartminski, "Polish Christmas Carols," 84.

26. Ibid., 89.

27. Ibid., 93–94.

28. It is important to distinguish, as Dell Hymes does, between perfunctory and authoritative performances of folklore, that is, performances by informants merely knowledgeable about a folkloric item and those who actually perform it. The distinction is especially true in the genres of folk music and narratives. But, as Hymes observes, that does not mean there is an original performance any more than there is an original text. Of the more than 150 Polish-Americans I interviewed, only a small handful could be considered authoritative performers of stories and folk songs. They were designated as such both by themselves and by others in the folk community. Hymes, "Breakthrough into Performance," 81–84.

29. Dorson, "Is There a Folk in the City?" 46.

30. Because kolędy are so widely available in song collections and on recordings, their musical scores will not be presented here. Examples are included in two collections edited by Josepha K. Contoski: *Treasured Polish Songs with English Translations* and *Treasured Polish Christmas Customs and Traditions*. Many LP albums and compact discs are available, including the CD Kolędy: *Christmas Carols*, PNCD 010 (Poland: Polskie Nagrania, 1991), which features performances by Poland's famed Mazowsze and Śląsk folk musical ensembles.

31. Interview with Steve Litwin, 30 Jan. 1993. A detailed account of one such tavern kolędy night, at Jumbo's in North Tonawanda, N.Y., was provided by Norman Skiba ("Kolendy at Jumbo's") in 1984. Members of the Kosciuszko Club of Dunkirk, N.Y., tried caroling from club to club, but the idea was abandoned after a few years because of a lack of interest, according to Ray Budniewski (taped interview, 6 Feb. 1993). At one time, Kosciuszko Club members went caroling at the Moniuszko Club, Dom Polski, Dunkirk Falcon Club, and the First Ward Falcons, all in Dunkirk. The singers, performing a cappella, would have a free drink and snack at each club for donating their time.

32. Taped interview with Mark Kohan at the Knights of St. John's Club Kolę-

dy Night, Cheektowaga, N.Y., 19 Dec. 1992. Kohan runs the Kolędy Night with the Polka Pals.

33. Interview with Edward Sabloski. The Mohawk Valley party songfest is led by a local choir director, with kolędy in Polish and American carols in English. A priest offers an invocation, and Santa Claus makes an appearance. The opłatek is blessed and distributed at a separate gathering earlier in December.

34. Interview with Kate Moch.

35. Interview with Gabrielle Merta.

36. Interview with Mary Miller.

37. Lawrence Kozlowski was selling the kits at the Cheektowaga, N.Y., Polish-American Festival, 19 Aug. 1995.

38. Knab, *Polish Customs*, 65.

39. Ibid., 67.

40. Ibid., 68.

41. Ibid., 71–74.

42. Ibid., 75.

43. Benet, *Song*, 46.

44. Ibid., 47; interview with Robert Hora.

45. Interview with Kate Moch.

46. The following account is based on Knab, *Polish Customs*, 129–32, and descriptions from taped interviews with several interviewees in Dunkirk, N.Y.: Lucy and Monica Sekula, 17 Jan. 1979, and Celia Purol, 13 Feb. 1979.

47. This description is based on Sokolnicki, "St. John's Eve," 1.

48. Benet, *Song*, 73; Knab, *Polish Customs*, 157–59.

49. Three feast days were celebrated during Advent in Poland and associated, respectively, with St. Barbara (Dec. 4), St. Nicholas (Dec. 6), and St. Thomas (Dec. 21), but these were not observed to any extent in Polish-American communities. For details on the Polish observances, see Knab, *Polish Customs*, 23–29; for further information on the Polish St. Nicholas Day, also see Benet, *Song*, 90–93.

50. Interview with Kate Moch.

51. Benet, *Song*, 89.

52. Interview with Lawrence Kozlowski.

Chapter 5: Rites of Passage

The epigraph could be interpreted as "good life, good death; mean life, mean death."

1. Rosten, *The Joys of Yiddish*, 91.

2. West, *Mexican-American Folklore*, 151.

3. Bianco, *The Two Rosetos*, 118; Malpezzi and Clements, *Italian-American Folklore*, 75.

4. Bianco, *The Two Rosetos,* 119.

5. Abrahams, "The Language of Festivals," 27.

6. Myerhoff, "Rites of Passage," 113.

7. Zand, *Polish Proverbs,* 10; Benet, *Song,* 191.

8. Interview with Gabrielle Merta.

9. Benet, *Song,* 191.

10. Knab, *Polish Customs,* 161.

11. Taped interview with Martha Steffan, Dunkirk, N.Y., 17 Aug. 1991.

12. These beliefs were obtained from the following sources, respectively: interview with Gabrielle Merta; interview with Ann Clark, Dunkirk, N.Y., 10 June 1978; interview with Rose Gibson, Dunkirk, N.Y., 15 Jan. 1979; interview with Martha Steffan; interview with Melania Rucinski, Dunkirk, N.Y., 15 Jan. 1979; interview with Adriana Anders, Dunkirk, N.Y., 17 July 1991; interview with Ann Clark; and Zand, "Polish-American Weddings and Christenings," 31.

13. These beliefs were obtained during interviews with the following individuals: Gabrielle Merta, Dorothy Mazur, and Monica Sekula, Dunkirk, N.Y., 17 Jan. 1979; Joe Rozen, 20 July 1991.

14. For further discussion of the baba, see Zand, "Polish-American Weddings and Christenings," 31; and Benet, *Song,* 195.

15. Interview with Martha Steffan.

16. Taped interview with Ted Miehl, Dunkirk, N.Y., 1 June 1991; Zand, "Polish American Childways," 74.

17. Benet, *Song,* 203.

18. Zand, "Polish-American Weddings and Christenings," 33.

19. Benet, *Song,* 204.

20. Taped interview with Felix and Delphine Jacobs, Dunkirk, N.Y., 30 Jan. 1979.

21. Interview with Gabrielle Merta.

22. Zand, *Polish Proverbs,* 16.

23. Benet, *Song,* 228.

24. Interview with Mary Miller.

25. Benet, *Song,* 234.

26. Knab, *Polish Customs,* 257; Benet, *Song,* 235.

27. These beliefs were mentioned by the following individuals: Mary Miller, Valerie Pawlak, Martha Steffan, Dorothy Mazur, Joe Rozen, Gabrielle Merta, and Adriana Anders.

28. Interview with Martha Steffan.

29. Interview with Gabrielle Merta.

30. Interview with Adriana Anders; interview with Gabrielle Merta.

31. Interview with Tom Gestwicki.

32. Knab, *Polish Customs,* 260.

33. Benet, *Song,* 236.

34. Zand, "Polish American Folkways: Cures, Burials, Superstitions," 101.

35. Interview with Tom Gestwicki; Knab, *Polish Customs*, 265; Zand, "Polish American Folkways: Cures, Burials, Superstitions," 101.

36. Knab, *Polish Customs*, 265; interview with Dorothy Mazur.

37. Interview with Alois Mazur.

38. Interview with Alton Nowak.

39. "Pusta noc" may refer to the fact that the house is empty (*pusta*) without the deceased individual (Knab, *Polish Customs*, 269) or because much of the home's furniture is removed and the night is spent in frivolity (Benet, *Song*, 240).

40. Interview with Alton Nowak.

41. Zand, "Polish American Folkways: Cures, Burials, Superstitions," 102.

42. Interview with Joe Rozen, 20 July 1991.

43. Zand, "Polish American Folkways: Cures, Burials, Superstitions," 102; Benet, *Song*, 243–44.

44. Benet, *Song*, 244.

45. Taped interview with Thela Nowak, Dunkirk, N.Y., 14 Dec. 1978.

46. Knab, *Polish Customs*, 273.

47. Zand, "Polish American Folkways: Cures, Burials, Superstitions," 102; Benet, *Song*, 245.

48. Benet, *Song*, 245.

49. Taped interview with Sophie Urbanik, Dunkirk, N.Y., 8 June 1991.

50. Benet, *Song*, 246.

51. Zand, "Polish American Folkways: Cures, Burials, Superstitions," 102.

52. Benet, *Song*, 246.

53. Knab, *Polish Customs*, 276.

54. Benet, *Song*, 246.

55. Ibid., 246–47.

Chapter 6: Faith, Love, and Community

1. Zand, *Polish Proverbs*, 13.

2. This sequence is described in Benet, *Song*, 151.

3. Ibid., 152.

4. An account of peasant Poland's courtship and wedding traditions in the late nineteenth and early twentieth centuries is contained in Benet, *Song*, 150–78. The discussion that follows will focus on those traditions that were continued or modified in Polish-American communities.

5. Zand, "Polish-American Weddings and Christenings," 24; Davis, "Old-Fashioned Polish Weddings," 90.

6. Zand, "Polish-American Weddings and Christenings," 25.

7. Interview with Melania Rucinski.

8. These dowry items were described by Rose Gibson, Melania Rucinski, and Kate Moch; also see Benet, *Song,* 156.

9. Zand, "Polish-American Weddings and Christenings," 30.

10. The first two items were from the interview with Alois and Dorothy Mazur; the final item was from the interview with Joe Rozen, 20 July 1991.

11. Interview with Celia Purol; similar descriptions of the prenuptial blessing were obtained from the interviews with Gabrielle Merta and Alois and Dorothy Mazur.

12. Interview with Alois and Dorothy Mazur.

13. Interview with Dianne Ziosk and Lynda Waszczuk, whose parents emigrated to Canada from Poland.

14. Interview with Martha Steffan.

15. Pacyga, *Polish Immigrants and Industrial Chicago,* 140.

16. Interview with Al Clark, 7 Nov. 1978; interview with Celia Purol.

17. Interview with Kate Moch.

18. Interview with Gabrielle Merta.

19. Interview with Alton Nowak, who played tuba in the White Eagle Band in addition to the piano in the Woodcliffe Orchestra, a group also including sax, clarinet, and violin that performed for weddings and other social functions both within and outside the local Polish-American community for more than fifty years.

20. Interview with Gabrielle Merta.

21. Interview with Alton Nowak.

22. Interview with Melania Rucinski and Rose Gibson.

23. Pacyga, *Polish Immigrants and Industrial Chicago,* 138.

24. Interview with Helen Sawka.

25. Telephone interview with Mark Kohan, 20 Nov. 1995. Kohan noted that a variant in Binghamton follows the dollar dance at some contemporary Polish-American weddings. Single men form a circle around the bride, and the groom must crash through in order to "take her away from them." The practice may derive from the ancient custom of locking the gate and barring entry to the groom. Knab, *Polish Customs,* 194.

26. Interview with Martha Steffan.

27. Interview with Gabrielle Merta.

28. The words *czerpiny* and *oczepiny* were used interchangeably by interviewees to describe this ceremony. Benet (*Song,* 151) and Knab (*Polish Customs,* 210) refer to it as "oczepiny." "Czerpiny" may be the Galician spelling and pronunciation of "oczepiny." Interview with Mark Kohan, 20 Nov. 1995.

29. Knab, *Polish Customs,* 210.

30. For descriptions of the unbraiding ceremony, see Benet, *Song,* 170–71, and Knab, *Polish Customs,* 210–11.

31. Turner, *Ritual Process,* 95.

32. Benet, *Song*, 171.

33. This song is cited in Knab, *Polish Customs*, 211.

34. Benet, *Song*, 172. The original Polish lyrics are not given in Benet.

35. Ibid., 175.

36. Interview with Celia Purol.

37. Information about these four songs was provided, respectively, from interviews with the following individuals: Rose Gibson, Melania Rucinski, and Helen Sawka; taped interview with Gertrude Kupiec, Dunkirk, N.Y., 28 Oct. 1978; interview with Robert Hora.

38. Interview with Melania Rucinski.

39. Taped interview with Buffalo native Florence Ruszaj, Forestville, N.Y., at the Eden, N.Y., Polka Festival, 21 July 1991.

40. Taped interview with James Griffin at the Chopin's Singing Society Dyngus Day party, Buffalo, N.Y., 12 April 1993.

41. Taped interviews with Valerie Pawlak, Dunkirk, N.Y., 13 July 1991, and Daniel Kij, Lackawanna, N.Y., 29 May 1995; conversation with Edward Silverman, formerly a member of the Lone Star Band, 20 Nov. 1995.

42. Taped interview with Belle Graminski, Dunkirk, N.Y., at the Kosciuszko Club Fourth of July weekend dance, Dunkirk, 7 July 1991.

43. Interview with Daniel Kij, who showed me both the songsheet and the videotape.

44. Information about these two American songs was provided by Mark Kohan, 20 Nov. 1995. His band performs at a number of Polish-American weddings both because the musicians can play for the oczepiny ceremony and because they perform rock-and-roll numbers.

45. Interview with Alton Nowak.

46. Taped interview with Rita Danner, Cheektowaga, N.Y., at the Cheektowaga Polish-American Festival, 20 Aug. 1995.

47. Interview with Gabrielle Merta.

Chapter 7: Spinning Tales, Weaving the Fabric of Identity

1. Benet, *Song*, 227.

2. Cezaria Baudouin de Courtenay Jędrzejewicz also contends that dances such as the extremely fast *oberek* and the *lenek* ("high flax" dance) were born of these spinning evenings, which took place from mid-November to February with the exception of the period from Christmas Eve to St. Stephen's Day (Dec. 26). Jędrzejewicz, "Polish Peasant Rituals and Seasonal Customs," 11.

3. For examples of these narratives translated into the English language, see *Polish Folk Legends*, ed. Florence Waszkelewicz-Clowes.

4. This account was collected by Helen Orze from Helen Smakosz Wagner,

"a lively and very devout little lady of about seventy-four" who came to the United States at age twenty-one and settled in Beaver Falls, Pennsylvania, Helen Orze's native town. Orze, "How St. Roch Came to *Lubotyń.*"

5. Interview with Dianne Ziosk, who heard the legend from her maternal grandparents, who had emigrated from Kraków.

6. For an in-depth discussion of this shift from complex to simpler narratives among today's ethnic American groups, see Stephen Stern, "Ethnic Folklore and the Folklore of Ethnicity," 20.

7. In earlier years, Polish-Americans still fluent in the Polish language also told proverbs dealing with everyday life: the weather, good and bad luck, the home, hospitality, love and marriage, children, friendship, and death were common topics. Now, however, such proverbs are rare because English is spoken by the majority of Polish-Americans. Zand, *Polish Proverbs.*

8. See, for example, West, *Mexican-American Folklore,* 65; Malpezzi and Clements, *Italian-American Folklore,* 165; and Hymes, "Breakthrough into Performance," 133.

9. Malpezzi and Clements, *Italian-American Folklore,* 166.

10. Dorson, "Is There a Folk in the City?" 45.

11. Zeitlin, Kotkin, and Baker, *A Celebration of American Family Folklore,* 2.

12. Ibid., 19.

13. Interview with Kate Moch.

14. Interview with Gabrielle Merta.

15. Interview with Martha Steffan.

16. Ibid.

17. Interview with Mary Miller.

18. Interview with Martha Steffan.

19. Interview with Peter Tofil.

20. Morawska, *Maintenance of Ethnicity,* 14.

21. Interview with Alois Mazur.

22. Interview with Kate Moch.

23. Interview with Adriana Anders.

24. Taped interview with Wolf Tombak, Buffalo, N.Y., 4 April 1993.

25. Interview with Kate Moch.

26. Written account of Raymond Roganski, nineteen, of Buffalo, N.Y., in 1964, in Ainsworth, *Polish-American Folktales,* 21. The legend was told at Roganski's home by his uncle, a Polish immigrant, in 1953.

27. Interview with Kate Moch.

28. Interview with Valerie Pawlak.

29. I am indebted to Charles Keil and James Leary for pointing to the existence of this in-group joke-telling tradition in taverns. See Leary, ed., *Midwestern Folk Humor,* 131–36. For other examples of the "dumb Polack" joke as a

genre, see Barrick, "Racial Riddles and the Polack Joke," 3–15; Clements, *The Types of the Polack Joke,* 56; Dundes, "Polish Pope Jokes," 219–22; Dundes, "A Study of Ethnic Slurs," 186–203; Fish, "Is the Pope Polish?" 450–54; Kerman, "The Light-Bulb Jokes," 454–58; Preston and Preston, "A Note on Visual Polack Jokes," 175–77; Preston, "Xerox-Lore," 11–26; and Welsch, "American Numskull Tales," 183–86.

30. Taped interview with Lucy Moch, Dunkirk, N.Y., 24 Jan. 1979.

31. Interview with Kate Moch.

32. See, for example, "Pelt Kid and His Grandmother" in *Finding the Center,* trans. Dennis Tedlock, 193–213.

33. Interview with Kate Moch.

34. Zeitlin, Kotkin, and Baker, *Celebration of American Family Folklore,* 15.

35. Interview with Kate Moch.

Chapter 8: "Guardian Angel, Stay by My Side"

1. A good discussion is provided in Ainsworth, "Polish-American Church Legends," 286–94.

2. Taped interview with the Rev. Cornelian Dende, O.F.M., Athol Springs, N.Y., 26 Jan. 1996. Dende was the director of "The Rosary Hour," a Polish-language weekly radio program, for thirty-six years until his retirement in 1995. The proverb also is found in Zand, *Polish Proverbs,* 17, and in a number of Polish-American homes that I visited.

3. Thomas and Znaniecki, *The Polish Peasant in Europe and America,* 276–77. The same idea is expressed in Pacyga, *Polish Immigrants and Industrial Chicago,* 112.

4. Falkowski, "Accommodation and Conflict," 139.

5. For details, see Pacyga, *Polish Immigrants and Industrial Chicago,* 114–15.

6. Bianco, *The Two Rosetos,* 85.

7. Interview with Cornelian Dende.

8. Like Polish-Americans, Italian-American Catholics have cultivated strong ties to the Virgin Mary and various saints. Such devotion could involve home altars anchored by holy pictures and flanked by candles and votive candles; yard shrines; special prayers and foods for a saint's feast day; medals and other amulets associated with a particular saint, pinned to clothing; vows fulfilled in return for the saint's response to a petition; and participation in summer feste honoring a certain saint. Malpezzi and Clements, *Italian-American Folklore,* 113–16.

9. Benet, *Song,* 28.

10. Kolinski, "Shrines," 36.

11. Benet, *Song,* 28–29; Kolinski, "Shrines," 34–36.

12. Kolinski, "Shrines," 36.

13. Statistics on western New York's Polish-American Catholic population were provided by Cornelian Dende. He noted that in 1959 there were approximately forty Polish ethnic parishes in the area; since then, a number have either closed or merged with other parishes.

14. Interview with Valerie Pawlak.

15. Jews, for example, used the phrase *kayn aynhoreh* (literally in Hebrew, "the evil eye," meaning "thank God") to ward off the evil eye, as in this response to a question about one's son or daughter: "My child? In perfect health, *kayn aynhoreh.*" Rosten, *The Joys of Yiddish,* 168–69.

16. Bianco, *The Two Rosetos,* 95.

17. Zand, "Polish American Folkways: Cures, Burials, Superstitions," 103–4.

18. Taped interview with Daniel Kij, Lackawanna, N.Y., 26 Jan. 1996.

19. Interview with Tom Gestwicki.

20. Corso, "The Evil Eye," 6. The writer, from Chicopee Falls, Mass., learned this cure from her parents, who came to America from Biecz in southwestern Poland.

21. Koperski, "Children's Guardian Angel Beliefs," 137. A belief in guardian angels is prevalent among Italian-American Catholics as well. Frances Malpezzi and William Clements note that informants believe guardian angels watch over each child, not only protecting their charges but also "hiding their heads under their wings" when the child misbehaves. *Italian-American Folklore,* 116.

22. Koperski, "Children's Guardian Angel Beliefs," 136–37.

23. Interview with Alois and Dorothy Mazur interview.

24. Interview with Mary Miller.

25. Interview with Kate Moch.

26. This prayer is contained in *Nowa Księga Przysłów,* ed. Krzyżanowski, 238. I am indebted to Daniel Kij for pointing out this work to me.

27. Interview with Martha Steffan.

28. Obtained from Józefa Zalewska Hodorowicz, Grand Island, N.Y., in a telephone conversation with Daniel Kij, 19 Jan. 1996.

29. Benet, *Song,* 74.

30. Interview with Martha Steffan.

31. Born in Poland in 1825, Angela Truszkowska was the eldest child of a wealthy lawyer. In 1855 she founded the Congregation of Felician Sisters, which later sent five nuns to the United States. She died in Poland in 1899 and was beatified by Pope John Paul II on April 18, 1993. When the Vatican certifies that a second miracle can be attributed to her, she will be elevated to sainthood.

32. Lillian Halasinski's usage of "doctored" means "went to a doctor."

33. Taped interview with Lillian Halasinski and her daughter, Geraldine Halasinski, Dunkirk, N.Y., 12 Jan. 1996.

34. Interview with Cornelian Dende.

Chapter 9: The Garden of Healing

1. Knab, *Polish Herbs,* 14–15.
2. Ibid., 15–16.
3. Ibid., 19. For a detailed discussion of individual Polish herbs and flowers, see Knab, *Polish Herbs,* 87–176, and Knab, *Polish Customs,* 159–77.
4. Knab, *Polish Herbs,* 19–20.
5. Wong, "Magic in the Mullein Stalk," 46.
6. Knab, *Polish Herbs,* 140.
7. This blessing used to be commonplace in Polish parishes in western New York state but is now observed only by a handful of parishes.
8. Knab, *Polish Customs,* 160.
9. Knab, *Polish Herbs,* 40–45. She notes that beginning in the Middle Ages, a number of Polish herbalists published books listing medicinal plants.
10. Ibid., 39–40.
11. Coleman, "Podhalan Plant Lore from Connecticut," 44–45.
12. Zand, "Polish American Folkways: Cures, Burials, Superstitions," 100.
13. This was one of several herbal medicines dating back to the 1920s that was shown to me by Daniel Kij during a taped interview, 29 May 1995.
14. Interview with Mary Miller, who is referring to the Seneca Nation, part of the Iroquois Confederacy, which has two large reservations in western New York state, the Allegheny Reservation at Salamanca and the Cattaraugus Reservation at Irving.
15. Taped interview with Rita Danner at the Cheektowaga, N.Y., Polish-American Festival, 20 Aug. 1995. She was sitting next to her mother, Rose Lehr, who noted that she preferred to add a dash of powdered garlic rather than raw garlic to her foods.
16. Interview with Mary Miller.
17. Taped interview with Al and Ann Clark, Dunkirk, N.Y., 10 June 1978. Because Ann Clark remembered many deaths in Dunkirk's Polish-American community during the flu epidemic, she questioned the effectiveness of the camphor bags as a remedy.
18. Interview with Celia Purol.
19. Interview with Kate Moch.
20. Interview with Rita Danner.
21. Interview with Martha Steffan.
22. I am grateful to Dennis Tedlock for pointing out that many different folk communities around the world have used human urine for medicinal purposes because of its sterility.
23. Interview with Martha Steffan.
24. Interview with Ann Clark.
25. Interview with Mary Miller.

26. Interview with Ann Clark.

27. Knab, *Polish Herbs,* 148.

28. Interview with Rita Danner.

29. Interview with Ann Clark.

30. This information was provided by, respectively, Mary Miller, Rita Danner, and Alois and Dorothy Mazur.

31. Knab, *Polish Herbs,* 115.

32. Interview with Stephanie Rozen; interview with Martha Steffan.

33. Taped interview with Sophie Hodorowicz Knab (formerly of Dunkirk), Grand Island, N.Y., at the Cheektowaga, N.Y., Polish-American Festival, 19 Aug. 1995.

Chapter 10: Polish Folk Songs

The epigraph is from the Polka Family Band, "We Are Family," composer Hank Guzevich, Polka Family Music, PF1004CD, 1991.

1. As Janice Kleeman has noted, Polish Christmas carols, wedding, and liturgical pieces have survived because they serve as life markers and repositories for old traditions representing important psychological ties to the past. See "Origins and Stylistic Development of Polish-American Polka Music," 5.

2. As his clarinet teacher in the late 1970s, I notated dozens of tunes, adding the correct rhythms to his accurate melodies to form a unique fakebook of Polish and American songs. "These are all simple to me, but I love them, I love every one of them," Al explained as we began the project. We developed an efficient methodology. With the tape recorder running, Al would play a tune on the clarinet and then sing the entire song in Polish, followed by a line-by-line translation. The resulting handwritten collection was eclectic, including Polish folk songs from Al's early years in Scranton's Polonia and polkas that he heard later on radio and television; German songs such as "Der Schnitzelbaum" from Al's later years in Buffalo, when he lived near a German bar; and mainstream American tunes in English such as "The Yellow Rose of Texas," "After the Ball," and "Red River Valley."

3. Taped interview with Al Clark, 6 Nov. 1979.

4. Wolska, *Dances of Poland,* 14.

5. Interviews with Helen Uszacki, Dunkirk, N.Y., 16 April 1995; and Chet Tarnowski, Dunkirk, N.Y., 17 April 1995. Tarnowski's parents and Helen Uszacki emigrated from southeastern Poland. Both informants remembered the wiejska sound as a carryover from the old country.

6. The verb *kosić* means "to mow," but informants and the editors of *Treasured Polish Songs* translated the word as "to sow." I am indebted to Robert A. Rothstein of the Slavic languages department at the University of Massachusetts at Amherst for pointing out this discrepancy.

7. Interview with Al Clark, 10 June 1978.

8. Sung by Lucy Moch, 24 Jan. 1979. The English translation appears in *Treasured Polish Songs with English Translations*, ed. Contoski, 27. Lucy Moch is one of dozens of the folklore interviewees who could recall at least a portion of this song as one they had learned from their family or friends.

9. The following is taken from a performance by Zespół Górali Giewont, a group of musicians from southern Poland's Tatra Mountains. Many people have emigrated to Chicago and the East Coast from this region. The performance is available on an album produced by Richard K. Spottswood: *Songs of Migration and Immigration*, vol. 6 of *Folk Music in America*, Library of Congress, 77–750125, 1977.

10. Pawlowska, *Merrily We Sing*, 157–58. This classic volume features songs by ten folklore interviewees, most of them first-generation Polish-Americans who learned the songs in Poland. As such, they are at least two generations closer to the immigration experience than my interviewees.

11. Interview with Lucy Moch; English translation by Martha Andrzejewski, Dunkirk, N.Y.

12. In *Treasured Polish Folk Songs with English Translations* (160), Josepha Contoski notes that the tune also was known as "Czemu Tęsknisz za Chatą?" (Why do you pine for your humble home?) or "Wrony Konik" (Little black horse).

13. Performed on 10 June 1978 by Al Clark. A literal translation of the verse, but not as metrical in English, would be: "An old woman had a rooster / Rooster, rooster, / She kept him in her shoe, / In her shoe, hey!" For a more complete version of the song, see *Treasured Polish Songs with English Translations*, ed. Contoski, 160.

14. Interview with Al Clark, 6 Nov. 1979.

15. Interview with Al Clark, 7 Nov. 1978.

16. Performed and translated by Al Clark, 10 June 1978. He explained that "łupu cupu" are nonsense syllables. Another version of the song, "Kuba," is available in *Treasured Polish Songs with English Translations*, ed. Contoski, 132.

17. Sung and translated by Al Clark, 10 June 1978. The words "jumptary, jumptary a," like "łupu cupu," are nonsense syllables in Polish.

18. Interview with Al Clark, 7 Nov. 1978.

19. Recorded by Al Clark on 10 June 1978. He did not translate the last line, although he wrote it in Polish. It probably should read "Sama niedawno" (Myself not long ago) and could be interpreted as a young man's boast that he had spent the entire night with his girlfriend, with sexual connotations.

20. Sung and translated by Paul Urbanik, Dunkirk, N.Y., during a taped interview, 6 Feb. 1979. Another common variant inserts four lines at the beginning as follows: "The grass is growing in the shade in the cemetery / You gave your hand to a man by the big altar, / You gave him your hand and then the priest gave him the wedding ring. / You burst into tears before his eyes."

21. Interview with Al Clark, 7 Nov. 1978.

22. Interview with Robert Hora.

23. Sung by Al Clark, 10 June 1978. In *Treasured Polish Songs with English Translations* (234), Josepha Contoski notes that the melody was previously sung as a national hymn, "Boże, Coś Polskę" (God, who held Poland), after the uprising of 1830 until Poland's conquerors forbade its performance. They continued to prohibit the song later when the lyrics of "Serdeczna Matka" were substituted.

24. Interview with Robert Hora, who recalled that the lyrics used to be printed on the back of the holy cards handed out at funerals so mourners would have the words at the cemetery. At many Polish-American funerals now, the hymn is performed as the recessional during the funeral mass because mourners no longer accompany the body to the cemetery.

25. Performed by Alton Nowak, Dunkirk, N.Y., 14 Dec. 1978; English translation by Martha Andrzejewski, Dunkirk, N.Y.

26. Interview with Al Clark, 10 June 1978.

27. The Kolipinski radio program theme song that follows was sung on WEBR Radio in Buffalo around 1930 by Mieczysław Jachimski, according to Irena Kolipinska-Malinowska, daughter of the store's owner. I am indebted to Daniel Kij for obtaining the Polish lyrics from her, providing an English translation, and performing the song in its entirety (taped interview, 29 May 1995).

28. Other individuals who sang portions of the commercial, usually the first or second chorus (because both are relatively short and easy to remember) included Al Clark (interview of 10 June 1978); Ted Miehl (taped interview, Dunkirk, N.Y., 1 June 1991); and James Griffin, who learned it growing up in his South Buffalo neighborhood of Irish and Polish families.

29. Even now, the polka is not well known in Poland. Both ethnomusicologist Charles Keil, on a trip there in 1979, and Sophie Urbanik, who visited Poland in 1990, reported that the polka was not a popular dance, although some bands attempted to play them to please American tourists. Keil, Keil, and Blau, *Polka Happiness,* 19; taped interview with Sophie Urbanik, Dunkirk, N.Y., 8 June 1991. Gabrielle Merta also told me that the polka was virtually nonexistent in Poland. A young Polish graduate student who spent a summer living with the Steve Litwin family in Binghamton, N.Y., however, told them that the Polish-American polka sounds much like the music she heard at weddings in her native village in northern Poland. Interview with Steve Litwin, 30 Jan. 1993.

Chapter 11: An American Original

1. Armstrong, *The Affecting Presence,* 90. Armstrong (10) notes that objects which are considered by a community to be affecting presences are those wor-

thy of "the kind of treatment which indicates an investment of feeling—whether it is held in awe, whether it receives sacrifice, protection, ritualized respect, or indeed disrespect."

2. An introduction to the polka music field is provided by Charles Keil, Angeliki Keil, and Dick Blau in *Polka Happiness*. I am indebted to Charlie Keil and Mark Kohan for suggestions that influenced my thinking about the evolution of Polish-American polka music.

3. Crease, "In Praise of the Polka," 78–79.

4. Falkowski, *Polka History 101* n.p.; Keil, Keil, and Blau, *Polka Happiness*, 10. Also see Keil, "People's Music Comparatively," 197–217.

5. See Kleeman, "Origins and Stylistic Development of Polish-American Polka Music," 33, for a discussion of this European urban "salon polka" adapted from the folk polka by trained classical musicians of the upper classes.

6. Taped interview with Steve Litwin at the St. Patrick's weekend polka festival, Hamburg, N.Y., 19 March 1995. The comments about high C culture are from a taped interview with Buffalo Common Council member David Franczyk, Buffalo, 12 April 1993; and Falkowski, *Polka History 101*, n.p.

7. Taped interview with polka promoter Stan Kozak at the St. Patrick's weekend polka festival, Hamburg, N.Y., 19 March 1995.

8. Kohan, *Polish Folk Roots in Today's Polka*, n.p.

9. This version is contained in Contoski, *Treasured Polish Folk Songs with English Translations*, 113.

10. Greene, *A Passion for Polka*, 11.

11. Keil, "People's Music Comparatively," 198; Greene, *A Passion for Polka*, 71–73.

12. Greene, *A Passion for Polka*, 73.

13. Keil, Keil, and Blau, *Polka Happiness*, 19.

14. Greene, *A Passion for Polka*, 89.

15. Keil, Keil, and Blau, *Polka Happiness*, 19.

16. For further information about this shift in instrumentation, see Greene, *A Passion for Polka*, 80; Davis, "Utica's Polka Music Tradition," 110; and Trojak and Kohan, "Celebrate the Polka," 6.

17. Keil, "A Short History of the Polka," n.p.

18. Kohan, *Polish Folk Roots in Today's Polka*, n.p.

19. Kohan, "The Accordion and Concertina in the Polish-American Polka," n.p.

20. For a discussion focusing on the interchange of ethnic musical styles in Detroit's Polonia since the 1920s, see Savaglio, "Big Band, Slovenian-American, Rock, and Country Music," 23–44.

21. Keil, Keil, and Blau, *Polka Happiness*, 57.

22. For example, Li'l Wally's ideas inspired many locally based polka bands in the Utica area to add traditional Polish songs to their repertoires. Davis,

"Utica's Polka Music Tradition," 116. Folklore informants also reported that the Chicago style was popular in the Buffalo area by 1965.

23. Keil, "People's Music Comparatively," 201.

24. Interview with Valerie Pawlak.

25. Interview with Steve Litwin, 19 March 1995.

26. Taped interview with Ted Szymanski and Ed Skoczylas, members of City Side, at the Eden, N.Y., Polka Festival, 21 July 1991.

27. Taped interview with Eddie Blazonczyk, Chicago, at the St. Patrick's weekend polka festival, Hamburg, N.Y., 17 March 1995.

28. "DP" stands for "displaced person," a term in vogue after World War II to describe the latest wave of immigrants to America, those displaced by the war. As the newest group of Polish immigrants, DPs were most likely to have Polish as their primary language, unlike earlier generations of Polish-Americans who by the end of World War II were either bilingual or spoke English only.

29. Taped interview of Walter Kapinos, Floyd, N.Y., 6 July 1978, conducted by Susan Davis, as contained in Davis, "Utica's Polka Music Tradition," 107.

30. Taped interview with Hank Guzevich and his parents, Gus and Nellie Guzevich, at the St. Patrick's weekend polka festival, Hamburg, N.Y., 19 March 1995.

31. Since the 1980s a number of polka albums have featured the old country sound. Among them are *PFC Players with Chet Kowalkowski—A Kolberg Sampler* (1990); Toledo Polkamotion's *Favorite Traditional Polkas and Waltzes; Chet Kowalkowski and John Jaworski Sing Original "Old Country Songs"* (Bel Aire Records, 1992); *Songs of Little Poland* by John Jaworski and the Keynotes (Chicago Polkas, LP-7102, 1981); and Po Staru Krajsku's *Eddie Blazonczyk and Chet Kowalkowski Sing Your Polish All Time Favorites* (Bel Aire Records, n.d.).

32. Interview with Eddie Blazonczyk.

33. Interview with Hank Guzevich.

34. Leary and March, "Dutchman Bands," 27. The influence of country-western upon the Polish-American polka as played in western New York state dates from approximately the mid-1970s. Janice Kleeman also notes the impact of country-western music upon the polka since the 1970s, when traditional Anglo-American fiddle music was introduced into polka tunes. "Origins and Stylistic Development of Polish-American Polka Music," 95.

35. Taped interview with Ray Budniewski, 6 Feb. 1993; taped interview with Willy Wisniewski, Buffalo, N.Y., 12 April 1993; conversation with Edward Silverman, Hamburg, N.Y., 23 April 1995. Also see Walser, "The Polka Mass," 188–89, for a discussion of the interaction between the country-western sound and the polka as demonstrated in the polka mass.

36. Jimmy Sturr, interview on "Music City Tonight," aired on TNN on 21 April

1995. Sturr also mentioned an upcoming polka–country music cruise featuring his and several other polka bands with "Whispering Bill" Anderson.

37. Comments from Jean Osora during a taped interview with her and her husband Frank at the St. Patrick's weekend polka festival, Hamburg, N.Y., 19 March 1995

38. Taped interview with musician Chet Kozlowski, leader of Centerpiece, Dunkirk, N.Y., 7 July 1991.

39. The term *polka roadie* is from Stan Kozak; *polka people* and *polka hoppers* are from Jean Osora.

40. Interview with Jean Osora.

41. Interview with Steve Litwin, 19 March 1995.

42. A discussion of the polka mass can be found in Walser, "The Polka Mass," 183–202. The historical information I present here is taken from Walser. Descriptions of polka masses come from my observations at several polka masses and my background as a folk mass musician.

43. Larry Trojak as interviewed by Bill Falkowski, in Keil, Keil, and Blau, *Polka Happiness*, 172. I am indebted to John Gutowski, Charles Keil, Steve Litwin, and Mark Kohan for additional information about the band.

44. Interview with Hank Guzevich. In discussing the continuing popularity of Polish-language polkas, Janice Kleeman argues that a large percentage of the audience still understands Polish well enough to comprehend polka texts; furthermore, because many polka "classics" are in Polish, people prefer to hear them in the original language for sentimental reasons. Kleeman, "Origins and Stylistic Development of Polish-American Polka Music," 165.

45. Interview with Edward Sabloski, president of the United Polka League of the Mohawk Valley since 1979.

46. Interview with Stan Kozak.

47. Taped telephone interview with Tom Warzecha, Syracuse, N.Y., 25 April 1993, following Syracuse's first Dyngus Day weekend polka event, which Warzecha promoted.

48. Interview with Denise Szatkowski, Alliance, Ohio, formerly of western New York state, at the St. Patrick's weekend polka festival, Hamburg, N.Y., 19 March 1995.

49. Interview with Nellie Guzevich.

50. Taped interview with Michelle Matthews of WDOE–AM Radio, Dunkirk, N.Y., 19 March 1995.

51. Interview with Fred Gordon.

52. Taped interview with Bob King, Buffalo, N.Y., at the St. Patrick's weekend polka festival, Hamburg, N.Y., 19 March 1995.

53. A thorough discussion of the International Polka Association is contained in Keil, Keil, and Blau, *Polka Happiness*, 73–125.

54. Interview with Edward Sabloski.

55. Interview with Florence Ruszaj.
56. Interview with Steve Litwin, 19 March 1995.

Chapter 12: Reinventing the Reel

"Hej, Mazurze" is a mazurka, a Polish folk dance in moderate triple time from the province of Mazovia in Poland.

1. Pack, *Costumes and Dances of Poland*, n.p.
2. Wolska, *Dances of Poland*, 18.
3. Ibid., 13.
4. Pack, *Costumes and Dances of Poland*, n.p.
5. Wolska, *Dances of Poland*, 10; Pack, *Costumes and Dances of Poland*, n.p. The following descriptions are based on those contained in Pack.
6. According to Charles Keil, the polonez is alive and well in the wedding ceremonies of the Celebes Islanders in Indonesia via Dutch transmission. Conversation of 13 Sept. 1995.
7. Wolska, *Dances of Poland*, 11–13.
8. Recorded interview with Daniel Collins, née Chojnacki, Grand Island, N.Y., 17 March 1995.
9. Recorded telephone interview with Janet Stanek, East Aurora, N.Y., 22 March 1995.
10. Interview with Janet Stanek.

Chapter 13: Games People Play

1. Tadeusz Delimat's comments are contained in his introduction to Czarnecka, *Folk Art in Poland*, 5. All subsequent references to Delimat are to the *Folk Art* introduction.
2. Benet, *Song*, 114.
3. Delimat, *Folk Art in Poland*, 6–8.
4. Knab, *Polish Customs*, 212.
5. Tyborowski, "Ritual Bread Baking," pamphlet handed out at the Cheektowaga, N.Y., Polish-American Festival, 19 Aug. 1995. Tyborowski notes that ritual breads also were baked for christenings, harvest, deaths, and such holidays as New Year's Trinity Sunday and various Marian feasts, including the Annunciation and Visitation. For an in-depth discussion of korowaj, see Knab, *Polish Customs*, 197–200.
6. Knab, *Polish Customs*, 200.
7. Benet, *Song*, 95. Alternatively, wycinanki were made just before Easter, as suggested in *Wycinanki Polish Cut-Outs* (n.p.).
8. *Wycinanki Polish Cut-Outs*, n.p.
9. Benet, *Song*, 95–96.

10. Contoski, ed., *Treasured Polish Christmas Customs and Traditions*, 122.

11. Benet, *Song*, 95; Kozlowski, *Christmas Ornaments, Polish Style*, 6.

12. Kozlowski, *Christmas Ornaments, Polish Style*, 6.

13. Benet, *Song*, 50.

14. Kozlowski, *Easter Eggs, Polish Style, and More!* 4.

15. Newall, "Easter Eggs," 8.

16. Kozlowski, *Easter Eggs, Polish Style, and More!* 4.

17. Newall, "Easter Eggs," 14.

18. The following discussion is based on Kozlowski, *Easter Eggs, Polish Style, and More!* 5–27.

19. *Pisanki* is the name generally given to all decorated Easter eggs by my Polish-American informants, regardless of the specific decorating technique used.

20. Kozlowski, *Easter Eggs, Polish Style, and More!* 50.

21. Folklorists working in other ethnic American groups also have noted the importance of games to the immigrants and their ancestors but not the American descendants. Mac Barrick, who conducted research among German-Americans, believes the replacement of one-room schoolhouses with larger, consolidated schools eliminated the opportunity for such game-playing. At about the same time, manufactured toys became more available. John West has observed the same phenomenon among Mexican-Americans since the 1950s. Barrick, ed., *German-American Folklore*, 124; West, *Mexican-American Folklore*, 194.

22. *Treasured Polish Folk Rhymes, Songs and Games*, 46.

23. Ibid., 48.

24. See *Treasured Polish Folk Rhymes, Songs and Games*, 49–50, for a complete description of the Father Virgilius and "On a Monday Morning" games. Other Polish games no longer played in Polonia also are featured in this collection.

25. Jackson, *Fieldwork*, 39.

26. Interview with Kate Moch.

27. Interview with Martha Steffan.

28. Interview with Gabrielle Merta.

29. Interview with Geraldine Halasinski.

30. Interview with Al Clark, 23 Nov. 1979.

31. Delimat, *Folk Art in Poland*, 9.

32. The following description is taken from Koperski, "Building Community," 42–57; and Boynton, "Community Murals and Religious Paintings," 30–41.

33. Koperski, "Building Community," 42.

34. Hardin, ed., *Folklife Annual 90*, 8.

35. Koperski, "Building Community," 55.

36. Interview with Sharon Tyborowski.

37. Recorded interview with Henia Makowski at "A Celebration of the Easter Egg in Eastern European Tradition," Cheektowaga, N.Y., 29 March 1992.

She was demonstrating how to make pin-style pisanki inscribed with wax and then dyed in onion skins.

38. Taped interview with Dick Makowski at "A Celebration of the Easter Egg in Eastern European Tradition," Cheektowaga, N.Y., 29 March 1992.

39. Taped interviews with Judith Krauza at "A Celebration of the Easter Egg in Eastern European Tradition," Cheektowaga, N.Y., 29 March 1992; and Lawrence Kozlowski and Sharon Tyborowski at the Cheektowaga, N.Y., Polish-American Festival, 19 Aug. 1995. According to Judith Krauza, the workshops in Poland cost about $550 plus airfare in 1992. Workshop participants live in college dormitories but travel widely around the country during their stay in Poland and have assistance from an English translator.

40. Interview with Sharon Tyborowski.

41. Ibid.

42. Interview with Judith Krauza.

43. Interview with Henia Makowski.

Chapter 14: Pierogi, Kielbasa, and Other Symbols of Ethnicity

1. See, for example, Kalčik, "Ethnic Foodways in America," 44; Magliocco, "Playing with Food," 107; and Malpezzi and Clements, *Italian-American Folklore,* 221.

2. Kalčik, "Ethnic Foodways in America," 39; Malpezzi and Clements, *Italian-American Folklore,* 221; Theophano, "'I Gave Him a Cake,'" 44; Toelken, *Dynamics of Folklore,* 73; and Stern, "Ethnic Folklore," 21.

3. Stern, "Ethnic Folklore," 21; Toelken, *Dynamics of Folklore,* 73; Malpezzi and Clements, *Italian-American Folklore,* 222.

4. Goode, Theophano, and Curtis, "A Framework for the Analysis of Continuity and Change," 69.

5. Royce, *Ethnic Identity,* 210; Kalčik, "Ethnic Foodways in America," 54–55.

6. Theophano, "'I Gave Him a Cake,'" 44–54.

7. Gutierrez, "The Social and Symbolic Uses of Ethnic/Regional Foodways," 170.

8. Dorson, "The State of Folkloristics," 89–92.

9. Magliocco, "Playing with Food," 108.

10. Benet, *Song,* 182.

11. *Treasured Polish Recipes for Americans,* 12. John West, Sabina Magliocco, and Mac Barrick also make the same point with respect to the regionalism of Old World foodways in other American ethnic groups. West, *Mexican-American Folklore,* 207; Magliocco, "Playing with Food," 109; Barrick, ed., *German-American Folklore,* 149.

12. Barrick, ed., *German-American Folklore,* 149–50, and West, *Mexican-American Folklore,* 218–20.

13. Interview with Mary Miller.

14. Interview with Kate Moch.

15. Benet, *Song*, 185.

16. The reference to barrels on a television show is apparently to "Petticoat Junction," a television program of the 1960s that opened with a view of three young women hanging their petticoats over the side of a wooden water tank.

17. Interview with Kate Moch.

18. Benet, *Song*, 183.

19. *Treasured Polish Recipes for Americans*, 102.

20. Taped interview with Jadwiga Dzięgielewska at the Cheektowaga, N.Y., Polish-American Festival, 19 Aug. 1995.

21. Taped interview with Ed Jeronczyk, Greenfield, Mass., at the Cheektowaga, N.Y., Polish-American Festival, 19 Aug. 1995. He was referring to a Polish immigrant in Greenfield who recalled her Sunday morning trips to the woods as a child in Poland.

22. Interview with Mary Miller.

23. Interview with Robert Hora. Also see *Treasured Polish Recipes for Americans*, 10, for a discussion of the use of butter in Polish cooking.

24. Douglas, *Natural Symbols*, 65–66.

25. See Douglas, *Natural Symbols*, 66, for a discussion of the distinction between serving drinks and meals. Drinks were shared by strangers, acquaintances, workers, and family in an atmosphere of relative distance, whereas meals were occasions for intimacy involving family, close friends, and honored guests. Sula Benet has noted that Polish peasants rarely had guests at meals, both because there was barely enough food for themselves and eating was considered to be an intimate, biological function (*Song*, 219). Frances Malpezzi and William Clements have pointed to the sacramental nature of the meal among Italians and Italian-Americans, with similar care taken to avoid wasting food (*Italian-American Folklore*, 224).

26. Benet, *Song*, 56.

27. Toelken, *Dynamics of Folklore*, 78.

28. Benet, *Song*, 97.

29. In Catholic nations such as Italy and Poland, bread in its many forms held a central role in rituals. Italians had numerous taboos about the baking of bread (Malpezzi and Clements, *Italian-American Folklore*, 226). Poles did also, particularly for ceremonial occasions such as weddings.

30. Benet, *Song*, 184.

31. Malpezzi and Clements, *Italian-American Folklore*, 227; Knab, *Polish Customs*, 208; Benet, *Song*, 167; Moore, "Metaphor and Changing Reality," 100.

32. *Treasured Polish Recipes for Americans*, 9.

33. Kalčik, "Ethnic Foodways in America," 37–39.

34. Nagorka, "Traditional Polish Cooking," 283.

35. Malpezzi and Clements, *Italian-American Folklore*, 239–41.

36. Interview with Joe Rozen, 20 July 1991.

37. Ibid.

38. Taped interview with Frank Grupa, Ray Budniewski, and Ed Tarnowski at the Kosciuszko Club, Dunkirk, N.Y., 10 April 1993.

39. Malpezzi and Clements, *Italian-American Folklore*, 234; Raspa, "Exotic Foods among Italian-Americans in Mormon Utah," 185.

40. Elizabeth Goldstein and Gail Green also have noted a decrease in the amount of time that Polish-American women spend in cooking. Goldstein and Green, "Pierogi- and Babka-Making at St. Mary's," 71.

41. Interview with Jack Pencek.

42. Raspa, "Exotic Foods among Italian-Americans in Mormon Utah," 185.

43. Interview with Joe Rozen, 20 July 1991.

44. Taped interview with Ed Tarnowski, Dunkirk, N.Y., at the annual Holy Saturday swięconka held at the Kosciuszko Club in Dunkirk for club members, 10 April 1993. Tarnowski serves as one of the cooks for the event.

45. Taped interview of Wanda Skup conducted by Edward Silverman at the Famous Horseradish stand at the Broadway Market, Buffalo, N.Y., 4 April 1993.

46. Taped interview with Stephanie Rozen, her son Joe, and her daughter Pauline Rozen Newman at Stephanie Rozen's family wigilia, Dunkirk, N.Y., 24 Dec. 1994.

47. *Treasured Polish Recipes for Americans* (23) refers to this soup as *żurek Wielkanocny* (Easter soup), but among Polish-American interviewees it was universally referred to as Easter barszcz. Barszcz prepared with beets is served as a soup at the Christmas wigilia.

48. Interview with Ed Tarnowski.

49. Interview with Robert Hora.

50. Taped interview with John Panowicz, Cheektowaga, N.Y., 29 March 1992. His family adds prunes but not raisins. A variant substitutes beef broth for the duck's blood, with red food coloring or beet juice added to give the czarnina its characteristic reddish-brown color. The substitution was made because the informant's family did not like the taste of duck's blood. Interview with Gabrielle Merta.

51. Interview with Rita Danner.

52. Taped interview with Mary Zachary, Dunkirk, N.Y., at the Kosciuszko Club Fourth of July weekend street dance, 7 July 1991.

53. Taped interview with Monike Poslinski of the E&M Bakery, Buffalo, N.Y., 4 April 1993.

54. The E&M Bakery is a case in point. During the 1990s its owners invested in special equipment to enable them to manufacture chrusciki more quickly and in greater quantity in order to sell them to supermarkets as well as at their food stand.

55. Taped interview with Joe Rozen, Dunkirk, N.Y., 24 Dec. 1994. This "hybridization" is also occurring among other ethnic groups; Malpezzi and Clements have found that traditional Italian foods are being "adulterated" by American ingredients. *Italian-American Folklore*, 238.

56. Interview with Dorothy Mazur.

57. Interview with Mary Miller, who was referring to her daughter.

58. Interview with Jean Brogcinski.

59. Interview with Emily Boruszewski.

60. Two women told me about saving recipes on their home computers and printing them out periodically for friends and relatives. Taped interview with Christine Kupiec Snyder, Cheektowaga, New York, 10 July 1991; interview with Dorothy Mazur.

61. Toelken, *Dynamics of Folklore*, 76.

62. Armstrong, *The Affecting Presence*, 90.

63. For a description, see Goldstein and Green, "Pierogi- and Babka-Making at St. Mary's," 71–79.

Chapter 15: Anchors and Passports to Polishness

Bishop Rhode's remarks to the forty-first Polish Roman Catholic Union convention are quoted in Wytrwal, *Behold! The Polish Americans*, 243; and Haiman, *Zjednoczenie Polski Rzymsko-Katolickie*, 433.

1. Information was obtained during a taped telephone interview with Patricia Wojcik, chair of the Cheektowaga, N.Y., Polish-American Festival, 21 Aug. 1995.

2. For a thorough description of the Onion Harvest Festival's early years, see Wright, "The Orange County Onion Harvest Festivals," 197–204. Also see Pirkova-Jakobson, "Harvest Festivals among Czechs and Slovaks in America," 266–80. Pirkova-Jakobson has analyzed the means by which Czechs and Slovaks in America improvised similar rituals based on Old World harvest celebrations.

3. Taped interview with Betty Saccone, a cook at the Chopin's Singing Society Dyngus Day party, Buffalo, N.Y., 12 April 1993.

4. Information about the festivals was provided in a telephone conversation with Steve Litwin, 16 March 1996. He noted that Chicago generally hosts the International Polka Association and United States Polka Association festivals in addition to the Bel-Aire Days.

5. Interviews with Ed Jeronczyk, Greenfield, Mass., at the Cheektowaga, N.Y., Polish-American Festival, 19 Aug. 1995; and Joe Rozen, past president of the Dom Polski Club of Dunkirk, N.Y., 20 July 1991. Ed Jeronczyk was videotaping portions of the 1995 Cheektowaga event for a presentation to his club in Massachusetts.

6. Interview with Robert and Jean Brogcinski.

7. Taped interview with Robert Ciesielski at the Chopin's Singing Society Dyngus Day party, Buffalo, N.Y., 12 April 1993.

8. Taped interview with Sophie Hodorowicz Knab, Grand Island, N.Y., at the Cheektowaga, N.Y., Polish-American Festival, 19 Aug. 1995, where she was exhibiting Polish herbs.

9. Interview with Lawrence Kozlowski.

10. For more on the "revival" of ethnic identity in Polonia, see Bukowczyk, *And My Children Did Not Know Me,* 104–24.

11. Several recent works examine the difficulties posed by the representation of folk traditions in new public contexts such as multiethnic folk festivals. See, for example, Baron and Spitzer, eds., *Public Folklore;* Feintuch, ed., *Conservation of Culture;* and Stern and Cicala, eds., *Creative Ethnicity.* A particularly fine treatment of the topic appears in Staub, "Folklore and Authenticity," 166–79.

12. Staub, "Folklore and Authenticity," 172.

13. Interview with Patricia Wojcik.

14. Telephone conversation with Linda Lemieux, Onion Harvest Festival committee member, 21 Aug. 1995. Kmieć and the dance instructor, Donna Kalinowska-Werter, both studied at the University of Marie Curie–Sklodowska in Lublin, Poland.

15. Sapir, "Culture, Genuine and Spurious," 314.

16. Dorson, "Folklore and Fake Lore," 335–43.

17. Handler and Linnekin, "Tradition, Genuine or Spurious," 273.

18. Royce, *Ethnic Identity,* 210; Barth, ed., *Ethnic Groups and Boundaries,* 35.

19. Myerhoff, *Number Our Days,* 10; Cadaval, "Making a Place Home: The Latino Festival," 208; Danielson, "St. Lucia in Lindsborg, Kansas," 192.

20. Dorson, "State of Folkloristics," 92; interview with Mark Kohan, 29 Dec. 1992.

21. Bukowczyk, *And My Children Did Not Know Me,* 112–14.

22. Ibid., 115. In their negative stereotyping of Polish-Americans, outsiders selected certain traits while excluding others. The same process is now occurring in reverse within the group.

23. Taped interview with Buffalo Common Council member David Franczyk at the Chopin's Singing Society Dyngus Day party, Buffalo, N.Y., 12 April 1993.

24. Interview with Alois Mazur.

25. Interview with Sharon Tyborowski.

26. Interview with Mark Kohan, 29 Dec. 1992; Lopata, *Polish Americans,* 3.

27. Gutierrez, "Social and Symbolic Uses of Ethnic/Regional Foodways," 171.

28. Handler and Linnekin, "Tradition, Genuine or Spurious," 282.

29. Bell, "Ethnicity and Social Change," 169; Smith, *The Ethnic Revival,* 157; Fischer, "Ethnicity and the Post-Modern Arts of Memory," 195–96; Royce, *Ethnic Identity,* 232.

30. Fischer, "Ethnicity and the Post-Modern Arts of Memory," 195.

31. Interview with Gabrielle Merta.

32. Interview with Ray Budniewski, 6 Feb. 1993. Anthropologist Paul Wrobel, who interviewed Polish-Americans in Detroit, also found that most described themselves as "Polish-American" rather than "Polish" (*Our Way,* 117).

33. Interview with Robert Hora.

34. Taped interview with Msgr. John Gabalski, pastor of St. Stanislaus Roman Catholic Church, Buffalo, N.Y., at the Knights of St. John's Club Kolędy Night, Cheektowaga, N.Y., 19 Dec. 1992.

35. Isajiw, "Definitions of Ethnicity," 121.

36. Interview with David Franczyk.

37. Bukowczyk, *And My Children Did Not Know Me,* 97–98.

38. Ibid., 109.

39. Lopata, *Polish Americans,* 6; Bukowczyk, *And My Children Did Not Know Me,* 110.

40. Lopata, *Polish Americans,* 171.

WORKS CITED

Abrahams, Roger D. "The Language of Festivals: Celebrating the Economy." In *Celebration: Studies in Festivity and Ritual*, edited by Victor Turner, 161–77. Washington, D.C.: Smithsonian Institution Press, 1982.

Ainsworth, Catherine Harris. "Polish-American Church Legends." *New York Folklore Quarterly* 30, no. 4 (1974): 286–94.

———. *Polish-American Folktales*. Buffalo: Clyde Press, 1977.

An Album of Polish Easter Hymns. The Lutnia Choir of Holy Mother of the Rosary Parish, Chicopee, Mass., conducted by Frank W. Curylo. Rex Heritage, LP 778, n.d.

Armstrong, Robert Plant. *The Affecting Presence: An Essay in Humanistic Anthropology*. Urbana: University of Illinois Press, 1971.

Barnett, Clifford. *Poland*. New Haven: Hraf Press, 1958.

Baron, Robert, and Nicholas R. Spitzer, eds. *Public Folklore*. Washington, D.C.: Smithsonian Institution Press, 1992.

Barrick, Mac E., ed. *German-American Folklore*. Little Rock: August House, 1987.

———. "Racial Riddles and the Polack Joke." *Keystone Folklore Quarterly* 15, no. 1 (1970): 3–15.

Barth, Fredrik, ed. Introduction. In *Ethnic Groups and Boundaries: The Social Organization of Culture Difference*, 9–38. Bergen, Norway: Universitets Forlaget, 1969.

Bartminski, Jerzy. "Polish Christmas Carols and Their Cultural Context." *Slavic and East European Journal* 34.1 (1990): 83–97.

Bauerle, Tom. "Breakfast with Bauerle." On WGR-AM, Buffalo, N.Y., 12 April 1993.

Bazielichówna, Barbara. "Further Notes on the Polish Guisers." *Folklore* 69 (1958): 254–61.

Bazielichówna, Barbara, and Stefan Deptuszewski. "The Guisers of Koniaków." *Folklore* 68 (1957): 497.

Bell, Daniel. "Ethnicity and Social Change." In *Ethnicity: Theory and Experience,* edited by Nathan Glazer and Daniel P. Moynihan, 141–74. Cambridge: Harvard University Press, 1975.

Benet, Sula. *Song, Dance, and Customs of Peasant Poland.* New York: Roy Publishers, 1951.

Bianco, Carla. *The Two Rosetos.* Bloomington: Indiana University Press, 1974.

Boynton, Mia. "Community Murals and Religious Paintings: Ethnic Images in Buffalo's Polish-American District." In *Folklife Annual 90,* edited by James Hardin, 30–41. Washington, D.C.: Library of Congress, 1991.

Brooks, Maria Zagórska. "The Bear in Slavic and Polish Mythology and Folklore." In *For Wiktor Weintraub: Essays in Polish Literature, Language, and History Presented on the Occasion of His Sixty-fifth Birthday,* edited by Victor Erlich, Roman Jakobson, Czeslaw Miłosz, Riccardo Picchio, Alexander M. Schenker, and Edward Stankiewicz, 107–11. The Hague: Mouton, 1975.

Brown, Linda Keller, and Kay Mussell, eds. *Ethnic and Regional Foodways in the United States: The Performance of Group Identity.* Knoxville: University of Tennessee Press, 1985.

Bukowczyk, John J. *And My Children Did Not Know Me: A History of the Polish-Americans.* Bloomington: Indiana University Press, 1987.

Cadaval, Olivia. "Making a Place Home: The Latino Festival." In *Creative Ethnicity: Symbols and Strategies of Contemporary Ethnic Life,* edited by Stephen Stern and John Allan Cicala, 204–22. Logan: Utah State University Press, 1991.

Carpenter, Niles, and Daniel Katz. "The Cultural Adjustment of the Polish Group in the City of Buffalo: An Experiment in the Technique of Social Investigation." *Social Forces* 6 (Sept. 1927): 76–90.

———. "A Study of Acculturation of the Polish Group of Buffalo, 1926–28." *University of Buffalo Studies* 7.4 (1929): 103–33.

Clements, William M. *The Types of the Polack Joke.* Folklore Forum Bibliographic and Special Series no. 3 (1969): 56.

Coleman, Marion Moore. "Introduction." *Polish Folklore* 1 (March 1956): 1.

———. "Podhalan Plant Lore from Connecticut." *Polish Folklore* 2 (1957): 44–45.

———, ed. *Polish Folklore.* Vols. 1–5. Cambridge Springs, Pa.: Alliance College, 1956–60.

Contoski, Josepha, ed. *Treasured Polish Christmas Customs and Traditions.* Minneapolis: Polanie Publishing, 1972.

————, ed. *Treasured Polish Songs with English Translations.* Minneapolis: Polanie Publishing, 1953.

Corso, Rose. "The Evil Eye." *Polish Folklore* 4 (1959): 6.

Crease, Robert P. "In Praise of the Polka." *The Atlantic* 264 (Aug. 1989): 78–83.

Curran, Bob. "Buffalo Has Dyngus Day Spirit to Match South Bend's Big Blast." *Buffalo News,* 12 April 1992, B-2.

————. "It's Tough to Pick Favorite Spot for Celebrating on Dyngus Day." *Buffalo News,* 4 April 1993, B-2.

Czarnecka, Irena. *Folk Art in Poland.* Warsaw: Wrocławska Drukarnia Naukowa, 1957.

Danielson, Larry. "St. Lucia in Lindsborg, Kansas." In *Creative Ethnicity: Symbols and Strategies of Contemporary Ethnic LIfe,* edited by Stephen Stern and John Allan Cicala, 187–203. Logan: Utah State University Press, 1991.

Davis, Susan. "Old-Fashioned Polish Weddings in Utica, New York." *New York Folklore* 4 (1978): 89–102.

————. "Utica's Polka Music Tradition." *New York Folklore* 4 (1978): 103–24.

Delimat, Tadeusz. Introduction. In Irena Czarnecka, *Folk Art in Poland,* 5–9. Warsaw: Wrocławska Drukarnia Naukowa, 1957.

Dorson, Richard M. "Folklore and Fake Lore." *American Mercury* 70 (1950): 335–43.

————. "Is There a Folk in the City?" In *The Urban Experience and Folk Tradition,* edited by Americo Paredes and Ellen J. Stekert, 21–52. Austin: University of Texas Press, 1971.

————. "The State of Folkloristics from an American Perspective." *Journal of the Folklore Institute* 19 (1982): 71–105.

Douglas, Mary. *Natural Symbols: Explorations in Cosmology.* Reprint. London: Barrie and Jenkins, 1973.

Dundes, Alan. *Folklore Matters.* Knoxville: University of Tennessee Press, 1989.

————. "Polish Pope Jokes." *Journal of American Folklore* 92, no. 364 (1979): 219–22.

————. "A Study of Ethnic Slurs: The Jew and the Polack in the United States." *Journal of American Folklore* 84, no. 332 (1971): 186–203.

Etzioni, Amitai. "The Ghetto—A Re-Evaluation." *Social Forces* 37 (March 1959): 255–62.

Falkowski, William G., Jr. "Accommodation and Conflict: Patterns of Polish Immigrant Adaption to Industrial Capitalism and American Political Pluralism in Buffalo, New York, 1873–1901." Ph.D. diss., State University of New York at Buffalo, 1990.

————. *Polka History 101.* Buffalo: Polish Community Center, 1980.

Feintuch, Burt, ed. *The Conservation of Culture: Folklorists and the Public Sector.* Lexington: University Press of Kentucky, 1988.

Fischer, Michael M. J. "Ethnicity and the Post-Modern Arts of Memory." In

Writing Culture, edited by James Clifford and George E. Marcus, 194–233. Berkeley: University of California Press, 1986.

Fish, Lydia. "Is the Pope Polish? Some Notes on the Polack Joke in Transition." *Journal of American Folklore* 93, no. 370 (1980): 450–54.

Flores, Richard R. "The *Corrido* and the Emergence of Texas-Mexican Social Identity." *Journal of American Folklore* 105 105, no. 416 (1992): 166–82.

Fox, Paul. *The Poles in America.* New York: George H. Doran, 1922.

Gimbutas, Marija. "Slavic Religion." In *The Encyclopedia of Religion,* edited by Mircea Eliade, volume 13, 353–61. New York: Macmillan, 1987.

Glazer, Nathan, and Daniel P. Moynihan. Introduction. In *Ethnicity: Theory and Experience,* edited by Nathan Glazer and Daniel P. Moynihan, 1–26. Cambridge: Harvard University Press, 1975.

Goldstein, Elizabeth, and Gail Green. "Pierogi- and Babka-Making at St. Mary's." *New York Folklore* 4 (1978): 71–79.

Goode, Judith, Janet Theophano, and Karen Curtis. "A Framework for the Analysis of Continuity and Change in Shared Sociocultural Rules for Food Use: The Italian-American Pattern." In *Ethnic and Regional Foodways in the United States: The Performance of Group Identity,* edited by Linda Keller Brown and Kay Mussell, 66–88. Knoxville: University of Tennessee Press, 1985.

Gordon, Milton. *Assimilation in American Life: The Role of Race, Religion, and National Origins.* New York: Oxford University Press, 1964.

Greene, Victor. *A Passion for Polka: Old-Time Ethnic Music in America.* Berkeley: University of California Press, 1992.

———. *For God and Country: The Rise of Polish and Lithuanian Ethnic Consciousness in America, 1860–1910.* Madison: State Historical Society of Wisconsin, 1975.

Gutierrez, C. Paige. "The Social and Symbolic Uses of Ethnic/Regional Foodways: Cajuns and Crawfish in South Louisiana." In *Ethnic and Regional Foodways in the United States: The Performance of Group Identity,* edited by Linda Keller Brown and Kay Mussell, 169–82. Knoxville: University of Tennessee Press, 1985.

Guzevich, Hank. "We Are Family." On Polka Family Band, *We Are Family.* Polka Family Music, PF1004CD, 1991.

Haiman, Mieczysław. *Zjednoczenie Polskie Rzymsko-Katolickie w Ameryce, 1873–1948.* Chicago: Polish Roman Catholic Union of America, 1948.

Handler, Richard, and Jocelyn Linnekin. "Tradition, Genuine or Spurious." *Journal of American Folklore* 97, no. 385 (1984): 273–90.

Hardin, James, ed. *Folklife Annual 90.* Washington, D.C.: Library of Congress, 1991.

Hobsbawm, Eric. "Introduction: Inventing Traditions." In *The Invention of Tradition,* edited by Eric Hobsbawm and Terence Ranger, 1–14. New York: Cambridge University Press, 1983.

Hymes, Dell. "Breakthrough into Performance." In *In Vain I Tried to Tell You: Essays in Native American Ethnopoetics*, 79–141. Philadelphia: University of Pennsylvania Press, 1981.

Isaacs, Harold R. "Basic Group Identity: The Idols of the Tribe." In *Ethnicity: Theory and Experience*, edited by Nathan Glazer and Daniel P. Moynihan, 29–52. Cambridge: Harvard University Press, 1975.

Isajiw, Wsevolod W. "Definitions of Ethnicity." *Ethnicity* 1 (1974): 111–24.

Jackson, Bruce. *Fieldwork*. Urbana: University of Illinois Press, 1987.

Jędrzejewicz, Cezaria Baudouin de Courtenay. "Polish Peasant Rituals and Seasonal Customs." In *Polish Civilization: Essays and Studies*, edited by Mieczysław Giergielewicz, 1–24. New York: New York University Press, 1979.

Kalčik, Susan. "Ethnic Foodways in America: Symbol and the Performance of Identity." In *Ethnic and Regional Foodways in the United States: The Performance of Group Identity*, edited by Linda Keller Brown and Kay Mussell, 37–65. Knoxville: University of Tennessee Press, 1985.

Kantowicz, Edward R. *Polish-American Politics in Chicago, 1888–1940*. Chicago: University of Chicago Press, 1975.

Keil, Charles. "Class and Ethnicity in Polish-America." *Journal of Ethnic Studies* 7 (Summer 1979): 37–45.

———. "People's Music Comparatively: Style and Stereotype, Class and Hegemony." In *Music Grooves*, edited by Charles Keil and Steven Feld, 197–217. Chicago: University of Chicago Press, 1994.

———. "A Short History of the Polka." In *A Celebration of Polish-American Traditions*. Buffalo: Panagraphics, 1991.

Keil, Charles, Angeliki V. Keil, and Dick Blau. *Polka Happiness*. Philadelphia: Temple University Press, 1992.

Kerman, Judith B. "The Light-Bulb Jokes: Americans Look at Social Action Processes." *Journal of American Folklore* 93, no. 370 (1980): 454–58.

Kleeman, Janice Ellen. "The Origins and Stylistic Development of Polish-American Polka Music." Ph.D. diss., University of California at Berkeley, 1982.

Klinkenborg, Verlyn. *The Last Fine Time*. New York: Alfred A. Knopf, 1991.

Knab, Sophie Hodorowicz. *Polish Customs, Traditions, and Folklore*. New York: Hippocrene Books, 1993.

———. *Polish Herbs, Flowers, and Folk Medicine*. New York: Hippocrene Books, 1995.

Kobielski, Milton J. *Millenium of Christianity of the Polish People: 966–1966*. Buffalo: The Millenium Committee of the Diocese of Buffalo, 1966.

Kohan, Mark. "The Accordion and Concertina in Polish-American Polka." In *Squeezebox Jam*. Buffalo: Panagraphics, 1992.

———. *Polish Folk Roots in Today's Polka*. Buffalo: Panagraphics, 1991.

Kolinski, Dennis L. "Shrines and Crosses in Rural Central Wisconsin." *Polish American Studies* 51 (1994): 33–48.

Koperski, Kate. "Building Community: Buffalo's Polish-American Mural Tradition." In *Folklife Annual 90*, edited by James Hardin 42–57. Washington, D.C.: Library of Congress, 1991.

———. "Children's Guardian Angel Beliefs in Buffalo's Polonia." *New York Folklore* 10 (1984): 135–44.

Koperski, Kate, and Judith Krauza. "A Polish Easter Basket." Pamphlet for "A Celebration of the Easter Egg in Eastern European Tradition Festival," Cheektowaga, N.Y., 29 March 1992.

Kosciuszko Foundation Dictionary. Volume 2. New York: The Kosciuszko Foundation, 1982.

Kozlowski, Lawrence. *Christmas Ornaments, Polish Style.* Pittsburgh: Polska, 1988.

———. *Easter Eggs, Polish Style, and More!* Pittsburgh: Polska, 1989.

Kruszka, Wacław. *A History of the Poles in America to 1908.* Part 1. Edited by James S. Pula, translated by Krystyna Jankowski. Washington, D.C.: Catholic University of America Press, 1993.

Krzyżanowski, Julian, ed. *Nowa Księga Przysłów I Wyrażeń Przysłowiowych Polskich* (New book of Polish proverbs and proberbial expressions). Volume 2. Warsaw: Państwowy Instytut Wydawniczy, 1970.

Kuniczak, W.S. *My Name Is Million: An Illustrated History of the Poles in America.* Garden City: Doubleday, 1978.

Leary, James P., and Richard March. "Dutchman Bands: Genre, Ethnicity, and Pluralism in the Upper Midwest." In *Creative Ethnicity: Symbols and Strategies of Contemporary Ethnic Life,* edited by Stephen Stern and John Allan Cicala, 21–43. Logan: Utah State University Press, 1991.

Leary, James P., ed. *Midwestern Folk Humor.* Little Rock: August House, 1991.

Lopata, Helena Znaniecka. *Polish Americans.* New Brunswick: Transaction Publishers, 1994.

Lukács, László. "Easter Whipping: A Festive Custom in Central Europe." *International Folklore Review* 3 (1983): 106–19.

Magliocco, Sabina. "Playing with Food: The Negotiation of Identity in the Ethnic Display Event by Italian Americans in Clinton, Indiana." In *Studies in Italian American Folklore,* edited by Luisa Del Giudice, 107–26. Logan: Utah State University Press, 1993.

Malpezzi, Frances M., and William M. Clements. *Italian-American Folklore.* Little Rock: August House, 1992.

"The Meaning of a Blessed Basket." *Am-Pol Eagle,* 12 April 1990, 15.

Moore, Willard B. "Metaphor and Changing Reality: The Foodways and Beliefs of the Russian Molokans in the United States." In *Ethnic and Regional Foodways in the United States: The Performance of Group Identity,* edited by Linda Keller Brown and Kay Mussell, 91–112. Knoxville: University of Tennessee Press, 1985.

Morawska, Ewa T. *The Maintenance of Ethnicity: Case Study of the Polish-American Community in Greater Boston.* San Francisco: R&E Associates, 1977.

Myerhoff, Barbara. *Number Our Days.* New York: E. P. Dutton, 1978.

———. "Rites of Passage: Process and Paradox." In *Celebration: Studies in Festivity and Ritual,* edited by Victor Turner, 109–25. Washington, D.C.: Smithsonian Institution Press, 1982.

Nagorka, Suzanne. "Traditional Polish Cooking." *New York Folklore Quarterly* 28, no. 4 (1972): 271–85.

Newall, Venetia. "Easter Eggs." *Journal of American Folklore* 80, no. 315 (1967): 3–32.

Obidinski, Eugene. "Ethnic to Status Group: A Study of Polish Americans in Buffalo." Ph.D. diss., State University of New York at Buffalo, 1968.

Obidinski, Eugene, and Helen Stankiewicz Zand. *Polish Folkways in America.* Lanham: University Press of America, 1987.

Oring, Elliott. "Ethnic Groups and Ethnic Folklore." In *Folk Groups and Folklore Genres: An Introduction,* edited by Elliott Oring, 23–44. Logan: Utah State University Press, 1986.

Orze, Helen. "How St. Roch Came to *Lubotyń.*" *Polish Folklore* 2 (Dec. 1957): 66–69.

Pack, Martin A. *Costumes and Dances of Poland.* N.p.: American Council of Polish Cultural Clubs, 1978.

Pacyga, Dominic A. *Polish Immigrants and Industrial Chicago: Workers on the South Side, 1880–1922.* Columbus: Ohio State University Press, 1991.

Pawlowska, Harriet M. *Merrily We Sing: 105 Polish Folksongs.* Reprint. Detroit: Wayne State University Press, 1983.

Pienkos, Donald E. "Research on Ethnic Political Behavior among the Polish-Americans: A Review of the Literature." *Polish Review* 21.3 (1976): 123–48.

Pieśni Wielkanocne: *Easter Hymns.* Buffalo: The Felician Sisters, 1962.

Pirkova-Jakobson, Svatava. "Harvest Festivals among Czechs and Slovaks in America." *Journal of American Folklore* 69, no. 273 (1956): 266–80.

Pogonowski, Iwo Cyprian. *Polish-English/English-Polish Dictionary.* New York: Hippocrene Books, 1993.

Preston, Kathleen A., and Michael J. Preston. "A Note on Visual Polack Jokes." *Journal of American Folklore* 86, no. 340 (1973): 175–77.

Preston, Michael J. "Xerox-Lore." *Keystone Folklore* 19, no. 1 (1974): 11–26.

Pula, James S. *Polish Americans: An Ethnic Community.* New York: Twayne Publishers, 1995.

Raspa, Richard. "Exotic Foods among Italian-Americans in Mormon Utah: Food as Nostalgic Enactment of Identity." In *Ethnic and Regional Foodways in the United States: The Performance of Group Identity,* edited by Linda Keller Brown and Kay Mussell, 185–94. Knoxville: University of Tennessee Press, 1985.

Raysman, Victor. *Say It in Polish*. New York: Dover Publications, 1955.

Rosten, Leo. *The Joys of Yiddish*. New York: McGraw-Hill, 1968.

Royce, Anya Peterson. *Ethnic Identity: Strategies of Diversity*. Bloomington: Indiana University Press, 1982.

Sandberg, Neil C. *Ethnic Identity and Assimilation: The Polish American Community*. New York: Praeger, 1974.

Sapir, Edward. "Culture, Genuine and Spurious." *American Journal of Sociology* 29 (1924): 401–29. Reprinted in *Selected Writings of Edward Sapir*, edited by David Mandelbaum, 308–31. Berkeley: University of California Press, 1958.

Savaglio, Paula. "Big-Band, Slovenian-American, Rock, and Country Music: Cross-Cultural Influences in the Detroit Polonia." *Polish American Studies* 54 (Autumn 1997): 23–44.

Schilling, Robert. "Lupercalia." In *The Encyclopedia of Religion*, edited by Mircea Eliade, volume 9, 53. New York: Macmillan, 1987.

Silverman, Deborah Anders. "The Folklore of Polish-Americans in Dunkirk, New York." Master's thesis, State University of New York College at Fredonia. 1979.

Skiba, Norman. "Kolendy at Jumbo's." Unpublished paper, State University of New York at Buffalo, 1984.

Smith, Anthony. *The Ethnic Revival*. New York: Cambridge University Press, 1981.

Sokolnicki, Alfred J. "St. John's Eve: Midsummer Night in Poland." *Polish-American Journal*, 12 June 1992, 1.

Sollors, Werner. "Introduction: The Invention of Ethnicity." In *The Invention of Ethnicity*, edited by Werner Sollors, ix–xx. New York: Oxford University Press, 1989.

Spottswood, Richard, ed. "Zrobił Góral Krzyż Na Czole." In *Songs of Migration and Immigration*, volume 6 of the Folk Music in America series. Library of Congress, 77–750125, 1977.

Staub, Shalom. "Folklore and Authenticity: A Myopic Marriage in Public Sector Programs." In *The Conservation of Culture: Folklorists and the Public Sector*, edited by Burt Feintuch, 166–79. Lexington: University Press of Kentucky, 1988.

Stern, Stephen. "Ethnic Folklore and the Folklore of Ethnicity." *Western Folklore* 36 (1977): 7–32.

Stern, Stephen, and John Allan Cicala, eds. *Creative Ethnicity: Symbols and Strategies of Contemporary Ethnic Life*. Logan: Utah State University Press, 1991.

Sturr, Jimmy. Interview on "Music City Tonight." On TNN, Nashville, 21 April 1995.

Szczepanski, Jan. *Polish Society*. New York: Random House, 1970.

Tedlock, Dennis, trans. *Finding the Center: Narrative Poetry of the Zuni Indians*. Reprint. Lincoln: University of Nebraska Press, 1978.

———. *The Spoken Word and the Work of Interpretation*. Philadelphia: University of Pennsylvania Press, 1983.

Theophano, Janet S. "'I Gave Him a Cake': An Interpretation of Two Italian-American Weddings." In *Creative Ethnicity: Symbols and Strategies of Contemporary Ethnic Life,* edited by Stephen Stern and John Allan Cicala, 44–54. Logan: Utah State University Press, 1991.

Thomas, William I., and Florian Znaniecki. *The Polish Peasant in Europe and America.* Volume 1. Reprint. New York: Octagon Books, 1974.

Toelken, Barre. *The Dynamics of Folklore.* Boston: Houghton Mifflin, 1979.

Treasured Polish Folk Rhymes, Songs and Games. Minneapolis: Polanie Publishing, 1976.

Treasured Polish Recipes for Americans. Minneapolis: Polanie Publishing, 1948.

Trojak, Larry, and Mark Kohan. "Celebrate the Polka: A Look at Polonia's Living Tradition." *Polish Heritage* (Winter 1983): 6–7.

Turner, Victor. Introduction. In *Celebration: Studies in Festivity and Ritual,* edited by Victor Turner, 11–32. Washington, D.C.: Smithsonian Institution Press, 1982.

———. *The Ritual Process: Structure and Anti-Structure.* Chicago: Aldine, 1969.

Tyborowski, Sharon. "Ritual Bread Baking." Pamphlet for Cheektowaga, N.Y., Polish-American Festival, 19 Aug. 1995.

Urdang, Laurence, and Christine N. Donohue, eds. *Holidays and Anniversaries of the World.* Detroit: Gale Research, 1985.

Walser, Robert. "The Polka Mass: Music of Postmodern Ethnicity." *American Music* 10, no. 2 (1992): 183–202.

Wandycz, Piotr S. *The Lands of Partitioned Poland, 1795–1918.* Seattle: University of Washington Press, 1974.

Waszkelewicz-Clowes, Florence, ed. *Polish Folk Legends.* Buffalo: Polish-American Journal Books, 1992.

Welsch, Roger L. "American Numskull Tales: The Polack Joke." *Western Folklore* 26, no. 3 (1967): 183–86.

West, John O. *Mexican-American Folklore.* Little Rock: August House, 1988.

Wolska, Helen. *Dances of Poland.* New York: Crown Publishers, 1952.

Wong, Celia. "Magic in the Mullein Stalk." *Polish Folklore* 2 (1957): 46.

Wright, Betty Jane. "The Orange County Onion Harvest Festivals." *New York Folklore Quarterly* 2, no. 3 (1946): 197–204.

Wrobel, Paul. *Our Way: Family, Parish, and Neighborhood in a Polish-American Community.* Notre Dame: University of Notre Dame Press, 1979.

Wycinanki: Polish Cut-Outs. Grosse Pointe Park: Friends of Polish Art, 1978.

Wytrwal, Joseph A. *America's Polish Heritage.* Detroit: Endurance Press, 1961.

———. *Behold! The Polish Americans.* Detroit: Endurance Press, 1977.

Zand, Helen Stankiewicz. "Polish American Childways." *Polish American Studies* 16 (July–Dec. 1959): 74–79.

———. "Polish American Folkways: Cures, Burials, Superstitions." *Polish American Studies* 17 (July–Dec. 1960): 100–104.

―――. "Polish-American Weddings and Christenings." *Polish American Studies* 16 (Jan.–June 1959): 24–33.

―――. "Polish Family Folkways in the United States." *Polish American Studies* 13 (July–Dec. 1956): 77–88.

―――. "Polish Folkways in the United States." *Polish American Studies* 12 (July–Dec. 1955): 65–72.

―――. *Polish Proverbs.* Buffalo: Polish American Journal, 1961.

Zeitlin, Steven J., Amy J. Kotkin, and Holly Cutting Baker. *A Celebration of American Family Folklore: Tales and Traditions from the Smithsonian Collection.* Cambridge: Yellow Moon Press, 1982.

INDEX

DEBORAH ANDERS SILVERMAN received a Ph.D. in English from the State University of New York at Buffalo and an M.A. in English and B.M. in music education from the State University of New York College at Fredonia. A fourth-generation Polish-American, her research interests are in ethnic folklore, particularly Polish-American folkways and the transmission of ethnic folklore in interethnic marriages. Recipient of the 1995 Bertrand H. Bronson Prize from the American Folklore Society's Music and Song Section, she has published articles on Polish-American folk celebrations, foodways, folk music, and the use of music in films and television programs.

FOLKLORE AND SOCIETY

Typeset in 10.5/13 New Baskerville
with New Baskerville display
Designed by Dennis Roberts
Composed by Celia Shapland
for the University of Illinois Press
Manufactured by Thomson-Shore, Inc.

University of Illinois Press
1325 South Oak Street
Champaign, IL 61820-6903
www.press.uillinois.edu